For the Sins
of My Father

* * * * * * * * * * *

BROADWAY BOOKS

New York

FOR THE SINS
OF MY FATHER

* *

A Mafia Killer, His Son,
and the Legacy of a Mob Life

ALBERT DeMEO

with

Mary Jane Ross

BROADWAY

Broadway Books titles may be purchased for business or promotional use or for special sales.
For information, please write to: Special Markets Department, Random House, Inc.,
280 Park Avenue, New York, NY 10017.

PRINTED IN THE UNITED STATES OF AMERICA

BROADWAY BOOKS and its logo, a letter B bisected on the diagonal,
are trademarks of Broadway Books, a division of Random House, Inc.

Visit our website at www.broadwaybooks.com

First edition published 2002

Designed by Nicola Ferguson

Library of Congress Cataloging-in-Publication Data

DeMeo, Albert, 1966–
For the sins of my father : a Mafia killer, his son, and the legacy of a Mob life / Albert DeMeo,
with Mary Jane Ross.
p.   cm.
1. Mafia—New York (State)—New York. 2. Criminals—New York (State)—New York—Biography.
3. Murder—New York (State)—New York. 4. Murderers—New York (N.Y.)—Biography.
5. Organized crime—New York (State)—New York. 6. DeMeo, Roy. 7. DeMeo, Albert, 1966–
I. Ross, Mary Jane. II. Title.

HV6452.N72 M343 2002
364.1'06'097471—dc21   2002066659

ISBN 0-7679-0679-9

1 3 5 7 9 10 8 6 4 2

For my father,
that he may find redemption

Acknowledgments

. . . .

A profound thank-you to our agent, Alan Nevins of Renaissance Agency, for being the first one to believe in this book, and for finding a way to make it happen. Thank you also to his assistant, Karima Ridgley, for her consistent helpfulness. To Charlie Conrad and Becky Cole, our editors, our gratitude for bringing the text to print in record time and with admirable attention to detail. Another thank-you to their support staff at Broadway Books; producing this book was truly a team effort.

On a more personal note, we are grateful for the practical support of friends and family: for Tommy, who shared his memories and his unflagging friendship; for Delores, who continues to demonstrate what it means to be a good neighbor; for Erma, the first to listen and the last to judge; for Joe and Maryann, who helped us put together the family puzzle; for Julie, who read the first draft and laughed and cried in all the right places; and for Christy, who spent countless hours listening to Mom talk about the book.

Every book is a collaboration. We are grateful to all who made this one possible.

Albert DeMeo
Mary Jane Ross

Contents

Roy Albert DeMeo was born in 1942 in Brooklyn, New York, to working-class Italian immigrant parents. In his late teens he started a small loan-sharking operation to supplement his after-school jobs. In the early 1960s, he became involved with John Gotti and other members of the Gambino crime family, rising rapidly through the ranks to become a Gambino soldier under Anthony Gaggi. When Carlo Gambino died in 1976, newly appointed successor Paul Castellano promoted Roy to the rank of *capo*, a made member of the family. Roy's business sense made him a valuable financial asset to Castellano, allowing him to develop lucrative enterprises in pornography, loan-sharking, smuggling, and car theft. Roy was the mastermind behind the biggest auto theft ring in New York history. By the late 1970s he had also become one of the most feared assassins in the city. He was murdered by his own associates in 1983 as part of Castellano's purge of family members who had attracted FBI scrutiny. In the years following his death, dozens of murders were attributed to him by former associates who sought plea bargains with the government. Though most of the allegations were never proven, Roy acquired a posthumous infamy through informants' lurid descriptions of the manner in which he disposed of victims' bodies to avoid detection. Roy DeMeo is survived by his wife, Gina; son, Albert; and two daughters, all of whom have gone on to pursue successful legitimate careers.

For the Sins of the Father shall be visited upon the children,

unto the third and fourth generation of them that hate me,

and walk not according to my commandments.

—Exodus 20:5

CHARON'S CROSSING

EASTER 1968: IN FRONT OF OUR FIRST HOME IN MASSAPEQUA

I come to lead you to the other shore,
Into eternal dark, into fire and ice.

—DANTE, *The Inferno*

So far everything had gone according to plan. Each afternoon for the last few weeks, I had ridden my bicycle past the surveillance vehicles in front of our house. A mile or two later I had stopped at various neighborhood hangouts for a soda or a snack, wound through the familiar Massapequa streets, and then disappeared onto the bike trails that weave through the green woods along the Sound. Just a local thirteen-year-old on a bike. The trails were too narrow for a car to follow. My only company was other bicyclists and the occasional jogger.

Every day my route varied, and every day I emerged from the woods in a different location to stand vigil beside a different neighborhood pay phone. That afternoon the call had finally come. I was relieved to be taking action at last.

I had told my mother that I would be spending a few days with Dad. She knew he was away on business, had been for over a month. More than that, she neither knew nor wanted to know. It was safer that way—safer for our family, safer for her sanity. She requested no details, and I offered none. She had long ago made peace with the fact that as the only son, I was the man of the family in my father's absence. I came and went as I chose. No questions asked.

After dinner that night I went to the cabinet in my father's study and removed the cash he'd asked for. Then I went to my room and began packing: enough clothes to last me for a couple of weeks, copies of the evening newspapers, and, of course, my gun. I'd been carrying it for months now, carefully concealed in my clothing. My father didn't like my carrying it, but as he'd explained to me, it was necessary. Our family couldn't hide in the house all day. So I hid the revolver from my sisters, and I hid the fear from myself. It's what a man does, my father had taught me.

I double-checked the items I'd packed, sealed them tightly inside a plastic garbage bag, slipped into my swim trunks, and lay down on top of the bed to wait. The alarm clock was set for 3:30 A.M., but I couldn't sleep. Instead I lay there in the warm darkness, damp with humidity, and watched the glowing dial on my bedside clock inch away the hours, millisecond by millisecond.

At 3:25 I turned off the alarm switch and rose silently, picking up the garbage bag from the carpet. I slipped down the hall in my bare feet, past my sisters' rooms, pausing only by the master bedroom to listen for my mother. I held my breath as seconds passed. Utter stillness. Good. Moving stealthily down the stairs, I made my way through the kitchen and down to the basement, past the target range and my sister's art studio to the boiler room.

The next part was tricky. I would need my flashlight. Turning on the small beam, I aimed it carefully at the windowsill. My hand did not shake. I slipped a flat clip onto the wire that triggered the alarm system; then, taking a deep breath, I unlatched the window and slid it open. To my great relief, the alarm did not go off. I climbed through the window, into the storage area under the backyard decking, and reached back through for the garbage bag filled with my belongings. I could smell the salt air on the wind. I closed the window, removed the clip, and crept toward the door. On the other side were the steps that led to the canal behind our house.

As I opened the door, I heard Major whine. Pausing for a moment,

I whispered, "It's all right, boy," as he put his muzzle out to lick my hand. Ordering him to stay, I paused once more, searching the night air for signs of intruders. Nothing. Down the ramp in the darkness, to the floating dock at the back of our house. I sat down on the edge of the boards, my ankles dangling in the water, and began to tie the garbage bag around my body.

It was beautiful that night. The summer air was velvet and warm, the darkness broken only by occasional pinpoints of light, shining down on the water from neighbors' back docks. Yet I was immune to the beauty that surrounded me, focused only on the task at hand. Jerking on the rope to make sure I had tied the bag securely, I slipped silently into the chilly water. I made certain there was no splash.

I began to swim, my muscles warming quickly to the exercise. The only sounds disturbing the stillness were my own breathing, the parting of the water as I stroked, and the faint roar of the Atlantic, less than a mile away. My eyes adjusted rapidly to the darkness, and I focused on the empty shoreline three hundred yards ahead. As I drew nearer, the outline of vegetation came into view, illuminated faintly by the carriage lamp in a neighbor's yard. Not much farther.

Finally my fingers touched sand, and I staggered onto the dim shore, the stirring reeds ghostly in the darkness. I untied the bag, wrapped my arms around it like a sleeping child, and climbed carefully up the embankment through the shoulder-high grass. A few yards later I emerged onto a small residential street that dead-ended onto the canal. In the darkness a car was waiting, lights out and engine purring smoothly. I climbed wordlessly inside, tossing the dripping garbage bag into the back seat as I did so, then turned to look at the driver. He had grown a beard to disguise his appearance, but even in the gloom of the car, the profile was familiar.

"Anybody see you?"

"No."

Driving quietly into the night, he reached across the seat and patted me, his arm resting on my shoulders.

"Good job, Al."

I leaned my head back against the soft leather upholstery, breathed in the familiar aftershave, and closed my eyes.

I was safe. I was with my father.

one

FAMILY

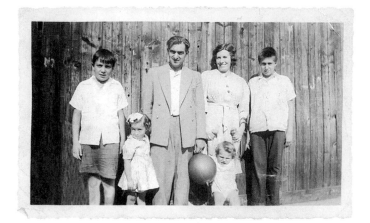

MY FATHER'S FAMILY IN BROOKLYN, CIRCA 1943

Let us go then, you and I,
When the evening is spread out against the sky
Like a patient etherized upon a table;
Let us go, through certain half-deserted streets,
The muttering retreats
Of restless nights in one-night cheap hotels
And sawdust restaurants with oyster-shells:
Streets that follow like a tedious argument
Of insidious intent
To lead you to an overwhelming question . . .
Oh, do not ask, "What is it?"
Let us go and make our visit.

—T. S. ELIOT, *The Love Song of J. Alfred Prufrock*

My earliest memory is of blindness. I was four years old when I woke up in a hospital crib with patches over my eyes, darkness all around, utterly alone. Confused and disoriented, for a moment I could not understand where I was or why my parents had left me there alone. Then I remembered: I'd had an operation to fix my crossed eye. Fear and loneliness whispered in the invisible room where I lay, and I cried out for my mother and father. When the bandages came off a few days later, the first image to emerge from the blur was my father's worried face. Looking back, it seems fitting. I have spent more than thirty years since then struggling to bring him into focus.

I was born in a quiet residential Brooklyn neighborhood in 1966, the second child of parents barely out of their teens. I had an older sister named Debra and a teenage stepbrother in my Uncle Joe. My grandfather DeMeo had died when Joe was a baby, and when Grandma DeMeo returned to her native Italy without Joe, my parents took him in as their own. The five of us formed a happy, traditional Italian-American family. A year later we moved to suburban Massapequa, where my younger sister Lisa was born. Grandma returned to Brooklyn shortly before Lisa was born and moved in with her closest friend, Mrs. Profaci—"Mrs. P," as I called her. Once again, the family was complete.

Mrs. P lived just down the street from the two-story brick duplex where my father had grown up. It was a green neighborhood in the springtime, with tall, well-established foliage and small shrines to the Virgin Mary in nearly every front yard. The Profacis' towering brick mansion dominated the quiet street. Twice a year until I was five or six, my father took me there to spend the night with my grandmother, down Flatbush Avenue, through a maze of side streets, and up to the corner lot where Mrs. Profaci's house stood. The Profaci home was like another world, a realm of elegant timelessness. The living room was filled with delicately curved gilt French furniture, always perfectly maintained. Pale satin drapes and lace panels covered the windows. Mrs. P was equally elegant in her high heels and pearls. The scent of Chanel No. 5 would wisp into my nostrils whenever she bent to kiss me. With her silver blond hair swept into a French twist, she seemed a human embodiment of the golden furniture that filled her home.

Mrs. P didn't own a television, so our evenings there were spent in quiet conversation in the kitchen after dinner. Grandma and Mrs. P spoke Italian to each other, but they spoke English to me. Grandma loved to talk about Mrs. P's brother-in-law, Joseph Profaci. Grandma admired everything about him—his custom-made clothing; his luxurious car; the lavish gifts he made to his family; and most of all, the way everyone looked up to him. "Your grandfather was just an ordinary working man, Albert," she would tell me. "But Joseph Profaci— he was something special. I pray God your father is half the man someday." One time I asked Mrs. P how her brother-in-law got so rich, but she changed the subject. Mrs. P didn't seem to like talking about him.

I lived in Massapequa, Long Island, for ten of my first eleven years. It was a wonderful place to grow up. The streets of our neighborhood were wide and clean, the sidewalks lined with children's bikes. It was the kind of place where you could sleep outside on a summer night and feel perfectly safe. My early years there were filled with joy and contentment. At the core of my sense of security was my father.

No one could have asked for a better father than mine. He was a husky man with dark hair and kind brown eyes, and though he was only five feet, nine inches tall, he was a giant to me. He could pick me up and toss me around as effortlessly as a cotton ball, and he often did. I loved to ride on his shoulders. He spent more time with me than any of the other fathers in the neighborhood spent with their kids. Most of the other fathers were firemen, policemen, teachers, or small business owners who worked on the island and had to be at work by nine o'clock every morning. My dad was different; he was home in the mornings, so he walked me to school while my mother cleaned the house and started lunch. When the other kids were kissing their moms good-bye, I was hugging my dad. Sometimes he brought me a doughnut when he came to pick me up a couple of hours later. I wasn't exactly sure what my father did for a living, and I didn't care. I just liked being with him.

On sunny weekends my father took my sisters and me for hikes in the nearby nature conservancy. Dad loved being outdoors with us. Dad; our German shepherd, Major; my sisters; and I would all head out after breakfast carrying bags of stale bread my mother packed for us. The path behind our neighbors' house led to a trail through the trees and about half a mile down to a preserve with woods and a small lake. The lake was filled with ducks and swans, and my sisters and I would crouch down near the water's edge and coax the birds with pieces of stale bread. Afterward we would hike through the woods until we got tired. When we were ready to rest, we headed for the big log near our favorite tree to sit down. My father always carried a switchblade. One afternoon my father took the knife from his pocket and carved all of our names on the tree, along with the date. After that we thought of it as our tree, and we visited it whenever we could. It was a DeMeo family secret, our special place in the woods.

Sometimes my dad took me for rides in the car with him on the weekends. One Saturday he told me he was taking me to the airport to meet someone named Uncle Vinny. "Uncle Vinny isn't a blood relation, Allie, just a friend of mine," he told me when we pulled into the terminal. I was too interested in watching the planes take off and land to pay much attention when my father introduced me to Vinny.

"How ya doin', Albert?" Vinny asked as he bent to shake my hand. He had on a blue uniform with his name embroidered on his shirt. We went back into the cargo section with Vinny so my father could talk to him, but I couldn't hear a word they said over the roar of the planes. I explored the dusty cargo area while Dad and Uncle Vinny talked. Vinny looked very earnest and waved his hands around a lot while my father shook his head the way he did when I was naughty. Finally Uncle Vinny gave my father an envelope, and we left.

It wasn't long until I saw Uncle Vinny again. Early the next Saturday morning Vinny drove up in a station wagon filled with crates of fresh fruit. My sisters and I lined up on the curb to watch as he carried the wooden crates into our house. We had never seen so much fruit. Along with the ordinary bananas and oranges, there were exotic fruits like guava that not even my mother had ever seen. My mother shook her head as she sorted through the crates, murmuring that there was enough here for half the neighborhood. Uncle Vinny smiled sweetly and murmured, "A little gift for you and the children, Mrs. DeMeo." The following Sunday he brought us boxes of imported chocolate. The weekend after that he brought beautiful London Fog raincoats for us kids. Trailing behind him back out to the car that afternoon, I asked him where he got all this stuff.

"They're F-O-T, Albert," he told me. When I looked blank, he winked at me and said, "You know, F-O-T. Fallen off trucks." I was amazed. How could the truck drivers be so stupid? This was a lot of stuff. It must be worth an awful lot of money. Uncle Vinny had brought more coats than we needed, so my mom gave the extras to Barbara and Jim, my parents' best friends on the block, for their kids. Jim was a policeman who didn't make much money, so Barbara was really excited to get the coats. Vinny continued dropping things off for us at least once a week, and after a while I started wondering why the truck drivers didn't just pick this stuff up if it wasn't damaged.

Finally I asked my father about it. He eyed me for a moment, then smiled and said, "Son, can you keep a secret? Man to man?"

Of course, I could. I was proud that my father trusted me.

"Your uncle Vinny steals things. He's a nice guy, but he steals just about anything he can lay his hands on. And he bets on horses a lot, so I loaned him some money, and he can't pay it back because he keeps betting. This is his way of repaying me. I don't ask him where the stuff comes from. I don't want to know."

Uncle Vinny was a thief? But he seemed so nice, and I could tell my father liked him. If my father liked him, he must be all right.

Saturdays were good, but Sunday was the best day of the week. My father got up early on Sundays to cook us breakfast. My Sunday alarm was the sound of the juice machine as my father squeezed fresh orange juice to go with the meal. I piled into the kitchen with my sisters one late spring morning to find the table loaded down with stacks of pancakes, butter and warm syrup, homemade hash browns, eggs to order, and bacon and sausage. We ate until our stomachs hurt as my father sat and watched, smiling to see our enjoyment. Afterward my mother chased us upstairs to get ready for church.

In half an hour, we were all back downstairs in our Sunday best. My sisters had lovely dresses and patent leather shoes, and I wore a nice suit and tie, with my shoes polished and my nails manicured. While Dad cleaned up from the morning's cooking, my mother drove us to the local Lutheran church and walked us each to our respective classes. Then she left to do errands while my sisters and I attended Sunday school and mass. She never came with us. Mom had been raised Lutheran, and Dad had been raised Catholic. Neither of them practiced their religion anymore, but they wanted us to grow up with a belief in God and good morals: conscientious, well mannered, honest, and respectful. I was polite and well behaved in church, but I found most of the lessons boring. Afterward, my mother picked us all up in the Cadillac and took us home to prepare for dinner and company.

Uncle Joe drove up in his limo and pulled into the driveway shortly after we got back from church. Joe had salvaged the limo from a junkyard for a hundred dollars and had done the body work himself. I'd sat with my father and sisters at the junkyard every Saturday for weeks, watching Joe work on the car. He used a crane to flip it on one side, worked on it a while, then flipped it on the other side and continued. We kids thought it was the coolest thing we'd ever seen. The limo was a shiny black 1960 Fleetwood Cadillac with all the luxuries: leather seats, radio, intercom, and phone. When Uncle Joe finally got it done, he used it to chauffeur us kids around on Sunday afternoons. One Sunday he took us to Coney Island Joe's for the best burgers and hot dogs in town; the next Sunday he piled us in with a dozen neighborhood kids and took us for ice cream. We all argued over who got to ride shotgun. We had double-scoop cones and then rode back home to eat Sunday dinner. My sisters had each invited a friend to eat with us. I didn't want to invite anybody. I liked to hang out in the workshop or yard with Dad and Uncle Joe, chatting about guy things like cars. Barbara and Jim walked over later in the afternoon and brought their children with them. Jim never pulled Sunday patrol. He came downstairs with Dad and Joe and me while Barbara went inside to help my mother.

Sunday was "sauce" day for our extended Italian family. My mother had been cooking for hours in the big downstairs kitchen by the time we got back with Joe: chopping ingredients for marinara sauce, mixing flour for homemade pasta, and grinding sausage for Italian meatballs. Barbara washed and mixed the salad greens and sliced the bread. Uncle Vinny had delivered several baskets of fresh bread that morning. Mom had made desserts the day before while we were out with Dad: brownies, pie, and three kinds of cookies. Dad had also made his specialty while we were at church—zabaglione, an egg custard made with muscatel wine and served warm over fruit. I came in the house every hour or so to sample the goodies. The aromas surrounding me in the warm kitchen gave me a heady rush. Mikey Hammer and his wife walked into the kitchen at about four o'clock. Like Uncle Vinny, Mikey wasn't really a relative, but he seemed like one. My parents knew him from the old days in Brooklyn. Uncle Mikey was one of my favorite uncles. He was stout and strong, with gray hair and hands like slabs. He was also nearly deaf. I had to shout at him to say hello. Mikey's wife and my mom started talking about gardening, so Uncle Mikey headed down to the basement where the men were talking cars.

Everything was perfect until my grandmother got up from her nap. Grandma DeMeo had arrived in state the afternoon before while I was out with Dad. My first hint that she was spending the night had been the sight of her huge undergarment hanging on the bathroom door at bedtime. My grandmother always wore a large girdle-brassiere combination made up of whalebone stays that was strong enough to stand up on its own. I could not understand why anyone would wear such a torture device. Her entrance cast a gloom over the cheery kitchen. She sat ramrod straight on the Naugahyde chair, her hair perfectly arranged and her face fully made up. Grandma was a statuesque woman, full busted and vain to a fault. She seemed to fill the room. Suddenly stricken with claustrophobia, I went out into the backyard to see my dad.

Just as my mother was finishing dinner, my aunt Marie arrived with my cousins. My father made me visit with them. Benny, the oldest, was ten years older than I was and had an attitude that made me uncomfortable. He was always looking around our house; and every time my father got a new car, Benny would look at me and smirk. I didn't understand why he watched me with that knowing grin. Sitting down on the bench by our big redwood picnic table that evening, he stared at my father as if he were fascinated. There was something about the way he looked at my father that I didn't like. I went back inside where my grandmother was setting the dining room table for dinner.

Grandma had brought a big casserole with her special lasagna, and as she placed it on the lace tablecloth, an idea came to me. When she went back into the kitchen, I ran to my room and got the rubber dog droppings I had bought from my favorite joke store. Creeping back down the hall, I arranged them carefully on Grandma's prized lasagna. She was nearly finished setting the table before she noticed. Clutching her chest, she turned purple and started screaming obscenities in Italian. Grabbing a wooden spoon, she raced down the stairs and into the yard in search of the dog. By the time I caught up with her, she had the poor creature by the collar, beating him as the dog whimpered in terror. My father shouted, "What the hell are you doing? Let go of that dog!" Letting go of its collar, she gave it one last kick and started back in the house.

"You see what he do!" she raged as my father followed her upstairs. Storming once more into the dining room, she pointed at the casserole. "The stupid animal, he poop all over my lasagna!"

I had been pulling on her sleeve for over a minute by then, and she finally noticed. "What you want, Albert?" she said, shaking me loose.

"Grandma, it wasn't the dog, it was me. I did it. I got fake dog poop from the store."

Her face twisted. "You do what? Why, you . . ." and grabbing me by the wrist, she sank her teeth into my forearm so deeply she drew blood and then began beating me over the head with the wooden spoon she still held in her other hand.

My mother had come out of the kitchen by that time, and I heard her cry out, "Mama, for God's sake!" The next thing I knew, my father was carrying me into the kitchen while my mother tried to calm my grandmother.

To distract Grandma from her hysterics over the ruined lasagna, Mom suggested we eat outdoors instead, as it was such a beautiful evening. Barbara and Uncle Mikey's wife quickly took the hint and began carrying the food and dishes outside to the picnic table where the men sat. It was a huge redwood table that Dad had had custom built for us. It was ten feet long and could seat nearly twenty people. My mother got Grandma settled in a chair in a warm spot and continued setting things up for dinner.

It was beautiful in the yard that evening. Barbara's kids were playing on the big swing set and slide; Lisa was in the playhouse Dad had built next to it, in the shade of the big tree. I wanted to go swimming, but Dad said the water was too cold. Dad and I had built a fifteen- by thirty-foot above-ground pool with a wooden deck the summer before. We'd also dug a rose bed for my mother around the front and sides of the house, so the entire yard smelled like roses in the evening air. Giant yellow sunflowers twice my height framed the picnic table. My grandmother was oblivious to all the beauty. She kept lamenting how sick she was, how unloved, how neglected.

"Albert," she said, "you almost kill me today with your tricks. You'll see. One of these mornings I'm gonna wake up, and I'll be dead!" She looked strong as an ox to me. I headed over to the slide and began climbing. My father went back in the house to bring out another bottle of wine.

I was halfway up the slide when I noticed a sick-looking squirrel at the base of the big tree nearby. Something about the animal didn't look right, so I went over to where the adults were sitting and said there was something wrong with the squirrel by the tree. Within seconds, all hell broke loose.

Everyone rushed over to look, and as soon as my grandmother saw it, she began screaming hysterically in Italian, "Roy, come quickly, there's a squirrel with rabies!" My aunt began shooing us kids away to the other side of the yard as my father ran back outside to see what all the yelling was about.

It only took a glance for him to see that my grandmother was right. He lunged for the big redwood table and pushed it over on its side, shouting at everyone to get behind the barrier. Food and dinnerware went flying in all directions. We all crouched behind the table as my dad ran into the garage and raced back out a few seconds later carrying his rifle. By then the squirrel was spooked by all the excitement and was running excitedly around the yard. My grandmother, who had been screaming the whole time, kept shouting at the top of her lungs, "Shoot, Roy, shoot!" as my father took aim.

Meanwhile my father was yelling, "Stay down! Stay down!" as he opened fire on the squirrel. The bullets caught the squirrel as it raced up the redwood decking toward the pool, going straight through the squirrel's body and into the side of the pool. As the squirrel went limp, water began pouring through the sides of the pool. Dad ran back into the garage to put the gun away and find something to stop the water while we children raced over to see if the squirrel was really dead. While we ran, my father kept shouting, "Stay away from it, kids! Don't touch it! It's still dangerous!"

All the time this was going on, my grandmother was screaming at the top of her lungs in a mixture of Italian and English, "He killed him! Oh my God, Roy killed him!"

Running back toward the pool with rags to stuff in the holes, my father shouted furiously, "You told me to shoot! You wanted me to shoot!" as my grandmother continued to wail.

Meanwhile my mother, who had been in the kitchen with Barbara, heard the gunfire and ran to the back door in panic just in time to hear Grandma screaming, "Roy killed him!" I looked up to see my mother standing in the doorway with horror all over her face, calling out to my father.

"Oh my God, Roy! Roy! Tell me you didn't shoot somebody! You wouldn't!"

My parents sent us kids inside while the adults cleaned up the mess, plugged the holes in the pool, and buried the rabid squirrel. Benny and I went downstairs to watch TV in the den while the girls watched the upstairs TV in the living room. There was a movie on called *The Valachi Papers*, starring Charles Bronson as Joe Valachi, one of the first men to inform on the Mafia to the FBI. I wouldn't have paid much attention to it if Benny hadn't kept looking over at me. I wondered what was wrong with him. About half an hour into the film, there was a scene where Joseph Profaci, the boss of the Mob family, is choosing the men who will work for him. Cousin Benny turned to me with a big grin on his face and said, "You know who that is, don't you? That's Mrs. P's brother-in-law!"

"Oh, uh-huh," I replied. "Grandma talks about him sometimes." I didn't know what he was getting at.

Benny started laughing. I knew that he was laughing at me, but I didn't understand what the joke was. I always felt like Benny meant something he wasn't saying. When he introduced me to someone, he never said, "This is my cousin Albert." He always said, "This is Albert, you know, Roy *DeMeo's* son, like I told you about," and the person would look me over like some kind of lab specimen.

A little while later Dad and Uncle Joe brought home hamburgers and hot dogs from the local diner, and we all ate in silence upstairs around the kitchen table. All except for Grandma, who couldn't eat a thing. She kept saying over and over that her heart was beating so hard, she was sure she was having another heart attack, that no one ever thought of her comfort and safety. For once even my father was too tired to try to talk her out of it. I was relieved when Aunt Marie said good night and took Grandma and my cousins home. Uncle Mikey and his wife left a short while later, with Jim and Barbara close behind.

Everyone looked tired and a little sad, so my father said, "How about some jokes, Albert?" Nearly every Sunday I told jokes in the living room after we finished eating. The ritual was always the same: Everyone would help my mother clear the table, and while she stacked dishes in the dishwasher, Dad would pop a huge kettle of Jiffy Pop popcorn and take it in the living room. By then I would be ready with my comedy box of items from the joke store down the street. I had all kinds of funny glasses in there: Groucho Marx glasses with a moustache and nose, X-ray glasses, glasses with eyeballs attached to coiled wires, even Chinese glasses with slanted eyes. That night I put on the moustache glasses and did my best impression of Groucho. Everyone laughed, even my sisters, and suddenly everyone felt better.

Then my father picked up Lisa's favorite teddy bear from its perch on the back of the couch and started teasing her, saying it was his bear now. It was her favorite game. She screamed, "Daddy!" and dove for the bear as my dad pulled it away. The chase was on, my dad running and dodging around the living room with Lisa in hot pursuit. When she got close, Dad grabbed her and tossed her in the air while my mother protested that he would make her throw up so soon after eating. He responded by picking me up in the other arm and tickling us both. Only when we had screamed and giggled ourselves into exhaustion did he put us down. By then it was time for *The Wonderful World of Disney*. Mom sent us to change into our pajamas, and when we came back, we dog piled on the couch with Dad to munch popcorn and watch TV. The excitement of the day was getting to me by then, and I found myself dozing on my father's broad chest. Lisa was already sound asleep on his other shoulder. I snuggled closer, Dad's chest hairs prickling my ear through his knit shirt. Picking us both up together, one in each arm, he carried us down the hall through the darkness. Still holding Lisa in the other arm, he placed me gently on the bed and pulled the covers up under my chin. I slept deeply that night, filled to the brim with food and contentment.

Most weekends we would all be together at home with my mother and sisters. Sometimes, though, my father had to get some business done on Saturdays. When I was about five years old, he started taking me with him on some of his Saturday errands. Most of them were on Long Island, to the car dealership Dad owned down the highway or to small shops and office buildings. I loved riding in the big car and meeting the interesting people he knew. It was on those Saturday outings that I gradually became acquainted with the long series of "uncles" that became an ongoing part of my life. They liked me, and I liked them, too. I was especially interested in their nicknames.

There was my uncle Frankie, also known as Frankie the Wop. He was perched on a wobbly wooden chair on a sidewalk in front of a grocery store the day I met him, drinking milk and eating Kit Kat bars. When my father introduced us, Uncle Frankie grinned at me and handed me an entire box of Kit Kats. I was thrilled. Uncle Frankie was the biggest man I had ever seen. A guy who knew him told me Frankie weighed four hundred pounds. Uncle Frankie did business with my father. Or so my father told me, though Frankie never seemed to do much of anything but eat. His favorite pastime was going to "all you can eat" establishments and staying there all day. My father told me Uncle Frankie would eat until his stomach touched the table. After a while, the restaurants where they knew him actually paid Uncle Frankie to go away.

One day Uncle Frankie went to the bathroom at one of the restaurants, and while he was sitting on the toilet, a mosquito flew in. Uncle Frankie panicked and tried to wave it away with a wooden toilet brush. When that didn't work, he reached for the spray cleaner and tried spraying it. That didn't work, either, and he really started to panic. He was afraid to even get up from the toilet, for fear it would attract the mosquito's attention, especially since he'd be stuck bare-bottomed in a stall where he could barely turn around. Finally, in desperation, he pulled out his .38 revolver and shot the mosquito. When the cops arrived a few minutes later to arrest him for discharging a firearm, they were astonished. He'd gotten the mosquito in a single shot.

I met another Uncle Frankie on our Saturday outings, too. This Uncle Frankie was nicknamed Frankie Elbows. My dad said that was because his arms were so long, everyone joked that his elbows dragged on the ground like a chimpanzee's. Frankie Elbows was a mortician who sometimes helped my father with his business.

One uncle who never came to our house was my uncle Nino. His real name was Anthony Gaggi, and he was a business associate of my father. I'd heard his name around the house from as far back as I could remember. Sometimes at night my dad would come home with a toy or a little money and say it was from Uncle Nino. I was about six years old when I finally got to meet him.

My father had taken me in the car to the city one Saturday, where he'd stopped to talk to a few people he knew. We were on our way home for dinner when my father stopped to make a call at a pay phone in Manhattan. When he got back in, he told me we needed to make one more stop before we went home. We drove a couple more miles to a tailor shop near the financial district. By the time my father parked the car and we got out, it was nearly dark.

As we walked toward the tailor shop, a man stepped out of the entrance onto the sidewalk. He was middle-aged, expensively dressed in an Italian suit, with black receding hair. There was a feeling of power surrounding him that I sensed right away. In spite of the deepening gloom, he wore black sunglasses that completely hid his eyes. I remember thinking how odd it was. I had never seen anyone wear sunglasses at night. How could he see when it was already so dark outside?

Nino turned as we approached and greeted my father warmly, embracing him and slapping him on the back. My father kept watching Uncle Nino's face and smiling at him. It was the first time I had seen my father seem anxious to please someone. Nino bent to me next and introduced himself as my uncle Nino. He was very nice, very friendly. I kissed him obediently on the cheek as I had been taught to do, the standard gesture of respect. Nino smiled at me, and I wondered if his eyes were smiling, too. Later I asked my father what color Nino's eyes were. Dark brown, he told me. I didn't see Nino's eyes that night, or any other night for that matter. He never once took off those dark glasses.

After laughing with my father and showing off the new coat his wife had had made for him, Uncle Nino and my father began strolling down the street, chatting in low voices as we walked. I walked quietly by my father's side, listening to their curious conversation without comprehension.

"Did you take care of that thing we talked about?" Uncle Nino asked my dad.

"It's done."

"And the other thing?"

"Just as we discussed."

"*Bene.*" Then, turning to me, Uncle Nino asked, "So Albert, I hear you started school. How is that going?"

I said it was going pretty good. After a few more minutes of polite chatter, Nino bid us good-bye and continued down the street.

Back in the car a few minutes later, I turned to my father. "Is Uncle Nino your boss, Daddy?"

My father considered the question for a minute. "Not exactly. He's more of an associate. We work for the same family."

This was interesting. "Uncle Nino works for our family?"

"Not our family, son, not the way you mean. Uncle Nino's been around a little longer than I have, so I pay attention to what he says. It's important to pay attention to more experienced men."

I nodded thoughtfully. Uncle Nino must be very important if my father turned to him for advice. My father knew everything.

two

PRIMARY LESSONS

MY FIRST GRADE PICTURE:
MY FATHER IN 1959 AFTER
HIGH SCHOOL GRADUATION

Train up a child in the way he should go;
and when he is old, he will
not depart from it.

—PROVERBS 22:6

When I was in the first grade, our teacher asked us to tell the class what our fathers did for a living. The other children got up one at a time and explained that their dads were doctors or businessmen. When it was my turn, to my great embarrassment, I didn't know what to say. I wasn't sure what my dad did. Worse yet, a couple of the kids from my block looked at each other and smiled funny when I went up to share. So I asked my mother to take me to the library, and I got one of those children's books on "What Daddies Do" and tried to find my father's job. But the more I looked, the more confused I became. My father carried a gun, but he wasn't a policeman. He must be doing something dangerous; else why did he carry a gun? He wore a suit, but he didn't work in an office. He didn't have an office, and the suits he wore weren't like the ones worn by other fathers. He wore custom-made suits, and he never wore a starched shirt and a tie. As I looked through the book, my stomach began to hurt, yet I didn't ask my mother.

I began to notice differences when I was at home, too. My playmates' fathers were referred to by their profession: Jimmy's dad was a policeman, Tony's a mechanic. But no one in the neighborhood ever said a word about what my father did for a living. Most fathers talked about what they did at the office or the precinct when they stopped by on a Saturday to chat. They asked each other how it was going at work. None of the other men asked my father about his work. I wondered why.

Even in our house, no one talked about Dad's business. One evening, at Sunday-night dinner, my aunt Marie asked me what I wanted to be when I grew up. I promptly replied, "I want to do what Daddy does."

She and my mother exchanged a look; and after a silence, my mother prompted me, "No, you don't, Al. You should pick something *you* want to do." Looking at my plate, I was at a loss for words.

So the next time someone asked me what my father did, I made something up. I was taking my first step toward the most basic survival mechanism in a crime family: lying. While other children were listening to fairy tales, I was learning to tell them. Since no one was giving me any answers, I provided my own and tried to believe they were true. If anyone asked, I said my father was a car salesman.

Other small oddities began to strike me as well. I wondered why my father left for work so late in the day, sometimes coming home long after midnight. I wondered why he always carried a big bag of change for pay phones. When we went out together, he nearly always stopped at particular pay phones to make calls. Sometimes one of the phones would ring while I waited in the car, and the call was always for my father. How did he know it would be for him? Why didn't he use the phone at home like other fathers? And why did he keep money in envelopes instead of in his wallet?

The neighbors were universally friendly. But if they thought I wasn't looking, they nudged each other when my father pulled into the driveway in a different luxury car every six months. No one else had new cars as often as we did. No one I knew had as much money as we did, either. My sisters and I got complete new wardrobes several times a year. We even had our nails manicured regularly. Still, people liked us, so perhaps it was just my imagination.

School itself went well enough in most respects. I had trouble learning to write, so my parents hired a tutor to work with me. Each day after school I would work with him at the big table in the small kitchen upstairs. Fortunately, I learned to read quickly and proficiently; by the time I reached second grade, I could read at a sixth-grade level. I was polite and well behaved, and the teachers seemed to like me. I got along fine with the other children, too, but I seldom invited them home to play. Somehow it didn't seem like such a good idea. I never made a best friend like most children do when they go to school. My father remained my best friend. It was with him that I spent my weekends, and as I grew older, he would begin the slow process of introducing me to his world.

Usually it was on Saturdays, when Debra was with her junior high friends and Lisa was at home with Mom. Dad and I would drive down Sunrise Highway and around Long Island, while my father pointed out the make and year of the cars we passed. By the time I was seven, I could accurately identify most automobiles on sight. We would stop occasionally at a barber shop or cleaner's while Dad went in, then returned a few minutes later and resumed the drive. He usually left me in the car because the stops were business and would only take a minute. Sometimes I saw him put an envelope in his jacket pocket as he came back outside. Our last stop was often his favorite place: one of those old-fashioned hardware stores that had everything you could ever want. The proprietor was an old man who had run the place for years, and my father loved talking to him. Dad would describe an item he needed for a home project we were working on, and within minutes the man would go into the back room and reemerge with exactly the right tool or fastener. I remember being amazed when my dad described a crystal doorknob to match one that had broken on a bedroom door and the owner came back with an exact duplicate. It seemed as if the owner had everything a person could want in that mysterious backroom.

Dad also began introducing me to more of his friends. One was

Freddy DiNome, a friend of my dad's from the old days in Brooklyn. Freddy was a drag racer who had an auto repair shop not far from the house where my father grew up. Freddy's racing name was Broadway Freddy. Freddy was semifamous, my father told me. Freddy raced his cars in Englishtown, New Jersey, and he was pretty good. Sometimes I heard his races mentioned on the radio when I went somewhere in the car with Dad, and my father had shown me pictures of Freddy's races in the newspaper. One Saturday afternoon Dad took me to meet Freddy at the car repair shop in Brooklyn.

It was a hot summer afternoon when we pulled into the driveway of Freddy's garage. Freddy was bent under the hood of a car when we got there, fiddling with the engine, and he didn't hear us when we first drove up. The person who looked up at my father's greeting was the filthiest human being I had ever seen.

Freddy was a husky guy about five feet, nine inches, a little shorter than my father, and every inch of him was covered with grease. He seemed to exude engine grease from his very pores. Freddy had dirty blond hair, a lopsided nose, and tattoos covering both arms. His teeth were stained and crooked, and his fingernails were filthy. My father had his own nails manicured every week, and I thought it was odd that he would have a friend with nails that black. Yet the face looking down at me had warm brown eyes, and when Freddy scooped me up to give me a hug, exclaiming, "So this is Albert!" I liked him immediately. I liked him even more when he began looking around for a piece of candy or a soda to treat me. When he returned a minute later with an ice-cold Coke in his hand, I settled down comfortably to sip it in the cool darkness of the garage while he and my dad talked.

"Got the truck all tagged up for ya, Roy," he said as they walked outside together. Freddy pointed at something down the street. A few minutes later another man pulled up in front of the garage in a well-kept Chevrolet. He got out of the car and walked over to Freddy and my father. The new man wore dark blue pants and a shirt that looked

like a gas station attendant's uniform, and his fingernails were almost as black as Freddy's. Freddy seemed to know the man; Freddy
nodded at him and said something to my dad. Dad and the man talked
a minute, then started down the street where Freddy had pointed. By
this time I had finished my soda. I wandered over to the corner
where Freddy and Dad had been standing. Halfway down the block I
could see a tow truck parked by the curb, across from an empty parking lot. The new man walked around the truck, nodded at my dad,
and took a white envelope from his pocket. Dad took the envelope,
slipped it inside his shirt pocket, and then shook the man's hand. I
heard the truck's engine start up, and the man drove away as Dad
and Freddy walked back to where I was waiting. Dad said it was time
to go.

"Thanks for the soda, Mr. DiNome," I said as we headed for my father's car.

Freddy grinned at me. "Call me Freddy," he told me, and my father told me to kiss Freddy good-bye. I planted a polite kiss on
Freddy's greasy cheek and got in the car with my father.

As we pulled into traffic, I asked my father, "Why is Freddy's nose
so crooked?"

"He broke it a few times," my father answered.

"In car races?"

"Yeah, that way. In fights, too."

Hmm. "Daddy, what did Freddy mean when he said the truck was
tagged? I didn't see any tag."

My father glanced at me, then replied, "Tagging means replacing
the identification tag that comes on a car. If you want to sell a stolen
car, you have to put a new tag on it so the police can't tell who it belonged to."

I absorbed this information in silence. I already knew my father
had a car lot on the highway not far from our house. He had taken me
there plenty of times. Now he was talking about stolen cars. Freddy

had changed the tag; I'd heard him say so. But the man who came and got the truck had given an envelope to my father, not to Freddy. What was in the envelope? Sometimes, when I sat with my dad while he undressed at night, I saw him take envelopes with money in them out of his pockets and put them in a drawer. Did this envelope have money in it? A small knot grew in the pit of my stomach. I ignored it. If my father was doing it, it must be all right.

I saw Freddy often after that. I could tell from the beginning that Freddy adored my dad. He looked at my father with the admiration of a faithful dog, and a few weeks later I found out why.

Dad had taken me by Freddy's house to play with Freddy's children while he and Freddy talked some business. I had never been to Freddy's house before, and I thought the whole place was incredibly cool. The house was set on nearly two acres, and Freddy's backyard was like a Hot Wheels racetrack. He kept race cars and motorbikes there, and he promised me that as soon as I was big enough, he'd let me ride one of the bikes. He also had a basement filled to the brim with electronic equipment. Hundreds of new electronic devices—televisions, VCRs, stereos, anything you wanted—covered his basement in stacks, all still in their boxes. It was great fun to go exploring there, for as I soon learned, the selection changed constantly. Wandering through Freddy's basement was like being set loose in an electronics store.

After my father and Freddy finished talking their business, Freddy's wife brought snacks and cold drinks into the living room for all of us, and Freddy started talking about what a great guy my father was. "Did you know your father was a hero, Albert?" he asked me. I just smiled at him as he continued, "Did you know your father once saved my life?"

Now that was interesting. "What did he do, Freddy?" I asked him.

"He saved me from a fire, that's what he did," Freddy went on. "Here, I'll show you. I got the tape." And he immediately went in search of something in the next room while my father protested in embarrassment. Ignoring him, Freddy returned a few minutes later and popped a videotape into the VCR. A few seconds later a picture crackled into view. It was news footage of one of Broadway Freddy's races.

The film showed Freddy's car veering out of control on a race-track, then slamming into a wall and bursting into flames as the watching crowd screamed in horror. A rescue team went running toward the car, then pulled back as the heat from the flames hit them. I could barely make out Freddy, slumped unconscious over the steering wheel inside. Suddenly another man rushed toward the door on the driver's side, shoving his hand into the fire and pulling the door open. The rescue team was shouting for the man to get away before the car exploded. I could see the man struggling with something inside as the newscaster explained that the unknown good Samaritan was cutting the seat belts off Freddy with a knife. In the time it took the newscaster to tell it, the man pulled Freddy from the flames and carried him away from the car, staggering under Freddy's weight. As the car exploded in the background, the man put Freddy on the ground and collapsed beside him, panting. When the man looked up at the camera, I could see my father's face.

It was the most amazing thing I had ever seen, like something out of a movie, except this was real life. Tears of pride filled my eyes. I listened as Freddy, his face glowing with gratitude, told me the end of the story. Freddy had suffered a concussion and minor burns that day, and my father had burned his hands and forearms pulling Freddy from the flames. Both had been taken to the hospital to have their wounds treated, but neither suffered permanent injury.

"If it wasn't for your daddy, Albert, I'd be dead," Freddy told me. Then turning to my father, "I won't never forget that, Roy. Never."

My father, clearly uncomfortable, announced that it was time to go. The glow of pride inside of me lasted all the way home. That night, when I went to bed, I drifted to sleep dreaming of heroic deeds. I was going to be just like my dad when I grew up.

One of my favorite trips with Dad was our visits to Uncle Frank in Greenwich Village. Unlike most of my other "uncles," Uncle Frank really was a relative, a great-uncle on my father's side. He was head chef at a restaurant called the Vineyard that my father owned in Greenwich Village. Uncle Frank's exploits in the war were a favorite family story. Uncle Joe loved to tell me the tale, and he never told it without laughing.

Uncle Frank had been General MacArthur's personal chef in World War II, stationed on a ship that transported the general from port to port. Like several of my ancestors, Uncle Frank was a little too fond of a good bottle of wine, and every now and then he would crawl into the 50-mm gun ports on deck to sleep off a bottle or two. On board his ship in Pearl Harbor one day, Uncle Frank decided to throw a little party for some visiting nurses. After they had eaten and drunk themselves into oblivion, Uncle Frank crawled into his favorite gun port to sleep. Unfortunately for him, this was not an ordinary day. It was December 7, 1941, and no sooner had he settled deep into a drunken slumber than the Japanese attacked. Startled out of his stupor, Uncle Frank held on to the huge gun for support and began firing wildly into the air. Entirely by accident, he happened to hit a Japanese kamikaze plane. Uncle Frank not only survived the attack but became a war hero, medals and all. What made the incident even more ridiculous was that afterward, he could barely even remember firing the gun.

I thought the story was hilarious, but I didn't care whether or not Uncle Frank was really a war hero. I was just happy eating his food. Every time I walked into the kitchen at the Vineyard, delicious aromas engulfed me like a warm embrace. Uncle Frank always had a fresh plate of antipasti or linguini and clam sauce waiting for me to nibble while he and my father talked business. When I finished my plate, I had the run of the kitchen. I picked my way through the kitchen where pots simmered with marinara sauce, lasagna baked in the ovens, and the walk-in refrigerator held shelves of pies and Italian custards. It was all mine to choose from. The undercooks smiled at me and offered me samples as I passed. As if that weren't exciting enough, my father also owned a pizza parlor across the street, and after talking with Uncle Frank, we usually wandered over there to sample the deep-dish pizza. Stuffed with pasta and sauce after an afternoon in the Village, I could barely keep my eyes open on the drive home.

A guy called Crazy Mark was usually hanging around the Vineyard when we visited there. Mark did odd jobs and errands for my father. Everyone called him Crazy Mark because he sometimes heard voices in his head. I think my dad felt sorry for the guy, since no one else would give Mark a job. To me Mark seemed a little weird but harmless. Crazy Mark was always eager to please my father and me. If I wanted anything, from a stick of gum to a candy bar, Mark would race off to fetch it. Within minutes he would be back, asking me if I wanted anything else.

For a long time our trips to see Uncle Frank were fun, but then something happened. An occult shop called The Dark Crystal opened across the street from the Vineyard, next door to my father's pizza parlor. The proprietors wore black robes, and the display windows were filled with strange-looking items that Uncle Frank said were used for witchcraft and devil worship. Weird-looking people in Gothic makeup and bizarre clothing began coming there all hours of the day and night. I heard people in the neighborhood say satanic rituals were performed there after dark. The whole place was creepy for a six-year-old, like something out of a horror movie, and it gave me the shivers. My father knew the store made me nervous, and he got a kick out of teasing me about it. The owners had erected a giant Ouija Board in the alley in back of the store, next to the pizza parlor's dumpster, and my father made me take out the trash so I'd have to go near the Ouija Board. The minute I stepped out the back, my father locked the door so I couldn't get back inside for a while. I didn't think it was very funny, but my father thought it was hilarious.

After a while, though, even my father didn't think the place was funny anymore. The neighborhood was largely Catholic, and many people were afraid to even pass the store. Business began falling off dramatically at both the Vineyard and the pizza parlor. Something had to be done.

One Saturday afternoon a couple of months after the store opened, I sat munching garlic bread in my uncle Frank's kitchen while my father's pie man complained about losing customers because of The Dark Crystal. Crazy Mark was sitting in the kitchen a few feet away, listening to the whole conversation. After a few minutes Mark left while Dad and the pie man continued to talk. About half an hour later, my father and I were ready to leave for the day. We stood on the sidewalk in front of the Vineyard, leaning on Dad's Cadillac, sipping cold drinks and bullshitting with Uncle Frank. Suddenly we heard piercing screams from the occult store. My father put down his drink and started toward the screams. A moment later the store owner came running out onto the sidewalk, black robes flapping, his face a mask of terror under the bizarre makeup. Seconds later Crazy Mark ran out after him. Mark was wielding a machete at the devil worshiper's head like a crazed Grim Reaper, screaming, "Out, Satan! I cast you out in the name of the Father, the Son, and the Holy Spirit! Begone and bother my friend Roy no more!"

I heard my father mutter "What the hell?" as they raced by. The man in black sprinted like he truly was possessed, gradually gaining distance from Mark as they disappeared down the street. No one in the neighborhood ever saw him again. The next day, the mystic merchandise was moved out and the store boarded up.

Mark was elated to have done this "favor" for my father. "I did it for you, Roy," he happily informed us when we saw him the following week. He was beaming with joy, clearly waiting for my father's approval. Dad listened quietly and gave Mark a few bills before sending him away. Then he looked at me and shook his head, muttering, "Crazy bastard." Dozens of people from the neighborhood also came up to us that day to thank my father. They all took it for granted that my dad had "taken care of the problem." As I watched them, I began to realize that my father wielded a power that I could not explain, and somehow, the realization disturbed me. I was proud of the respect everyone showed my dad. Yet as young as I was, I knew it wasn't normal to commit the sort of extreme act Crazy Mark had done just to please my father. What was it about my father that made everyone so eager to gain his favor?

The Christmas before I turned seven was one of the most memorable of my childhood. That year my father imported several cars from Italy to exhibit at the auto show in Madison Square Garden a few days before Christmas. I was thrilled when Dad told me he'd take me with him, and when he told me that Adam West and Burt Ward (Batman and Robin) from the television series were going to be there with the real Batmobile, I was too excited to sleep the night before.

It was a beautiful drive into Manhattan. The Macy's Thanksgiving parade had been held only a few days before, and I was wide-eyed as we passed the Christmas windows at Macy's and crossed the street to Madison Square Garden. Inside the huge lighted building, it was like a giant toy store with adult-size toys. Cars of every color and description gleamed from the exhibits as people milled through the aisles and jockeyed for a good vantage point to look at them. Dad led me through the maze toward his own exhibit.

A friend of his was waiting for us when we got there. Dad introduced the man to me as Chris Rosenberg. I'd heard Chris's name around the house, but I hadn't actually met him before. I could tell that my father was fond of Chris by the way Dad slapped him on the back as he introduced us. Chris bent down to shake my hand warmly, man to man, saying "How you doing, Albert?" He couldn't have been more than twenty at the time, athletically built, with dark blond hair and green eyes. He wore designer blue jeans, a polo shirt, and expensive-looking athletic shoes. He had on a leather jacket exactly like my father's and was as meticulously groomed as my dad. His left arm was in a sling.

"What happened to your arm, Mr. Rosenberg?" I asked him.

"Nothing much. I hurt it doing some work the other day. Call me Chris, Albert."

The three of us toured the exhibit together. The Garden was filled with gleaming new cars that glowed and twinkled like the holiday display at Macy's. There was a whole section dedicated to vehicles from television and the movies. Dad and Chris took me to meet Batman and Robin, and I stood in line to get their autographs. Batman was very nice, taking a moment to chat with me as he signed his photograph, but I didn't get to sit in the Batmobile. Afterward we went to another exhibit, where I met Roddy MacDowell and a nice woman with a familiar voice. My father explained that they were the actors who played Cornelius and Zera in *Planet of the Apes*, one of my favorite movies. I already knew the apes weren't real, so I wasn't disappointed to meet the actors without their ape makeup, just very excited. Finally we went to see the exhibit for a movie I hadn't seen yet, called *The Godfather*. I could see the movie when I was a little older, my father told me. The car from the movie was there, a 1948 Lincoln Continental filled with bullet holes. My father picked me up so I could see better and walked around the car, carefully explaining how the movie stunt had been done. The movie people had gotten an old Lincoln, he told me, and then taken it to the state police and asked them to shoot it full of holes, just as in a genuine police assault. The cameraman filmed the police while they were shooting the car. Once the police had riddled the car with real machine gun bullets, the movie people had taken it to the studio. Back at the studio, the special effects people had carefully filled each real bullet hole with blasting caps, then repainted and polished the car to make it look like new. For the shooting scene in the movie, the blasting caps were set off in the same pattern the police had used in the real shooting. That way the scene looked completely real, but nobody got hurt. I was fascinated. What a clever idea. Dad and Chris obviously thought so, too. When we finished inspecting the car, we went over to the booth where they had props from the movie. There were many things there, but the only thing I remember is the horse's head. It was a real head, stuffed and mounted for the onlookers to see. I shivered in delicious horror. This would be a great story to make my sisters sick when I got home. Afterward we went to the part of the exhibit that was showing Dad's car. Dad showed me how the roof on the Lamborghini could be lifted back so the driver could get in and out of the low-slung sports car. It was incredibly cool. By the time we got back in the Cadillac to head home, I was worn out with the excitement of the day.

With Christmas only a few weeks away, Dad and I started decorating the outside of the house the following Saturday. We draped every tree, fence post, window, and empty piece of wall with Christmas lights, the old-fashioned kind with multicolored one-inch bulbs. We wrapped the posts on both sides of the front porch with red and white lights, to look like candy canes. When we ran out of places to put lights, we started setting up the Christmas cut-outs. We put big plastic Santas, elves, and reindeer all over the roof and yard and tacked plastic candy canes to every post on the picket fence that bordered our property. Mom had Dad wire speakers for the front porch and kept the stereo playing Christmas carols into the yard all day long. She and my sisters decorated the inside of the house with wreaths and garlands, and together they baked literally hundreds of cookies for the neighbors to come by and sample. Mom's ginger cookies were my favorite. They made the whole house smell like Christmas.

Debra was in charge of the presents we kids got for Mom and Dad. All three of us had saved our allowances for weeks. One clear afternoon Debra led our little procession of bicycles on the half-mile trip to the shopping center. We went to May's first, to the chinaware department. Mom loved figurines, especially the pale blue-and-white Lladros from Spain, so we got her one and had it gift wrapped. They were expensive, so we pooled our money. Dad was next. My sisters got him a nice sweater, but I preferred buying him tools. It really didn't matter what we got, for Dad was sure to like it, but we wanted something special for him anyway.

Debra was also in charge of the gifts for us, though my parents didn't know it. I hadn't believed in Santa Claus since I was five; Debra had initiated me young into the mysteries of "Santa gifts." She knew that our parents kept our gifts locked in the big closet in their bedroom, and having discovered the hiding place, she rose to the challenge. A few days before Christmas, while Dad was at work and Mom was running an errand, we made our raid. Creeping into Mom and Dad's room, Debra shushed Lisa and me while she expertly ran a bobby pin into the lock on the closet door and popped it open. My sister could pick that lock like a pro. One by one, she quietly removed the presents while I set them on the floor nearby. Then, using a straight-edged razor from her craft box, she slit open the wrapping paper so carefully that I couldn't see the line and removed the gifts for us to look at. We giggled and whispered with excitement as we peeked at them; afterward Debra replaced each one in its wrappings and sealed it carefully with tape overlaid on the original adhesive. The final trick was putting them back in the same order we had removed them so that Mom and Dad wouldn't be able to tell they had been tampered with. Then Debra locked the closet, and we all crept out to practice our innocent expressions before Mom got home. If my mother suspected, she never let on. And all three of us gave Oscar-worthy performances on Christmas morning, exclaiming with happy surprise as though we'd never seen the presents before.

The most exciting part of the official preparation was the trip to the tree lot to buy the Christmas tree. One evening a few days before Christmas, my mother bundled us all up in our warmest clothes and sent us out with our father to pick the perfect tree. There was something magical about the outing. We settled back in the big, warm car and stared through the windows at the Christmas lights twinkling in the frost along Sunrise Highway. I put my mouth up to the cold glass and watched the mist form like faint snowflakes on the car window. Once we got there, the three of us kids scattered, tramping through the sawdust in every direction to point excitedly to the best tree. My cheeks burned with the cold, and the smell of pine filled my nostrils. It was exhilarating. When we finally finished arguing and agreed on a tree we all liked, my father picked up the seven-foot beauty and tied it in the Cadillac's big trunk. Then it was home again, where Mom was waiting in the living room with hot cocoa and decorations.

As always, we put the tree in front of the big bay window in the living room. Dad strung the tree lights, and then everyone decorated the tree with the ornaments my mother had collected. Each of us children hung the special homemade ornaments we had made for my mom over the years. We nibbled at the homemade popcorn strands while we draped them over the branches, and Mom half-heartedly scolded us for eating the decorations. Every year she made big balls of popcorn and marshmallows for us to wrap in plastic wrap and tie on the branches with ribbon. We weren't allowed to unwrap them until Christmas morning. Mom hung the antique glass ornaments herself. They were very fragile. When all the ornaments were on the tree, Dad lifted Lisa high to place the gold-and-white angel on the very top of the tree. And then came the grand moment. My mother turned out the living room lights, and Dad plugged in the tree lights.

Everyone gasped, oohing and ahhing at the beauty before us. That year's tree was the best ever.

The only thing that marred the festivities was a small incident two days before Christmas. During the night someone stole all the plastic candy canes Dad and I had tacked to the fence posts around the house. My father was really irritated that someone had taken our decorations, and he asked around the neighborhood to see if anybody had seen the thieves. On Christmas Eve morning when my mom opened the door to get the newspaper, a strange thing had happened. Someone had brought back every one of the stolen candy canes, nearly a hundred in all, and carefully stacked them on our porch with a note saying, "Really sorry." I was so surprised that someone would do that. I thought it must be the Christmas spirit.

That evening my mother served the traditional Italian dinner for Holy Night: lobster and shrimp with fish sauce, homemade pasta, piles of side dishes, and more cookies than I could count. Dad made his special Christmas dessert that year, too—*strufale*, deep-fried dough balls rolled in sugar and drizzled with warm honey. They were incredibly sticky but delicious. Grandma was there, and Aunt Marie and her children, Uncle Louis (my father's older brother) with his kids, and of course, my uncle Joe, all of us dressed to the teeth in new Christmas clothes. After dessert, the kids all changed into their pajamas, and we gathered in the living room with our parents. My father always set up toy train tracks around the Christmas tree, and my youngest cousins and I stretched out on our stomachs under the tree and took turns making the train go around. The adults and older children, too full and relaxed even to talk much, settled down on the gold velvet couches and watched Christmas specials on television. *March of the Wooden Soldiers* was first, and then the Yule log came on. My dad had made a cardboard cut-out of a fireplace to fit around the television set, and when the Yule log came on, he put the cut-out around the TV to make it look like a real fireplace. In the silence and beauty of the flickering lights, I could almost believe the fire was real.

A little before ten o'clock, we kids were sent to bed. My boy cousins stayed in my room, the girls with my sisters. I fell asleep almost immediately, but a little after midnight, I woke to hear my mother's voice shouting from the hallway: "Santa came! Get up, everybody! Santa came!" We all went racing for the living room as fast as our feet would carry us. Sure enough, Santa had come. The living room was filled with presents. It didn't lessen my enthusiasm at all that I knew where they really came from.

Nearly all of our presents were special ordered, and mine were amazing. That year I got a safari kit, complete with an outfit, a light gun, and a two-foot plastic lion that would charge until I hit it with a beam of light. The minute the light touched it, the lion fell down and stopped moving. But the best gift of all was a white Jaguar convertible, just my size. It was the most beautiful thing I had ever seen, an exact replica of the real car. The motor was electrical and ran on distilled water. My dad charged it up for me, and I drove it all around the living room. I was so excited, I could hardly breathe. My cousins had a lot of gifts, too, but none as wonderful as my car. When my dad insisted they have a chance to drive it, one of them deliberately smashed it into a railing and then glared at me in triumph. I started crying, but my father reassured me that he would fix it in the morning. I was still crying when Dad carried me to bed. My aunts and uncles, meanwhile, packed up to go home.

The next morning I woke up to the smell of ham and sausage frying. All the sorrows of the night before were forgotten as I threw on my robe and raced down the hall to the kitchen. Dad was there, preparing a huge meal. One of the neighbors had given my parents a big basket of specialty meats, and Dad had sliced them into big slabs and was frying it all up for us to eat so my mom could relax for a while. After stuffing ourselves on pork, eggs, pancakes, and anything else we wanted (Dad took orders), we changed into our play clothes and went back to the living room to explore our new toys. By late morning we could already smell ham and turkey baking in my mother's double oven. Christmas Eve dinner was Italian; Christmas day dinner was American. We had the best of both worlds.

All day long we played while company dropped by to visit. Barbara and Jim came with their kids, chatting in the living room while we kids compared presents and made deals to share the good ones. Freddy came by in the afternoon with his kids. They got miniature motorbikes from Santa, the only gifts so far that could compare with my Jag. Freddy told me not to worry, that he'd teach me to ride the bikes the next time I came over. I generously offered to let his kids drive my car.

An hour or two before dinner, Uncle Mikey and his wife walked through the living room door. Uncle Mikey was dragging the biggest Christmas stocking I'd ever seen in my life. It must have been nearly eight feet long and was filled with teddy bears and Christmas toys. The only other stocking I'd seen that was anything like it was hanging in the main display area of a department store. In fact, this stocking looked almost exactly like the one I'd seen in the store. Uncle Mikey said it was for me and my sisters. We all ran to give him a hug and then began unloading the booty as he watched us with a beaming smile. Later I whispered to my dad privately, "Where did Uncle Mikey get that stocking, Daddy?"

Dad replied, "He told me he won it in a game of craps." Dad looked into my eyes and smiled.

I looked at him a minute and finally said, "Oh." A minute later I had forgotten all about it.

Just before dinner started, I heard a car pull up in front of the house. Peering out the bay window in front, I called out, "Here's Chris!" He was driving his beige Mercedes 450 SL convertible. The polished hood almost glowed in the streetlights. It was the first Mercedes I had seen outside a car lot.

The doorbell rang, and a minute later Chris bounded up the stairs with his usual ebullience. His wife was right behind him, her face covered with smiles, carrying an armload of gifts. Chris's left arm was still in a sling, but he had a holiday basket for my mother in his right hand.

Chris's arrival was followed almost immediately by another ring of the doorbell. My father went down to answer it and returned a couple of minutes later with a tall dark man that he introduced to us as Dominick, Uncle Nino's nephew. Dominick's wife was a pretty brunette, and each of them was carrying a baby girl. My mother introduced herself and made them welcome. I saw her lead Dominick's wife down the hall to put the babies down for a nap.

By that time I was starving; a day of excitement and the amazing aromas drifting from the kitchen were making my stomach growl. When my mother called out that dinner was ready a few minutes later, I couldn't get to the table fast enough.

Dad poured wine in the adults' glasses and soda into ours, then raised his hand for a toast. "To good fortune and friendship!" Everyone clinked their glasses and murmured, "Bona fortuna!" in reply. Dad touched his glass to his lips and then set it down. My father rarely drank alcohol. He said it dulled a man's senses. We children filled our plates at the big table and then went into the adjoining kitchen to eat.

Later that evening, after dinner, I went down the hall to the upstairs bathroom and opened the door to go inside. I jumped when I saw that Chris and his wife were already in there. Chris had taken his bad arm out of the sling and was resting it on the bathroom sink. Gauze and tubes of medicine lay on the counter, and Chris's wife was just throwing a dirty piece of gauze with traces of blood on it into the bathroom trash. What startled me wasn't the blood, though; it was Chris's arm. There was a small hole about half an inch wide on the outside of his upper arm. With the light from the bathroom counter shining right behind it, I could see straight through the hole and out the other side. I froze in fear, staring at the hole. Chris and his wife exchanged a brief glance; then Chris smiled at me and said reassuringly, "It's all right, Albert. She's just fixing up the bandage where I hurt myself. I'll be fine."

I nodded and tried to say something back to him, but I couldn't find my voice. Backing quietly into the hall again, I shut the door behind me.

Uncle Mikey was the first one to take his leave. At sixty-something, he was already exhausted from the long day. Freddy wasn't long behind him; his wife was anxious to get the kids to bed. Chris and his wife kissed everyone good-bye, and I knew Dominick's wife was ready to go. The babies were fussing, and she was starting to give Dominick that look that wives get when their husbands are ignoring them. Dominick told her to be patient, that he just had to speak to Roy for a minute; then he went downstairs to talk to my father in the foyer. My mom sent us kids to our rooms to get ready for bed.

I heard Dominick and his wife say good-bye as I went back to the living room. Dad was smiling. As soon as all three of us kids were back in the living room, he told us to sit down on the couch. He had presents for us from Uncle Nino. All three of us sat down in a row while Dad handed us each an envelope with our name printed on it. An envelope? That didn't seem very interesting. It was kind of plump, though.

I heard Debra scream with excitement as I opened mine. Inside was a bundle of hundred-dollar bills, more money than I had ever seen in my life, far more than I could count at that age. "Oh, my gosh," Debra kept exclaiming. It must have been enough to pay our allowances for the rest of our lives.

My mother's eyes nearly bugged out of her head. "For God's sake, Roy, how much is in there?" she asked.

"Five thousand each," Dad told her. Five thousand dollars? How much was five thousand? It didn't matter. I knew it was a huge amount of money.

"Oh, for cripes sake," I heard my mother mutter. I couldn't tell whether she was pleased or not.

My father picked up on her reaction. "Now kids, that's a lot of money for anybody, especially for a kid. Tomorrow I'm going to let you take one of those bills, and we'll go to the shopping center. You can each pick out one thing. Then we're going to the bank and putting the rest in a savings account for your college."

My mother looked mollified. We were all a little disappointed, but we knew better than to moan and groan. After all, *five thousand dollars.* Wow. Dad collected each of the envelopes from us and told us he'd put them in a safe place until tomorrow.

That night I asked Dad to carry me to bed. As he tucked the covers around me, I said, "Daddy? How did Chris get that hole in his arm?" And I told him what I had seen.

Dad finished tucking the covers around me in silence. Then he looked me matter of factly in the face and said, "He got shot. We can't take him to a hospital because the police will come if we do." That was all he said. Then he kissed me good night, turned off the bedroom light, and shut the door behind him.

I was too exhausted to move. For a little while I lay there quietly, images of the last twenty-four hours swirling through my head. Christmas stockings and Santa Claus and bullet holes and a white Jaguar just my size were still spinning in my brain when I fell asleep.

One Sunday afternoon a few days later, I was cleaning out my father's car. One of my regular chores after church was to clean his Cadillac. He was very particular about keeping it nice. I never minded cleaning it, for I often found interesting things inside, sometimes under the mat or in the box he kept in the trunk. The box with a gun inside was hidden under the spare tire, but I had long since discovered it. I already knew my father carried a gun to work; he even slept with a gun under the bed, but that didn't seem unusual to me. Lots of people we knew had guns. On this day, though, I found more than his gun. Hidden under the floor mat by the driver's seat was a knife. And when I opened the box under the spare tire, I found a fake beard and moustache, several hats, and three pairs of Isotoner gloves. My head started spinning. Why would anyone take these things to work? What did my father do with them? And why were they hidden?

That night my father was out late again. Instead of cuddling up on his chest and drifting off to sleep, I went upstairs at bedtime and crawled into bed alone. Lying there in the darkness, I kept seeing the gun and the knife and the box of disguises and the bullet hole in Chris's arm. For the first time, an inarticulate fear began to form in my chest. What was my father doing out there in the darkness? What was so dangerous that it required weapons and disguises? What if something bad happened to him while he was doing it? What if he never came home?

three

· ·

LITTLE MAN

MY FATHER WITH UNCLE ALBERT AND UNCLE DOMINIC: MY MAFIA CARD

Shades of the prison-house begin to close
Upon the growing Boy.

—WORDSWORTH, *"Ode: Intimations of Immortality*
from Recollections of Early Childhood"

It was my father himself who slowly began cracking the window to give me glimpses of the world he inhabited outside Massapequa. Just as other fathers took their sons for a tour of the fire station or insurance office, so my father began showing me the way his business functioned, the tools of his trade. Neither my mother nor my sisters shared in the knowledge he began to impart to me. It was a man's thing, passed on from father to son.

I started learning about guns when I was six. My father imparted these lessons as matter of factly as he taught me to build shelves or install decking. My dad bought and sold guns regularly, and he was an educated collector. He particularly liked the antiques, pistols from the Civil War and before. Sometimes he would bring home an entire bag of guns and empty them onto the workbench to disassemble and clean in the garage workshop. The mechanics fascinated me; and by the time I was eight, I could disassemble and reassemble virtually any gun like an expert. Dad was careful and precise when handling a gun, and he made certain I never touched one carelessly. He always wore gloves when he handled a weapon. Isotoner gloves were the best, he told me, for it enabled a person to work efficiently without leaving fingerprints.

My father also taught me utter respect for the power that a gun implied. I learned to assume that a gun is probably loaded, that if I picked one up, I should point it down away from others, that I should never point a gun at anybody unless I was prepared to use it, that using a gun was a serious thing. If it became necessary to shoot someone, the safest thing was to aim for the head and get off at least two bullets. If you aimed for the torso, the other person might shoot you back before you got off a second shot. I understood the gravity of what he was telling me, and it never occurred to me to aim a gun at a human being myself. I knew that Jimmy's father used a gun at work, and I sensed that shooting must form some part of my father's job. I never handled a gun without my father's permission. I knew that my dad kept a gun under the bed all the time, but it never occurred to me to touch it. It was a given that the weapon was off limits. My father got me my first gun when I was six, a little .22, and took me upstate to a friend's farm to teach me how to fire it. I was allowed to shoot only at targets. One day I shot a chipmunk while I was practicing in the brush, and my father was furious. "What did that chipmunk ever do to you?" he asked me. "You don't shoot nothing without a good reason."

My father began taking me with him into the social clubs in Manhattan, especially in Little Italy about the time I entered the third grade. His business was taking up more and more of his time by then. I would kiss him good-bye when I left for school in the morning, but I was often in bed long before he got home at night. So the weekends became more important than ever. When there was business to conduct on a Saturday or Sunday afternoon, I would make the long drive across the bridge and into the crowded streets of the city with him.

The first social club I remember going to was in Manhattan. I was about eight years old at the time. I don't remember its name. What I do remember is the sense of overwhelming noise and confusion as the men who guarded the entrance opened its doors for us. The place was crowded with small tables where men were playing cards; in a corner another group watched a horse race on a TV mounted above the bar. They were all screaming at the television, either cheering or cursing the horses they had bet on. Almost everyone seemed to know my dad. Guys called, "Hey, Roy!" as my father shook the occasional hand and said hello. Within moments of our arrival other men started approaching my dad to ask him about balloons. The one who got to us first said, "Roy, how ya doin? I need to borrow fifty balloons. Think you could help me out?"

Dad replied, "Sure, no problem, I got fifty with me. Let's take a walk."

All three of us went back outside and started walking down the sidewalk as Dad and the man chatted vaguely about their families. I stretched my legs to keep pace with them, filled with curiosity. Balloons? Dad had balloons? Where were they? In the trunk? Or were we going someplace else? A few blocks away we came to a small café and went inside to sit down. Dad ordered espresso and pastry for all three of us. I grimaced as I sipped the hot, bitter liquid, proud to be included as one of the men. Dad and the man continued to chat about their families, the weather, how the Yankees were doing that year. Finally Dad said, "The usual arrangement."

The man replied, "Sure, no problem." Dad signaled the waitress for the check, and as he reached in his pocket to peel off a twenty from the roll he carried, I noticed him pulling out some envelopes. As he laid the twenty on the check with one hand, I saw him deftly pass five envelopes under the table with the other. The other man, also without looking at them, slipped the envelopes inside his jacket pocket as we rose to go. Back out on the sidewalk, Dad and the man shook hands good-bye, and we walked back toward the car.

Puzzled and a little disappointed, I reached up to touch my father's sleeve.

"Daddy?"

"What, Son?"

"Could I have one of those balloons?"

My father burst out laughing and then stopped walking and turned to me. Bending down, he said, "We weren't talking about real balloons. We were talking about money. A 'balloon' means one thousand dollars. That man wanted to borrow money."

So that was it. Those envelopes had money in them. Dad was lending money to the man, just like he loaned it to Uncle Vinny. It made sense. I knew Dad owned part of a credit union in Brooklyn; I'd been there with him once or twice.

"Why didn't he come to your bank, Dad?"

"Sometimes people have problems and they need money, but they don't own enough property to get money from a bank. You need to own things if you want money from a bank. And sometimes people need money in a hurry, and it takes a while to get it. So I loan it to them myself, and they pay it back with a little extra. It costs them a little more cause I'm taking a chance on them, but it usually works out pretty good for everybody."

It sounded fair to me.

Going into the business district was okay, but I much preferred going to Little Italy. So many interesting things went on there. Little Italy was well named, for it was a microcosm of a Mediterranean nation in a few square blocks. The streets were narrow, teeming with vehicles, merchandise, and people. The signs on the buildings seemed to fall over each other as they competed for attention: restaurants, Italian delis, cigar stores, sidewalk bins of movie posters, and clothing—anything and everything to attract a buyer or to fascinate an eight-year-old boy. Trucks filled with merchandise waited to be unloaded, clogging the streets. The storefront windows reflected a thousand faces, of every age, most dark eyed and rapt in conversation. I almost never saw any policemen there like I did when

we went to other parts of Manhattan. There was no one to direct traffic when the streets got full. Pedestrians wound along the crowded
sidewalks, dodging stalls of merchandise and café tables. Most people, however, remained restlessly stationary, leaning against cars to
bullshit, crowding their chairs around outdoor tables. Restaurants
outnumbered other businesses by far, all of them crowded on a
sunny weekend afternoon. The occasional tourist snapped pictures,
but no one paid attention.

Little Italy was a magical place for me in those days. I loved walking down the street next to my father. On warm days, the air was always filled with scents of garlic, olive oil, and warm bread as we
passed by. The sidewalk tables were at eye level for me back then, and
I could see what everyone was eating as I strode down the street next
to my dad. I always wore my best clothes on these trips: dress shirt,
nice slacks, my shoes carefully polished. I did my best to look just
like my dad when we went out together, hair slicked back and a roll of
dollar bills rubber banded in my pocket like my dad. That was the way
a man carried his money. Many children that age would hold their
parent by the hand, but not me. I kept my chin up, eyes straight
ahead, chest out in a miniature version of my father's swagger. At
home I was still a little boy, but in Little Italy we were two men—big
man and little man—doing business in the city together.

I loved trucks, and there seemed to be one on every corner we
passed. All of them were open in the back, and when I peeked in, I
saw racks of suits or boxes of electronics. There was always a man
leaning up against the truck or watching it from a few yards away
while other men came in and out of stores or alleys, unloading whatever was in the back. Sometimes they took the boxes out of one truck
and put them into another. The most exciting part of it was that I was
almost sure to get something from a truck whenever we went visiting
that part of the city. The first time Dad took me to Mulberry Street,
there was an open truck being unloaded just a few yards from where

my father parked. The minute we got out of the car, the man watching the truck noticed us and came running over to see my dad. "Hey, Roy! We got some good VCRs over here! Let me get ya a couple." Then turning to the men unloading the truck bed, he shouted, "Hey, boys! Grab a couple of VCRs for Roy!" Within minutes the trunk of our Cadillac was filled with boxes of VCRs. Dad shut the trunk and smiled at me as we started back down the street.

"Just a little gesture of respect, son," he told me. Everyone, it seemed, respected my father. I thought it was wonderful that everyone seemed to know my father and that they all wanted to give us gifts. I could tell my father was proud to have me see how much everyone seemed to like him.

Dad and I soon developed a ritual on these trips to Mulberry Street. First we would stop at one of our favorite cafés, where my dad would buy me a treat. I never chose a child's dish; my favorite was my father's: a cup of espresso and a San Giuseppe—a rich creamy dough, deep-fried and then drenched in cinnamon honey. When it came time to pay, the owner of the establishment would always refuse to bring us a check, saying he didn't want my father's money. And every time we walked out the door, my father would throw a twenty on the counter as we passed.

Afterward we went to see Uncle Nino at the Ravenite Social Club. He and my father did business there. There were always a lot of beautiful cars nearby, shiny black Cadillacs, BMWs, and Mercedes parked on the sidewalk and the street in front of the entrance. A guy on each corner and across the street kept an eye on the cars. There were usually several young guys hanging around out front, washing and polishing the cars or offering to run errands for the men who went into the club. They always rushed forward to pay their respects to my father and me. The entrance was guarded by big men in ugly suits who opened the door for some men and frowned at others to stay away. Once I saw a man at the entrance take a camera from a tourist and

break it when the man wouldn't stop taking pictures. The men guarding the door would nod at my father and reach for the shiny brass
handle to open the door for us. They always glanced around first to
make sure no strangers got a look inside. The doors were dark green
with glass on top covered by lace curtains blocking the view from the
street. The windows on either side, also curtained, were always shiny
clean, with gold letters spelling out "Members Only" in each corner.
It made me feel important to know that I was welcome in a place most
men weren't allowed to enter. I never saw another child there.

The moment I crossed the threshold, time always seemed to slow
down. Walking into the social club always felt slightly surreal to me,
like entering another world. As the doors shut behind me, I was
plunged into a dusky world filled with strange sights and sounds.
Bare bulbs with mushroom glass covers dangled from the ceiling,
giving just enough light to see.

Straight ahead of me was the bar, with its large espresso machine
towering above, almost as tall as my father. The machine was huge,
glowing brass with an eagle on the top, its wings spread in flight. It
was the most beautiful thing I had ever seen. I gazed up at it in awe.
The aroma of the coffee beans washed over me as I drew near. Mixed
with the aroma of espresso were the scents of food, much like Uncle
Frank's restaurant. A table near the bar was covered with Italian pastry, piles of cannoli and other rich delicacies. Large platters of antipasti were laid out, heaped with cold cuts and a variety of cheeses.
Every couple of hours the restaurant down the street would deliver
hot food—pasta, meat dishes, whatever anyone wanted. Servers from
the restaurants laid the food out on the tables and quietly disappeared back outside. Next to the bar was an old-fashioned candy
counter with display cases at eye level for me. To my disappointment,
no one ever put any candy in it. The only candy I ever saw there was a
dusty roll of Neccos that remained untouched week in and week out.
There was a cigarette machine next to it, also empty. I asked my dad

for quarters for the machine, just for the fun of punching the buttons, but my dad said there wasn't anything in it.

There were usually fifty or sixty men gathered around plain wooden tables in groups of five or six on a weekend afternoon. The chairs they sat on were red Naugahyde with brass studs. Like everything else in the place, the chairs were worn but clean. The dark floors were made of wood, scuffed from generations of men walking their boards. The white walls were bare except for some pictures of saints. The only decorations were a painted wooden statue of the pope, about three feet tall, and another of the Virgin Mary and the Christ Child.

There were two main rooms at the Ravenite: one in the front where people ate and played cards, another in the back where private business was conducted. There were no women there, and I never saw anyone in a uniform. Everyone wore nice slacks or a suit, and most of the men were swarthy and dark haired like my dad. The main room was filled with activity, dozens of men eating or playing cards. The front of the room was crowded with men watching a television mounted on the wall inside the entrance. Just as in the club near the business district, there was always a horse race showing, and the shouting and cursing of the onlookers made it hard to hear. In a smaller room in the back, the atmosphere was quieter. This room was much darker than the room out front. This was where we met Uncle Nino to do business.

People came and went continually, and everybody seemed to have something to buy or sell. The negotiating was ordinarily fast and furious. Three or four guys would sit at a table doing deals. One had a truckload of electronics to sell, another had cases of fine watches, another exotic fruit. Sometimes the buying and selling was outright; other times it was a series of elaborate trades. One guy would hook the other guy up with a buyer in exchange for something he needed. Occasionally one of the men would leave for a few minutes and come back with a sample of his merchandise. Other men would be talking money. "Joe over here needs fifty thousand, he's got a little union problem he needs to take care of." Or "Tony needs a little start-up money for his shop." Someone usually wanted to talk to my dad about getting a little help. After a while I would get bored and go looking for something to do.

I usually gravitated toward the old men who gathered at the club. While my father conducted boring business, I sat at the table with them to eat and play cards. I loved listening to their stories about the old country. My father taught me to have respect for older people; he told me that they were living history books, full of wisdom. I got to know many of them after a while. They liked me, for I was a polite boy. I would kiss them in greeting, call them "Uncle" or "Mister," and always remember to say "please" and "thank you." Some of them had no grandchildren, and as I was the only child in the club, they looked forward to seeing me. I felt like a lucky boy, for though both of my own grandfathers had died before I was born, the social club gave me a roomful of grandfathers to tell me stories, give me treats, and pat me on the head. I felt comfortable with them, more comfortable than I did with the kids at school.

One afternoon at the Ravenite, my father stuck his head out of the back room and called me over to him. "Go out to the car and bring in that package for me. You know the one. It's for Uncle Nino." He handed me the keys to the Cadillac.

I went outside and got the package out of the trunk. I knew there was a gun in it, because I had watched my father wrap it. I put the package inside my shirt, as I had seen my father do with other packages, and carried it back inside to Uncle Nino. He sat at the table with my father and two men I didn't know. As he took the package, Nino said, "So Albert, what do you think of the gun?"

I instinctively replied, "What gun?" Somehow I knew that I shouldn't acknowledge what was in the package.

Uncle Nino smiled at me and nodded his approval.

A few minutes later my father told me he wanted to introduce me to someone very special. We into the back room again, and I saw an elderly man seated at the table next to Uncle Nino. He was average height, with receding white hair and a lined tan face. He looked like an ordinary old grandfather, the kind I saw feeding pigeons in the park near home. The only thing that set him apart was his grooming. He was expensively dressed, with an Italian suit and shoes like my father's. He wore a diamond on his pinky finger, and his nails were beautifully manicured. My father introduced him to me as Mr. Dellacroce. I kissed him politely, and he said something to my father and patted me on the head. Then my father said, "Tell Mr. Dellacroce what you do if you have to shoot somebody, Al."

I knew the answer; my father had taught it to me when we were cleaning guns one day in the workshop. I promptly recited, "Two in the head, make sure they're dead."

I paused, and my father prompted me with a nod. Remembering the rest, I finished, "Then slit their fucking throats!"

Mr. Dellacroce guffawed, then said, "Good boy!" and bent over to give me a kiss. All the men were laughing. My father ruffled my hair and beamed with pride. I loved getting laughs. I'd even gotten to say a dirty word right out loud. Dad and I never used dirty words around my mother, only when we were alone. I started laughing with them. It was good to be in on the joke. In the car on the way home, my father talked to me about Neil Dellacroce.

"You can't always tell a man's importance just by looking at him, Al. That frail old man is very, very powerful. All he has to do is nod his head and hundreds of men will kill for him. That's why you must always be careful and respectful. You don't always know who you're really talking to." I was very surprised. To me Mr. Dellacroce seemed like just another grandfather telling stories.

I found out years later that he was the last surviving member of

Lucky Luciano's Murder, Inc., the most dangerous gang in the 1930s. He was also the underboss of the Gambino family.

In the dozens of trips I made to social clubs with my father, no one ever asked me to leave so they could talk. The moment someone approached my father, I walked away, but invariably I would be told, "No, no, you can stay, Albert. It's okay." I usually retreated to a distance anyway; though on the occasions I did stay, I seldom understood the discussion. I heard a great deal that I didn't understand, but I instinctively knew that the conversations were meant to be secret. Unless somebody was selling something, everything they said was so vague that it didn't mean anything to me. I couldn't have repeated anything meaningful if I'd wanted to.

Usually I didn't say a word during the conversations between my father and Uncle Nino at the Ravenite. One afternoon, however, I found myself drawn into their conversation for the first time. They were talking about a trial. Somebody they knew had been arrested, and the police had tapes of the guy committing the crime. Apparently the police were also helping Uncle Nino because he was talking about a cop who had brought him copies of all the reports. Uncle Nino was reading the cop's reports as I sat there. He handed the sheets to my father as he finished each one, and they spoke about what they were reading. Uncle Nino seemed pretty worried.

"We can't afford to have him go down for this. We gotta make those tapes disappear."

"I thought you had a guy on the inside," my father replied.

"I do. I could have him lift the tapes from the evidence room, but then they might be on to him. He's too valuable to lose. Besides, he might sell me out if he has to deal."

"There has to be a way to get rid of those tapes without getting caught."

As the men pondered out loud, throwing out ideas, I remembered something I'd learned at school. We were studying magnets, and the teacher had showed us what happened when you put a magnet next to an electronic tape. The magnet lifted the particles and erased the tape. I waited until he and Uncle Nino paused for a minute, and then said to my father, "Why don't you just put a magnet next to the tapes? That would erase them, wouldn't it?"

My father stared at me a moment; then he and Uncle Nino started to laugh. Finally Nino said, "The kid's right, Roy." Then turning to me, "You're one smart kid, you know that, Albert?" My heart swelled with pride. Uncle Nino ordered ice cream for me while my father went down the street to a hardware store and bought a big magnet. He returned a few minutes later and handed it to Nino. All the men slapped me on the back as we left that day. My father beamed with approval.

That evening when we pulled into the driveway at home, I saw Lisa sitting on the front steps waiting for us. Her small face was pale and worried as we got out of the car. The moment my father saw her face, he went over and sat beside her, putting his arm around her and looking into her eyes.

"Are you all right, honey? Is everything all right?"

Lisa's face was serious as she replied, "Daddy, I need to tell you something. Something bad."

"What is it, sweetheart?"

"I broke the basement window in the back. I didn't mean to do it. I was playing with my ball. I wanted to tell you because you told me it's always better to be honest, and I promised never to lie to you. You can take the money to fix it out of my allowance. Are you mad at me, Daddy?"

My father drew her onto his lap and held her tight. I saw his eyes fill with tears. "No, sweetheart, I'm not mad at you. It was an accident. You're my honest girl." Looking at my little sister's sober face, I suddenly didn't feel quite so proud of myself. I caught my father's eye, and he looked away. I felt as though a rock had formed in my stomach as we went inside to have dinner.

A couple of months later I asked my dad what ever happened to the tapes. He said a policeman put the magnet next to the tapes in the evidence room, and it erased everything on them just like I'd expected. When the lawyer played them in court, there was nothing but silence. The lawyer was furious, but no one could figure out how it had happened.

From then on, I enjoyed a new status among my father's associates at the social club. I had proven myself to be more than just Roy's son. Each time I went downtown with my father, men competed for the honor of giving me things. I could choose whatever I wanted from the trucks being unloaded on Mulberry Street. Guys from the club carried food back from restaurants for me. I could have the best food in Little Italy any time I wanted, in any amount I wanted. If I said some ice cream or a candy bar sounded good, someone would rush off to get it. If they got the wrong flavor, they went right back out the door to buy the right one. At school I was a well-behaved third-grade kid learning my multiplication tables in a back-row desk, but in the social clubs I was a little man who basked in my father's power.

That spring, with the return of warm weather, my father spent more time at home on the weekends, preparing the soil for my mother to plant. I started working in the small garden my father had dug for me, planting vegetables for the summer. It felt good to be outside instead of cooped up in a smoky room. My mother's bulbs were already sprouting, and daffodils and narcissus peeked through the gaps in the picket fence. As Easter approached, I prepared to take my first communion in the Lutheran church where my sisters and I attended Sunday school. My mother took me to May's to buy me a new suit for the occasion and told me Easter dinner would be extra-special that year in honor of my communion. My father brought home a whole pig from the butcher's to cook for Easter dinner, and my relatives and Uncle Mikey were invited to share the occasion.

The pig was stuffed with fruit and was rotating on a spit in the upstairs kitchen by the time we got up on Easter morning. The Easter

Bunny always came the night before to hide our baskets, and though I had outgrown believing in the bunny, I hadn't outgrown the basket. Even my older sister, who was nearly fourteen, loved the annual basket hunt. All three of us tumbled out of bed to begin the search before we even had breakfast. The "Bunny" was fiendishly clever when it came to hiding baskets, and that year it took us over an hour of determined searching to find them. We spread out all over the house, opening cupboards and ransacking every possible hiding place. Debra finally found her basket hidden among boxes of memorabilia in the attic. Mine was stashed behind a box of my father's tools in the basement workshop, but Lisa's was nowhere to be found. After we found our own, Debra and I pitched in to help her find it, but it was no good; we couldn't find it anywhere. Finally Lisa started crying and ran to my father for comfort, saying the Easter Bunny had forgotten her.

My father picked her up in his arms and reassured her that the Bunny would never forget a girl as good as she was. Then he took her upstairs and hinted that she might see it in the yard if she looked out the upstairs window. Lisa stuck her head through the open window and there, suspended from a hook on a rope from the attic, hung her basket. She screamed with joy as Dad pulled it up to the window for her. Everything in our baskets, even the chocolates, was homemade and absolutely delicious. We were happily covered in sugar syrup and chocolate when Mom called us to the breakfast table, already too full to eat. My mother just laughed when she saw us and sent us down the hall to wash off and get dressed for Sunday school. A while later we lined up for inspection, me in my new suit and my sisters in beautiful pastel dresses. Then it was off to church and Easter services.

The relatives had already started arriving by the time we got home, but my father had an errand to run in Little Italy before dinner, and he took me with him. He had given me a small diamond pinky ring that matched his for a communion gift, and when we got downtown, he had me show it off to the men at the Ravenite. When I showed it to the first man and told him what it was for, he immediately got to his feet, congratulated me on this holy occasion, and gave me a fifty-dollar bill. All around him other men began getting to their feet to fall in line behind him and pay their respects to me. One after another, they blessed me and put one-hundred-dollar bills into my hand. No one else gave me less than a hundred dollars, and some of them gave two hundred. By that time, the first man to congratulate me had noticed with embarrassment the amounts other men were giving me. So he got in line again and gave me another hundred, calling it "an additional gift." I looked at the growing pile of bills with amazement, politely thanking each man as he handed me the cash and bent to kiss my cheek. When it was all over, I had added nearly three thousand dollars to my little roll of bills. I shoved it deep into my pocket for the ride home.

By the time we got back, Uncle Joe and Uncle Louis and Aunt Marie and all the cousins were there. I put my money on the top shelf in my room, in the box where I kept my trick cards and other treasures, and went outside to play. High from the sugar we'd been eating all morning, we kids ran around the backyard and ruined our new clothes while the women finished preparing Easter dinner. My grandmother made her Easter bread from a secret recipe. It was heavy and rich with eggs and butter. My mother made grain pie from a traditional Italian recipe that called for soaking whole grain overnight and then mixing it with ricotta cheese and sugar. She had already made two kinds of pie and cake and her anisette cookies, another Easter specialty. My aunt made pizza rustica, a kind of deep-dish pie made with ham and a mixture of Italian cheeses. The roast pig was served whole on a big platter in the center of the dining room table. As everyone sat down, my mother made a little speech congratulating me on my first communion, and everyone offered me blessings. My father had me show everyone my new ring. I saw my older cousin Benny roll his eyes and look at his sister, but everyone else complimented me politely on my ring when I proudly told them it was just like Dad's. Then my mother announced, "Let's eat," and everyone forgot about anything but the food.

Uncle Mikey had just gotten back from a vacation in Italy with his wife, and he kept everyone entertained with stories of his travels while we ate. Dad had arranged for them to visit our family's ancestral town, and they toured in style. Mikey's wife talked about the villas and the gardens, but Uncle Mikey had better stories to tell. He'd found out the hard way that some of the bathroom facilities were pretty crude in the area, so he was caught unprepared when there was no toilet paper. The only thing he had with him was his wallet, stuffed with Italian lira, so he took out a handful of bills and used them to wipe his backside. When he told his hosts about it afterward, expecting them to laugh, they were amazed that anyone could be wealthy enough to do that. Word circulated through the village that Mikey was fabulously wealthy. And even though the lira were worth far less than American dollars, some enterprising teenagers went excavating in the facilities and managed to dig up the lira. Uncle Mikey roared with laughter as he told me about it. I could tell from my mother's face that she didn't think it was an appropriate story to tell at the dinner table, but I didn't care. I laughed so hard, I spit my food out.

That night, when my father came to my room to tuck me in, I was still smiling about Uncle Mikey's story. As my father tucked the covers around me, I said, "Dad?"

"What, son?"

"Why does everyone call Uncle Mikey 'Mikey Hammer'? Nobody calls his wife Mrs. Hammer."

My father replied, "Well, you know, Uncle Mikey was kind of a tough guy when he was younger. He used to collect cash from people who owed me and some other guys money. Sometimes the people wouldn't pay what they owed. Now Uncle Mikey's a real gentle guy, but if someone won't pay up, what are you gonna do? So every now and then Uncle Mikey would break a couple of their knuckles with a hammer as a kind of reminder they'd better pay. After a while people started calling him Mikey Hammer."

I felt my fingers flinch involuntarily. Uncle Mikey? Break people's knuckles? He was one of the nicest guys I knew. It didn't make sense. I shoved the image out of my mind and turned over to go to sleep. I drifted off dreaming of chocolate bunnies, hundred-dollar bills, and broken knuckles.

School was out at long last, and my sisters and I returned to the freedom of daily swims and evening barbecues. That summer Dad and I put laid concrete in the area behind the workshop, around the barbecue pit. That was also the summer my father rescued a small frog, left abandoned by its family in the backyard. My father was always rescuing wild creatures. My uncle Joe told me that when they were kids, he and my dad would go out in the backyard when the birds settled in the trees. He said my dad would stand very still, and the sparrows would come and land on his arms and hands. He'd never seen anything like it. My father dug a space for the tiny frog in the damp soil under the back porch, and every morning he would bring out a palm leaf filled with food and hand feed the small creature before he left for work. The frog wouldn't let the rest of us near him, but it had no fear of my father and would hop onto his hand to be stroked. Soon the frog would come hopping out from under the porch as soon as he heard my father's footsteps. My dad warned the man who mowed our lawn to be extra careful in the area around the porch, so that the frog would come to no harm.

One morning I woke up to hear my father screaming at someone outside. I ran downstairs and into the backyard to find my father yelling at the gardener. Dad's face was purple with rage. I had never seen him like that. I heard him shout, "You fucking idiot, what did I tell you? Now get out of here and don't come back! You're fired!" In

Dad's hand was a small misshapen green thing. When I looked closer, I could see that it was his pet frog, the lower half cut off by the lawn mower. It was dead. Dad's hand was shaking, and there were tears in his eyes.

Dad said nothing to me. Instead he walked past me into the work-shop and came out a few moments later carrying a small garden trowel. He walked over to the big tree near the swing set, then knelt down to dig a hole six inches wide and almost as deep. Ever so care-fully, he bent over and placed the mangled remains of the small frog in the hole. Then he filled the hole with dirt, gently smoothing the mound with his hand and scattering grass over the top. When he went back in the house, I touched his hand as he passed by. He did his best to smile at me.

Freddy brought his kids over to swim in our pool that August, and the following weekend my dad asked me if I wanted to go with him to Freddy's house to ride the motorbikes. I was very excited. I loved going to Freddy's house. I sat in the kitchen drinking coffee with Mrs. DiNome while Freddy and my dad went down to the basement to talk. A few minutes later I heard my father's voice from the room below. He sounded angry. I went downstairs to the basement to see what was going on.

My dad was talking about the new wide-screen television and VCR that Freddy had set up in the living room. He was yelling at Freddy, "What do you think you're doing, you idiot? How many times do I got to tell you, you never keep the merchandise for yourself. The police come here, they see the ID tags, they're going to know it's stolen. It's bad enough you got all this stuff in the basement. You should keep it in a warehouse. You're going to get caught." Freddy looked embar-rassed, and a few minutes later we left without riding the bikes.

For the first time it dawned on me that the boxes Freddy always kept in his basement weren't his.

"Dad?" I said. "Where does Freddy get all that stuff?"

"Give-ups, mostly. The truck drivers park the trucks where

Freddy can find them and then leave them there while he cleans them out. Sometimes the stores are in on it, too. The managers get greedy or the owner wants the insurance money. They get a double cut that way. Every now and then he hijacks them, but mostly they're give-ups."

I felt a twist of anxiety. Freddy was stealing things, just like Uncle Vinny, but Freddy wasn't taking only fruit or janitors' uniforms. He was stealing big things, expensive things. That's what the men at the Ravenite meant when they said things had fallen off trucks. And the people who drove the trucks and ran the stores were helping him do it. It seemed like everyone was mixed up in stealing things. Did the police know what was going on? And how did my father fit into all of this?

That fall I started the fourth grade. For Halloween that year my mother made me a leopard costume that felt like real fur. She always made all of our costumes herself on the sewing machine downstairs. For trick-or-treat night she decorated the house inside and out with ghosts and skeletons and baked treats for the kids in the neighborhood. Dozens of homemade caramel apples dried on waxed paper on the kitchen counter, and she made taffy and fudge as well. Neither of my parents liked us to go out trick-or-treating, for fear we would get a razor blade or poison in one of the treats. Instead we had a big costume party and invited all the kids for blocks around. We ate piles of goodies and bobbed for apples and sat in the dark with flashlights while my father told ghost stories. They gave me delicious shivers. He looked scary telling creepy stories in the dark, not like my father at all.

Though I continued to do well in school, I felt more like an alien among my schoolmates with every month that went by. My world centered around my father; and bit by bit, I was becoming more comfortable in his environment than with other fourth-graders.

Sometimes I felt like an adult surrounded by children at school, and though I didn't like it, I didn't know how to change it. Other boys my age were joining the Boy Scouts or Little League, but my free time was spent in the workshop with my father or visiting his friends in the city. My whole world was wrapped up in his.

Each morning before school, I sat in my parents' master bedroom and watched my father turn from a suburban dad into a wiseguy. It became a type of ritual between us. Freshly showered and shaved, my father would put on the expensive tailor-made suits and silk shirts that were the trademarks of his profession. He would slip on his Italian loafers, always impeccably shined, and then go to his dresser for his jewelry. He always wore the diamond on his left pinky finger, and on his left wrist a platinum watch with a smooth band and a circlet of diamonds around the crystal. Fastening his watch and checking his appearance one last time in the mirror, he would scoop me up in his arms for a hug. I always hated to let him go. I had the uneasy feeling he might not return.

I turned ten that January. I was learning more week by week about how my father made his living, but I still had no name to put to what he did. Dad was patient and gentle at home and always polite in his business dealings. In spite of the things I heard and saw on my outings with him, the line between legal and illegal was blurry for me. The social clubs I visited contained many legitimate business people, and I knew that Dad and Uncle Nino worked with the police all the time. I knew Freddy stole things, but he was a regular visitor on Sunday evenings, where he chatted happily with my father's best friend, the policeman. My father loaned people money in clubs in the city, but he also loaned money the usual way from a credit union in Brooklyn. Freddy put tags on stolen cars for my father, but my dad sold cars from a lot on the highway just like all the other car dealers in the neighborhood. It was hopelessly confusing.

I was halfway through the fourth grade when I finally put a name to what my father did for a living. The first two *Godfather* movies had been released while I was in kindergarten and first grade, and by the time I was ten, every kid in school had heard of the Mafia. One day during a visit to the joke store, I saw some fake ID cards that said, "Member of the Mafia," with a place to sign your name. I thought it would be funny to buy one and carry it around to show the other kids.

I showed the card to my father that Saturday. I expected him to chuckle and say, "Pretty funny, son," but instead he roared with laughter. My mother didn't seem to think it was so funny. Their reactions puzzled me. That afternoon, when we left for a trip to Mulberry Street, my father told me to take my ID card with me. When we found Uncle Nino at the Ravenite, Dad told me to show him my card. It was the first time I had heard Nino laugh really loud. Something strange was going on. I liked the card, but it wasn't that funny. Nino told me to go show it to my friends in the other room. Every time I showed it to someone, he started laughing like it was the funniest thing he had ever seen and handed the card to a friend. One of the men told another guy, "Hey, Tony, maybe we should get ourselves one of these. Whadda ya think?" An idea started to dawn on me. I had to find out if I was right.

I was reading at the eighth-grade level by then, and I had begun reading the morning newspaper along with my dad that summer. Usually I preferred the comics. Now, however, I started paying attention to what my father read. Each day he pored over the *New York Post* and the *Daily News* religiously. I noticed he always went to the obituaries first, then to the crime section. I began to read the same sections of the paper when I came home from school every afternoon, holed up in my room after I finished my homework. The papers were filled with detailed descriptions of murders and robberies, along with references to "reputed mobsters," sometimes by name. The descriptions of the murders were often frightening. But what frightened me far more was the familiarity of some of the names they mentioned. Some of the men I knew from the social clubs had the same last names. Could they be the same guys? I didn't dare ask anyone, not even my father. Once the idea began to germinate, however, it started putting down roots, deep poison roots of terror. I had to know the truth. And no one could find it for me, but me.

My father was gone more than usual the next couple of days, and he seemed preoccupied. He didn't smile as much as usual, and when I talked to him, his mind seemed to be a million miles away. When he left the house late one afternoon, I saw that he was dressed in a black suit and tie. Every instinct told me that something had happened, and my suspicions were further heightened when my mother abruptly turned off the television in the den before the evening news came on. I was already in the habit of watching the news, but on this night, my mother told me to go to my room and leave the television off. I went through the motions of obeying, but the minute she went back upstairs, I crept down the hall to the den and turned the TV back on with the volume down low. The news broadcast showed a church with tall brass doors and a circular stained window, and the broadcaster's voiceover informed viewers that they were watching the funeral mass of Carlo Gambino, godfather of New York's most powerful Mafia family. While the cameras rolled, the doors opened and the mourners filed out of the church, ducking their heads to avoid the cameras. Suddenly time stopped. My heart rose up and choked me as the camera caught two men emerging from the church: Uncle Nino, wearing his sunglasses like always, and right behind him—my father. My entire body went numb. I hurriedly switched off the television and rushed back down the hall to my bedroom. Images from the newspapers swirled through my head, a kaleidoscope of brutality, of swift and brutal death. Somewhere in the blur of those images, everything I had heard and seen for the last five years came into focus. My father was a mobster. He was part of the Mafia. I was dizzy with fear.

I had always made a point to tell my father good-bye when he left the house. Each time I would put my arms around his neck to kiss him and say, "I love you, Daddy."

And he would scoop me up in his arms and reply, "I love you too, Al." Now, however, the ritual took on a new urgency. From the night I saw his face on the television set, I lived in constant terror of losing my father. My greatest fear was that I would never see him again, and he would die without knowing I loved him.

I lay alone in the darkness that night, watching the dial on my clock creep around until three in the morning. When my father's headlights finally hit the wall beneath my window, I cried with relief. I would lie awake the next night, and the night after that, always waiting to hear my father's car in the driveway.

I never slept through the night again.

four

GEMINI

POSING FOR THE CAMERA

Though nothing can bring back the hour
Of splendor in the grass, of glory in the flower.

—WORDSWORTH, *"Ode: Intimations of Immortality from*
Recollections of Early Childhood"

From the moment I saw my father's face on the evening news, I began an agonizing process of gambling with eternity to keep my father alive. At night I lay awake, straining to hear the sound of my father's car in the driveway, bargaining with the Angel of Death. Sometimes I flipped a coin: If I got heads twice in a row, my father would come home alive. Other times I made small offerings to the Almighty, like a gambler offering up his best poker chips. I would get better grades, stop swearing, help my mother more, anything God wanted if He would only protect my father. And each time I heard the Cadillac's engine and ran to my bedroom window to look down at my father's figure in the half-light below, I would press my face against the glass and fervently thank whatever power had brought him home to me one more time.

As the only son, I was gradually being initiated into my father's rituals. My mother and sisters would never meet the people I met with my father, never enter the door of rooms reserved for men only. They did not even know that these rooms, these people, existed. My father went out of his way to protect them from that knowledge. Part of the task of keeping them safe in their ignorance now fell to me.

The horses were one small example of this. My older sister,

Debra, loved to ride, a passion she shared with my father. On sunny days when Dad was free from business for a few hours, he would take Debra to a stable on the shore of Long Island. The two of them would gallop down the beach together, joined by the exhilaration of the moment. I, on the other hand, was taken to the trainers and the tracks to watch the betting and learn how to fix a horse race. My father explained that the most common method was for the trainer to put cotton up a horse's nose so it would get winded in the backstretch and fade at the end. The jockeys and even the owners were often involved in these scams, betting against their own horses if it meant making money. It was always about the money. My father had contempt for people who threw their money away gambling on the races. Much of his loan-sharking business came from gamblers. My father believed in a sure thing. He never bet on a horse unless the race was fixed for the horse to win.

Bringing me into the family business meant educating me. By the time I entered the fifth grade, my father was teaching me the specifics of the various operations he ran. Some of them were legitimate. But many were conducted on the wrong side of the law, and my father made no attempt to hide that fact from me. He began to educate me in the way the world he knew functioned, complete with the rationalizations that allowed him to move comfortably within its structure. As he saw it, business was business. Everyone knew the rules, and no one was there against his will. You did what you had to do to make a living.

His oldest operation was his loan-sharking business. Occasionally, he explained, force had to be used to make certain the customers made their payments on time. This was unfortunate, he told me, but sometimes unavoidable. Many of his customers were bad risks; and since my father had no legal means to enforce payment, his collectors sometimes had to use physical injury to get the client to pay up. My father was sorry it had to be that way, but the clients knew the risks when they borrowed the money. It was all part of doing business. I learned that my father, who never so much as raised his fist to any of us, sometimes inflicted injuries in the course of business. Unable to process this contradiction, I tucked the information away in a separate compartment of my brain. I was rapidly developing an intricate network of such compartments. I had to keep the information separated, or I wouldn't be able to function.

I was away from home with my father nearly every Saturday and during school breaks, and I knew that my mother didn't much like it, but she had no real say in the matter. More and more, I was spending my spare time in the Flatbush area of Brooklyn, not far from the house where I'd visited Mrs. P when my grandmother still lived there. My father had bought a bar on Flatbush Avenue and gotten a retired fireman to run it for him. The bartender's name was Jackie. He was a hulking pink-cheeked man, a stereotype of the Irish bartender. The name of the bar was the Gemini Lounge. It was a nondescript building on the corner, faced with whitewashed brick. It was a workingman's bar, not so much a social club as an in-between place where my father could hang out during the day, a place where people could get in touch with him or drop off payments. If someone walked in off the street, it seemed like any other neighborhood hangout. It served drinks and snacks, and there was a jukebox and a small wooden dance floor where young couples did the Hustle on Saturday nights. There was a long wooden bar with a television set over it and tables where people could sit. I would sit on a barstool on Saturday afternoons, sipping Grenadine and soda and talking with Jackie while my father did business. Sometimes I'd go behind the bar and play with all the interesting gizmos I found there. A few feet to the rear of the bar was a little storage room where my father had a safe. He kept money for his loan-sharking business there and occasionally guns or other valuables.

In the back of the Gemini was an elevated area with a table where my father sat. It was a private place to talk, and my father could watch whatever was going on in the rest of the bar. He could see whoever came in before they saw him, and if necessary, he could slip out the rear exit without being noticed. I had already learned to sit with my back to the wall. It was always dim in the lounge. You had to look carefully to make out faces.

The Gemini was never a wiseguy hangout like the Ravenite was. Many of the customers were local firemen and cops. I quickly learned to recognize them, even out of uniform. My father was always telling me, "Keep your eyes and ears open, Al. You can tell a lot about a person just by looking." I could already spot a policeman by the way he walked, the way he looked around a room. And I could tell by his shoes. It was surprising how much I could tell about somebody by his shoes—how much money he made, what he did for a living. Wiseguys wore expensive Italian shoes, maybe top-of-the-line Nikes if they were young guys. My dad had shown me the finely stitched leather on the Italian shoes he wore. Cops all wore the same cheap, black, ugly lace-ups with thick soles. Some of the cops were just there for a drink after work, but many were there to see my father. Some had gambling problems and needed to borrow a few hundred; others were on his payroll. I would watch my father go into the back room with them and count hundreds into their hands. Other times they would simply hand an envelope to Jackie at the bar, and I would see Jackie slip a couple of hundreds under the cocktail napkin when he served their drinks. They were usually older cops, burned-out middle-aged men who gladly accepted the thousand dollars a week my father paid them to supply him with information and deflect unwanted attention. To me they were just more of my father's associates. The line was never clear.

When Dad bought the Gemini, he also rented the apartment attached to it for an elderly second cousin named Joe. Cousin Joe had just gotten out of prison for bank robbery. My mother rolled her eyes whenever my father talked about Joe, and she didn't like him coming to the house. My dad felt sorry for Cousin Joe and knew he wouldn't survive on his own, so he kept Joe around as a sort of resident care-taker and watchdog. Tall and gangly with a grayish, sad sack face, Cousin Joe was the most inept human being I ever knew. According to my father, he was also the world's stupidest bank robber. A few years before, he had decided to rob a bank in broad daylight, so to disguise himself, he got the bright idea of dressing up as a woman. He put on a woman's dress, shoes, wig, and makeup, and went off to rob the bank. He must have been the ugliest woman who ever darkened a teller's window. He stole a getaway car, held up the bank in the mid-dle of the afternoon, and then flipped the stolen car in his hurry to get away. Running from the scene of the accident, he peeled off his dress and wig as he fled. Since there was a long line of witnesses watching his remarkable progress down the street, the police didn't have much trouble finding him. They cuffed him and took him back to the bank for the manager to identify. The manager had no diffi-culty pointing him out to the officer. Cousin Joe, who hadn't even thought to wipe off the makeup, immediately responded, "How the fuck do you know it was me? I was dressed like a woman!" Joe had been sent to jail for a long, long time.

By the time I knew him, Joe was out of jail and living next to the Gemini. His apartment was as bare as a hotel room. I never saw any personal effects there. I did notice, after a while, that it got repainted a lot. I wondered why. Most of Dad's friends called him Dracula. I as-sumed it was because of his tall body and gray complexion. Joe looked like a walking corpse in his baggy sweaters and pants. Dad said it was because Joe looked like Bela Lugosi hunched over his big pot of steaming pasta. Joe was a tired old crook who was happy just to have a bed, three meals a day, and a steady supply of liquor next door. He was a great cook, and whenever Dad and I visited the Gemini, Cousin Joe would cook something for us. There always seemed to be a pot of

meat sauce simmering on the stove. Joe also delivered bread to our
house. Every morning he would come by our house with a delivery of
bread from a baker who owed my father money. He was such a bad
driver that it was a miracle he managed to get there with the bread.
Sometimes Joe told my father that there was some juice in the box
with the bread. One morning I was thirsty, so I went looking in the
box for the juice Cousin Joe had mentioned. To my disappointment,
all I found was an envelope of cash. When I asked my father where the
juice was, he laughed. It dawned on me that "juice" meant interest on
loanshark debts.

My father's operation was growing; and as it did, he started building his own crew. Henry Borelli came into the crew as my father's
accountant, keeping track of the money that changed hands continually. Henry was well educated, a suit-and-tie kind of guy. He
seemed better qualified for Wall Street than for the Gemini. Chris
Rosenberg was there a lot, and Freddy and his brother Richie
dropped by often. Uncle Nino's nephew Dominick came by every
couple of weeks to pick up Nino's share of the money my father
made. Dominick was Nino's eyes and ears at the Gemini. My father
felt sorry for Dominick. He told me that Dominick had never been
quite right since he came back from combat in Vietnam. Dominick
wanted to be a wiseguy, but he used heroin and had psychological
problems, so Nino didn't trust him to do anything dangerous or
complicated. Nino kept Dominick employed much the same way my
father employed Cousin Joe.

Shortly after he got the Gemini, my dad took on a guy from another crime family as a favor. The guy's name was Anthony Senter.
He was the nephew of another family's *capo*, the word for a Mafia
higher-up. It was the equivalent of an upper management position.
Anthony was an accomplished car thief who brought in a lot of
money, but I didn't like him. There was something slick and phony
about him. I didn't trust him. Anthony was a stereotype of a young

wiseguy. He was very handsome, very Italian looking, with dark brown eyes and black wavy hair brushed straight back off his forehead. He wore clothes well and was obsessed with his appearance. Everything on his body was expensive, from the Italian leather slip-ons, to the tailor-made slacks, to the Rolex and large diamond on his pinky finger. He always had a gold chain around his neck, the cross tangled in his chest hair. Anthony drove or wore every dime he made. What he didn't spend on cars or clothing he spent on women. He could get nearly any woman he wanted, from waitresses to supermodels. The only thing that didn't fit the image was his breathing. Anthony had a collapsed lung, and he chain smoked. He was always pressing his hand against his chest and complaining that he couldn't breathe. My father sent him to every lung specialist in town, and they all told Anthony the same thing: Stop smoking. Of course, he never did.

Anthony's best friend was Joey Testa. Joey was like a duplicate of Anthony, except his hair was a little straighter and he was an inch taller. Joey's complaint was his bad back. When Anthony wasn't complaining about his breathing, Joey was complaining about his back. People started calling them the Gemini Twins because they were always together at the Gemini and because they looked so much alike. Even their cars were alike. Both owned black Mercedes 450 SLCs. Anthony always drove. There was a subtle difference in power between them. Anthony took the lead in most things. I always suspected that Joey was jealous of Chris. Everyone knew that Chris was my father's favorite on the crew. Joey never said anything, but he looked at Chris sometimes the way my cousin Benny looked at me when I got a cool new toy. I had a feeling Joey would be happier without Chris around.

Cousin Joe's apartment became the main gathering place for the crew. I sat at Joe's kitchen table on Friday nights, eating pasta and watching my father count out everybody's cut from the car theft

operation. There was a definite pecking order in the crew. It was subtle, but it was there. Whenever we gathered at Cousin Joe's apartment, the positions were always the same. My father sat in the
middle, with Chris on his right. I was the only other person who ever
sat on my father's right. Anthony sat next to Chris, and then Joey. Joe
never sat with us; he cooked or watched TV, ready to come if my father called him for something. Freddy never sat, either; he stood or
paced, keeping an eye on my father like a watchdog.

One evening I sat in Cousin Joe's apartment with my father and
Chris while Joe cooked dinner. We were playing cards at the kitchen
table. A .38 revolver lay on the table next to me where my father had
set it. The aroma of garlic drifted through the air. After a few minutes
Chris went into the living room to watch TV, and my father went to
the bathroom. Joe went into the living room to watch TV with Chris.
Suddenly someone kicked open the door from the street with an
echoing crash. A man I didn't recognize rushed into my line of vision
with a gun aimed at me. Without pausing to think, I scooped up the
revolver and fired at the intruder. There was a click, and I realized
the gun wasn't loaded. I stiffened, but within seconds the intruder
put down his gun and laughed as my father and the others came into
the kitchen.

Everyone crowded around me, congratulating me on a job well
done. "You passed the test, Al! You're gonna go all the way!" my father said, beaming with pride.

The whole thing was a setup. My father had gotten some guy he
knew to stage the home invasion with an empty gun. None of us had
ever been in danger. He just wanted to see if I could handle myself in
an emergency. I'd passed the test.

Trying to control my shaking voice, I said, "Well, what did you
want me to do? I'm sitting here all alone and the guy was going to kill
us all!" Everyone in the room seemed to think it was all very funny,
that I had done a wonderful thing by firing at the man. I tried to play
along with them. I didn't want anyone to know how I actually felt.

My entire body had gone numb. I had been target shooting since I was six, but I had never shot at any living thing except the chipmunk I killed on my first hunting trip. I'd been handling guns all my life, and I had a shelf filled with GI Joes and other battle figures. But this wasn't play; this was real, horribly real. It didn't matter that it had all been a setup. All I could think was, "I could have killed somebody. Really killed somebody. I am capable of taking someone's life." That realization didn't make me feel powerful. It made me feel sick.

That night my mind spun as I lay sleepless at home. I replayed the scene in Cousin Joe's apartment over and over in my mind. I had actually fired a gun at somebody. I had done it believing I was defending myself and my family. But still . . . I was terrified by what I had done, desperately in need of some kind of explanation. But whom could I tell? Certainly not my mother. And my father seemed to think I had done a good thing. I struggled once again to shove the painful thoughts into the back of my mind. What other choice did I have?

Most of the time, life was still good that year. My parents seemed happy together, and my father was attentive and affectionate with my mother. Though she loved to cook for other people, my mother rarely ate her own cooking. She preferred a hamburger and fries from her favorite diner down on the highway. Nearly every night while we still lived in that house, my father went by the diner on the way home and picked up a burger and fries for my mom. Even when he came home late, he always carried a white paper bag from the diner in his hands. She rarely ate it all, but I could tell that it pleased her, not so much because of the food, but because it showed my father had been thinking of her.

The Fourth of July celebration we held that summer was the biggest we'd ever had. It was 1976, the year of the nation's bicentennial, and the streets downtown were all draped in red, white, and blue bunting. There was a reenactment of the colonizing of America in the New York harbor, complete with replicas of sailing ships parading around the Statue of Liberty. The market even sold special bottles of Coca-Cola for the occasion. My father went all out that year to host the neighborhood celebration. Panel trucks pulled up in front of the house all day, loaded with fireworks that the delivery men carried into the garage and workshop until there wasn't room for another box. There were freezers full of burgers and hot dogs, and my mother spent days making cold salads and desserts with Barbara and her friends from the neighborhood. The neighbors from blocks around came to the party; Freddy came with his wife and kids, and Chris was there with his wife. The Gemini Twins came and brought Cousin Joe with them. I could tell by my mother's stiff hello that she didn't like them. I saw Anthony whisper something in my father's ear. He nodded and then went on with the celebration. Everyone drank Coke and beer and ate until they couldn't hold another bite, and the kids swam in the pool and ran around on the grass screaming and giggling. When the sun began to set, Chris and Freddy cordoned off the street at either end with sawhorses.

It took nearly an hour just to move the boxes of fireworks from the garage to the front lawn and get set up: There were rockets, flares, sparklers, everything you could imagine. Jim was too drunk to stand up straight by then, so Dad asked Barbara to go home and get his uniform. I watched as Dad and the crew helped him into his NYPD uniform and propped him up against a car in front of the house. When the neighborhood police cruised by half an hour later and asked what was going on, my dad said, "We already got a cop here," and Jim pulled himself together enough to smile and wave. The officers recognized him and waved back, reminded us to be careful, and told us to have a good time. The only thing to do then was to wait until it got really dark.

Half the neighborhood had set up lawn chairs on the sidewalk and street around our house by then. It looked like a group of fans at a football stadium, waiting for the halftime show. Freddy and Chris cordoned off the area around the fireworks for safety while my father checked all the children's feet to make sure we were wearing shoes. A few of the kids were barefooted or wearing sandals, and Dad sent them home to put on sneakers for protection against stray sparks. There was a table set up with sparklers for the kids, with a trash barrel that my father filled with water for safety. He always worried that one of the little ones would get burned. When everything was finally ready, he started lighting the fuses, and the sky lit up above our house. It was glorious: red, white, blue, silver, gold, all filling the night air, rockets exploding with deafening noise, filling us with joy. Afterward he lit the sparklers for the little ones. I helped him watch the kids, and the minute a sparkler burned near a child's fingers, we would take it and drop it in the water barrel. By that time it was well past the small children's bedtimes, and their parents carried them home over the ashes, most of them draped sound asleep over their parents' shoulders.

Barbara helped Jim stagger home, but a few neighbors stayed behind to help us clean up. While the women wrapped the leftover food, the men took brooms and swept up the litter and ashes from the explosives. I helped my father with the sweeping. The crew had already left. About midnight a truck came and picked up the garbage. When the garbage trucks left and everything was clean once again, my father told my mother he had to go out for a while. I didn't want him to go, but he said he had to and told me to go upstairs to bed. It was nearly sunup when I finally heard him come in.

Whenever he could, my father would get me out of the city for the weekend. I think he needed the change of scene as much as I did. Dad had been an Eagle Scout in his teens; and though I never joined the Boy Scouts myself, these trips gave me a wonderful education in all of the outdoor skills that Scouts learn. The only difference was that instead of going on overnights with a Scout leader and a band of boys, I went with my father—and sometimes with the crew.

Some of the outings were strictly family trips. The "men" of the family—Dad, me, and Uncle Joe—would pack up the Cadillac with camping gear and head north. Sometimes we went to visit relatives in Connecticut. Other times we took my cousin Benny with us and headed out to the woods to camp. We would pack up tents and sleeping bags and rough it, living off the fish we caught and a few basic food supplies. I hated it when Benny came. Dad said we should bring him because he didn't have a father. Benny's father had been a policeman, but he'd died of a heart attack when Benny was very young. Dad and Joe and I loved roughing it, but Benny was another story. Even though he was ten years older than I was, he whined like a baby. *Why do I have to pee in the woods? Why can't we stay at a hotel with a real bathroom? I don't want hot dogs; I want lasagna.* By the end of the trip, we could hardly wait to take him home. Grandma was living with Aunt Marie and Benny by then, and I thought he and Grandma deserved each other.

One time my father's zeal for camping nearly got him killed. In a burst of temporary insanity, Dad took me and Joe to the sporting goods store and spent a small fortune buying state-of-the-art camping equipment, complete with cellophane survival blankets and astronaut-style freeze-dried food. Our first night out was cold, and we quickly discovered that the odd, shiny blankets offered little in the way of warmth. Worse, the food we had brought was anything but filling, and my father got up in the middle of the night and ate all of the freeze-dried packets we had with us. What he didn't realize was that the food was designed to expand in the moist environment of the stomach, eventually filling you up with a small portion.

The next morning he got up, and no sooner had he started moving around than the food expanded. The result was incredible. My father's stomach blew up like a cartoon figure before our astonished eyes, and within minutes he was doubled up in agony, his insides almost exploding. Realizing what had happened, we got him into the back seat, and Uncle Joe took off driving at nearly a hundred miles per hour to the nearest hospital.

As we roared down the highway, Uncle Joe looked in the rearview mirror and muttered, "Oh, shit."

"What's wrong?" I asked him.

"We picked up a cop."

My mind immediately went to my father's gun and the box he kept hidden in the trunk, and Uncle Joe and I exchanged a glance. Joe said, "Let me handle this." My father just groaned in response.

Uncle Joe pulled off the highway and stopped. The cop came to the window and asked for Joe's driver license. "Did you know you were going over a hundred miles per hour?" he asked Joe. The officer glanced at the car as he did so. A new Cadillac wasn't exactly common in that part of the woods.

"I'm sorry, officer," Uncle Joe replied, gesturing toward the back seat, "but my brother's really sick. I have to get him to the hospital as soon as I can."

The officer looked in the back, then opened the door near my father's head. "What seems to be the problem?" My father was in too much pain to talk, drenched in sweat, his stomach grossly distended. It only took a glance for the officer to see what bad shape he was in. "Follow me," he said to Uncle Joe, and jumped back on his motorcycle. With lights and siren going, he led us at maximum speed down the rural highway to the nearest hospital. My father had his stomach pumped and spent the night in the hospital for observation. The policeman never knew he had just saved the life of a Mafia *capo*.

Our most memorable camping trips with Uncle Joe were to upstate New York, where a friend of his lived in isolation on a piece of rural property. Russell was a Vietnam veteran who was unable to adjust to life when he returned from combat. Joe said Russ had battle fatigue, a mental problem that men sometimes suffered from after going to war. Russ used his discharge money to buy a piece of land in an isolated area, and when I first knew him, he was living in a tent while he slowly constructed a house for himself in the woods. We would go camping in the area, and over a period of time, we became good friends with Russell. My father always related to the outcasts of the world, so soon we started going up on the weekends to help Russ build his house. Dad's skills as a carpenter were invaluable, and the house was soon coming along nicely.

Late one afternoon, after a long day working on the man's house, Uncle Joe took Russ to the nearest town to buy food and other supplies. Dad and I stayed behind and built a campfire. As the shadows lengthened toward dusk, Dad and I were talking quietly when out of the silence, a shot pierced the air just over our heads. We dove away from the fire into the shadows as voices rang out. "Hey, ya'll, you hear that? That was just a warning. You take your crazy friend and get the hell out of there, or next time we won't shoot over your heads." Then we heard drunken laughter and a few more shots. It was like a scene out of *Deliverance.* We later learned that the men owned property nearby and wanted to get the "crazy guy" out of there so they could have the whole area to themselves.

They had shot at the wrong campers. My father had brought along a small arsenal of weapons for target practice, and as the voices came down to us, he tossed me a Mac Ten and nodded at the ridge. "See where they are?" he asked me as he pulled out extra rounds of ammunition for both of us. I looked up the ridge, in the direction the voices were coming from, and nodded.

"Yeah, Dad."

"Good. Okay, son, start firing in that direction when I do, and aim high. We don't want to hit anybody. We just want to scare the shit out of them."

On his signal, we both began firing, emptying round after round of ammunition into the growing darkness above the ridge. Finally we emptied the last clip, and quiet fell. After a moment a voice floated back down, a shaky one. The bravado was gone; this voice was stone sober.

"Anybody dead down there?"

Dad replied, "No, but you'll be if you keep fucking around."

That was the last we ever heard from them.

You haven't lived until you've gone camping with the Mob. Every now and again my father decided to bring the whole crew from the Gemini along with us. He'd rent a big Winnebago, and everyone would pile in, guns and all. On family trips we didn't shoot any living creature; except for the fish, no animal needed to fear when the DeMeos went to the woods. Apparently, however, no one explained this principle to the crew the first time they came with us. My father was horrified when Anthony and Joey came back from cruising the area, bragging that they'd whacked a cow in a Winnebago drive-by. Dad said, "What the hell did you do that for?"

We all got in the Winnebago, and Dad made the guys show him where the cow was. The farmer had called the police by then with a description of the shooters. The state police showed up to investigate, and things started getting complicated. I climbed on the fence and looked at the cows while Dad apologized to the farmer.

"Look," Dad said, "I'm really sorry about what happened. Those guys are idiots. They've never been hunting before. I'm not even sure they knew it was a cow. I don't want any trouble. Let me reimburse you for your loss. What was the cow worth?" my father asked as he peeled hundred-dollar bills off his cash roll into the farmer's hand. Somewhere around two thousand the farmer started to feel forgiving. He told the officers he'd decided not to press charges. There was nothing the police could do at that point but go away.

Back at the campsite, my father chewed out his crew. "What were you thinking? You want to go to jail over a fucking cow?"

My father was philosophical when he saw that the crew had brought virtually their entire arsenal of weapons to shoot at targets in the woods. He just didn't want them shooting animals. All went well for the rest of the expedition, with the guys happily eating hot dogs and firing off rounds to their hearts' delight. Late Sunday afternoon we headed for home. On the way everyone got hungry, so we pulled into a roadside diner for something to eat before continuing into the city.

We had finished eating and were waiting for the check when my father became aware that two state police officers had entered the diner. They were standing warily in the entrance, hands resting on their holsters, clearly surveying the area in search of a suspect. Glancing out the window, we could see more law-enforcement vehicles pulling up, surrounding the diner. When one of the crew noticed what was going on, his first impulse was to reach for his gun, but my father frowned and shook his head. Suddenly very quiet, my father said, "Everybody just hold still. Act as though nothing unusual is happening. When they get here, I'll tell them I'm calling my lawyer." I felt my heart stop, and as the officers drew near our table, the tension was palpable. No one said a word. I stared down at my plate, afraid to look up, trying to act normal as I picked at the remains of my food.

The two men drew adjacent to our table, paused a moment, then said, "There." My father placed his hands in clear sight on the tabletop and was just beginning to say something when the officers moved swiftly past our table and surrounded two men in the corner booth.

We all turned to look where they'd gone. Sitting at the booth were two confused, frightened, dark-skinned men who stared at the police officers and struggled to communicate in broken English. I heard them say, "No, no! We hunting. Kill deer. Is okay. Is okay." Then they lapsed into Spanish, shaken and clearly desperate to make their point. When the two officers escorted them outside, my father paid the bill, and we all trailed out after them, overcome with curiosity. The two dark-skinned men were walking toward a beat-up old pickup truck that had become the center of attention for a ring of incredulous officers. With worry written all over their faces, the two suspects pointed frantically at something in the bed of the pickup, repeating, "See! Deer! Deer! We shoot deer!" As I trailed toward the vehicle behind the rest of the crew, I could see four hooves sticking upright over the sides of the truck. There was something odd about the deer.

I walked up a few feet behind the officers and finally saw what was going on. In the back of the pickup was a mule, shot and gutted like a deer, roped down on the bed of the truck with its legs rigidly in the air. I couldn't believe my eyes. The crew was doubled up laughing, and even my father was having trouble keeping a straight face. He motioned us to get back in the motor home, and we all piled in before the officers even noticed us. A few moments later we pulled out of the parking lot as the officers cuffed the hapless poachers, who continued to insist with pathetic sincerity that they had shot a deer. As we passed the exit, the crew waved out the window at the officers standing by as backup. The officers waved back and smiled as half the New York Mob drove merrily back onto the highway, our load of illegal weapons stowed safely with the camping gear.

My father and I did some home projects together that summer, too, extending the back patio and bricking in the barbecue area. Dad taught me how to lay bricks and frame concrete. One hot afternoon, as we sat together in the basement workshop at home, he also taught me how to build a homemade silencer.

"If you ever need to quiet a gun down," he told me, "you'll need a silencer. You can get silencers for pretty much any gun, but if you have to, you can make your own. It's easy. I'll show you."

He picked up a plastic Coke bottle from the garbage can and began to work. He used the knife he always carried to slice the top off the bottle, where the neck widens about two inches down. Then he took some chicken wire, coiled it tightly, and slid it inside the bottle. He repeated the process until he had a thick coil of wire, with an empty core just big enough to admit the barrel of a .38. When he finished, he picked up the bottle top he'd cut off earlier and reattached it, winding duct tape around the bottle until it was secure. Finally he took the contraption, slid it carefully over the barrel of his gun, and handed it to me.

"Go ahead, Al. Try it."

I pointed the gun down toward some rubbish where the bullet would bury itself safely and pulled the trigger. It made a popping sound that I could hear clearly but would be difficult to hear from any distance. I nodded at Dad and handed back the gun. He pulled the coke bottle off the barrel and tossed it back in the garbage.

Another evening I found my father in the basement examining something that looked like a ratchet screwdriver. "What's that, Dad?" I asked him.

"I just got it. Ordered it from a guy. Here, I'll show you how it works. You know the wings that stick out on either side of the car ignition, kind of like ears?"

"Yeah."

"If you want to start a car without a key, the first thing you have to do is pop those off. You can use pliers for that. But the hard part is getting past the wheel and ignition lock. That's what this is for." He held up the ratchet-looking thing and demonstrated. "You can slide this thing in the ignition and give it a quick twist, and it will break the locks real easy. Then all you have to do is put a screwdriver in and it'll start right up. See?"

"What if you get caught?" I asked.

"Oh, that's no problem if you use your head. Only an idiot would drive around with a screwdriver sticking out of the ignition. Once you get it going, you stick the ears back on and replace the screwdriver with a fake key. That way if the cops stop you for a traffic ticket or something, they won't suspect a thing."

I knew by then that the crew made their living by stealing and that my father helped them do it. The lessons I'd absorbed at Sunday school taught that stealing was wrong, yet my father made it seem ordinary, harmless. The black-and-white lines of childhood were already gray for me. To me, my dad was primarily a businessman who sometimes went about matters in an unusual way. As long as I was with him, life seemed normal. It was only in his absence that the anxiety crept in.

The year I turned eleven was a landmark year for the men in our family. I was confirmed in the faith and became a man in the eyes of the Lord. The occasion was celebrated with a special dinner, attended by our relatives, and a beautiful Bible—a gift from my mother. It was called the Good News Bible, a new modern translation. The cover was gold, with black letters and a flyleaf inscribed, "To my dear son Albert, God bless you—Love, Mom." An avid reader, I read it from cover to cover, flaked out on my bed in the afternoons after school. It didn't always make sense to me, but I liked the idea that God cared about what happened to people. It gave me hope that there was a purpose somewhere in the confusion of my life.

Not long after my mother gave me my Bible, my father gave me a commemorative book as well: Machiavelli's *The Prince*, advising me to read it from cover to cover. He said it would help me understand his life. My father had been passing along books to me for years, and I dutifully studied every page of the Italian statesman's cynical treatise on political survival. It was an interesting counterpoint to the Bible I had just read. Unlike the scriptures, the precepts Machiavelli taught seemed both realistic and familiar. Where the Bible encouraged readers to expand their horizons to find greater meaning in life, *The Prince* reduced human existence to a bleak Darwinian struggle. The Mafioso scriptures spoke not of hope but of resignation, not of transformation but of survival. I nicknamed it the "Mafia Bible." It seemed to fit.

The same year I became a man in the eyes of God, my father finally

achieved the dream he had been chasing since adolescence. In spite
of misgivings, Paul Castellano inducted my father into the Gambino
family as a made man. My father did not share this information with
me, but I knew something was different. For one thing, his schedule
changed, and he was gone more of the time. The weekend outings my
sisters and I had once taken with him became rare events.
Sometimes he even missed Sunday dinner, and on weeknights he
came home later than ever. He didn't take me to see Nino Gaggi very
often anymore; and when he did bring me along, I noticed a new intensity in the conversations between him and Uncle Nino. There was
a lot more money, too. My father began talking of building a big new
home in one of the most exclusive neighborhoods in Long Island and
furnishing it from the ground up. We were even going to get a small
yacht. From my sisters' point of view, Daddy's business was doing
really well, and he was happy about it. I knew he had somehow moved
up in the organization, but the only thing I knew about getting made
was what I'd seen in the movies. It was not a secret men shared, even
with their sons.

That fall my father told me that he was taking me to the White
House. To any other fifth-grader, this would have meant that we were
going to Pennsylvania Avenue to see where the president lived. Yet I
already knew that there were two White Houses in America. One was
the White House we talked about at school, where President Carter
lived. Anybody could visit that place. The White House my father was
taking me to was the place where Paul Castellano lived. Paul
Castellano was *il capo di tutti cappi,* the boss of bosses, godfather and
chosen heir to Carlo Gambino. Big Paul was at least as powerful in the
underworld as the president was in the world of international politics. The Castellano White House was a private place, and only the
inner circle could go there. My father was now a part of that circle.

My father prepared carefully for the trip. I watched as he put a case
of the finest wine in the trunk of the car, then counted out tens of

thousands of dollars in cash and put it in an envelope for Big Paul. Dressed in my very best clothes, I sat quietly next to my dad as we wound through the streets of Massapequa to Staten Island toward the great white mansion on a hill. As we drove, my father talked about Paul Castellano and his role in the Gambino family.

"I don't have much use for Big Paul myself. He doesn't like to get his hands dirty, so he has other people do the dirty work for him. Remember when Uncle Nino introduced you to Mr. Dellacroce at the Ravenite? Now that's a powerful guy. That old man can do more with a wink or a nod than Big Paul ever did. But Mr. Gambino named Big Paul to replace him when he died, and I got to respect Mr. Gambino's wishes." Tradition said that tribute was due to the head of the family every week. Usually my father sent it up to the White House through Nino, but now that Dad was a *capo*, he took it himself every now and then. My father was bringing tribute that week, and he wanted me to witness the ritual.

The house hidden behind the armed steel gates that opened before us was a dead ringer for the White House on Pennsylvania Avenue, columns and all. This was no coincidence, as Castellano wanted a home that reflected his new power. My father had contempt for this need for display. Carlo Gambino had lived much more simply, in a rambling yellow house on the shore of the Sound. He would never have drawn attention to himself in this way, but Castellano, my father explained, wanted to be named among New York's rich and famous. Big Paul wanted people to think of him as an executive, a white-collar corporate leader. If you really had power, my father told me, you didn't need to show off.

I approached the towering front door of the mansion by my father's side. A strikingly beautiful young maid answered the bell. My father went inside, but I hung back, knowing that protocol required I keep my place. My father murmured, "My son, Albert," and the woman smiled and waved me in. My father disappeared into another room on the way down the hall. The maid took me to the kitchen and served me espresso. It was the worst espresso I had ever tasted, and it took all my courtesy not to register this on my face. But she was a nice woman, and we chatted while I waited for my father to come back. The maid's English was terrible, so we talked about the weather and smiled at each other in between silences.

About half an hour later my father returned and said it was time to go. As we walked back down the hall toward the front entrance, I could see Paul Castellano sitting behind a desk in the room my father had gone into. When Mr. Castellano saw me, he waved us both in; but once again, I hesitated. He called out, "Come in, come in, Roy; let me meet your son."

Entering the study, I approached the elegant white-haired man seated behind an elaborately carved desk and reached out to shake his hand. His hands were huge. The room itself was beautifully decorated, with oil paintings and dark, glowing wooden furniture. I leaned over to kiss Big Paul on the cheek as a gesture of respect, as my father had instructed me. Castellano seemed pleased by my manners and smiled approvingly at my father. He remained seated throughout the encounter. When you are the boss, people come to you. You never go to them. When it was over, I walked quietly back down the carpeted hall by my father's side.

My father was unusually preoccupied on the way home. When we came to the Brooklyn Bridge, I finally broke the silence by asking him why he was so quiet. "Politics, Al, politics." Then he turned to me and asked, "What did you do for that half hour with the maid?"

I said I talked to her and drank the worst espresso I'd ever had. My father laughed at this.

"You can make lousy espresso when you're banging the boss." When I looked startled, my father said that Mr. Castellano did not keep her in his employ because he liked her coffee. The woman was Big Paul's mistress. Most of the important men in the Mafia had mistresses, he informed me. I thought about my mother. Did she know that?

I still read the papers every day after school, and I knew that the Mafia killed people, but I had never seen my father do anything remotely violent. I knew that he helped the crew steal things, but it had never entered my mind that he was capable of murder. The father I knew was tender, warm, a man who nurtured the lives of animals and children alike. He carried his gun for self-defense, to protect himself in the dangerous world he lived in. I knew that he made much of his money outside the law, but I had no idea that doing hits was part of his function as a Gambino man. I discovered his secret accidentally, as the result of a simple schoolyard quarrel.

I was small for my age and got teased quite a bit by the bigger boys at school, but my parents didn't want me starting fights at school. One kid in particular was always harassing me, and for a long time I just brushed it off. But one day the abuse became physical, and he pushed me into a trophy case in the gym. I knew how to box, and even though I was half his size, I beat the living hell out of him, throwing him into the glass case. The boys' PE coach saw the whole thing. He knew that the other kid had started the fight. Neither of us was seriously injured, but we were both taken to the principal's office to be disciplined. The principal called our parents, and there was a conference in his office to decide our punishment. My father came to pick me up.

Driving home afterward, my father asked me to tell him exactly what had happened. I explained that the other boy just wouldn't quit hitting and shoving me. Dad listened carefully, then patted me on the knee and said, "You did the right thing, Al. A man has the right to defend himself. If this is the worst thing you ever do, you've got nothing to be ashamed of."

Relieved to find that my father wasn't angry with me, I asked in the camaraderie of the moment, "What's the worst thing you ever did, Dad?"

He looked away from me and concentrated on the road. I realized uncomfortably that he couldn't meet my eye. His voice was husky as he replied, "Someday you'll know, son."

In one horrible instant it came to me, as clearly as if I'd heard him speak the words. I knew what he was referring to. My father was a murderer. My dad, the person I loved most in the world, had killed people. Photos I had seen in the newspaper and movies, of bodies lying on streets in pools of blood, flashed through my mind. Had my father killed any of those people? A wave of pain and nausea washed through my body. In that endless moment I sat by my father, trapped with him in silence.

five

··

INFERNO

THE NEW HOUSE

Between the acting of a dreadful thing
And the first motion, all the interim is
Like a phantasma or a hideous dream.

—SHAKESPEARE, *Julius Caesar*

For the first twelve years of my life, my father worked to keep our family in a glass bubble. As long as we stayed inside that bubble, we would be safe. From the inside, the bubble was a very convincing microcosm of the real world. My parents had a traditional marriage in most respects, and my sisters grew up like the daughters of policemen and stockbrokers, worrying about grades and party dresses. Inside the bubble, my father was a regular dad. Bad guys are not bad guys twenty-four hours a day. Like other fathers, our father liked movies and music, good food, and Sunday nights in front of the TV. For twenty-three of every twenty-four hours, he was just like any other father. But in the early summer of 1979, something happened that shattered the bubble, and my father was never able to piece the fragments of glass together again.

As I prepared to enter the seventh grade, our family was planning for another change. With his income expanding exponentially, my father began building his dream house on the southern shore of Massapequa. The neighborhood we were about to enter was among the wealthiest on Long Island, with wide, curving tree-lined streets and mansions that housed an assortment of lawyers, doctors, stockbrokers—and mobsters. Carlo Gambino's house is there. Building such a house was the pinnacle of the American Dream for a Brooklyn boy like my father. Moving there was the beginning of a nightmare for our family. From the day we moved into the mansion by the water, our lives began to swerve out of control.

The new neighborhood was only a few miles from the old one, but it was light years away psychologically. The old neighborhood was largely middle class, tight-knit, and unpretentious. Kids rode their bikes on the sidewalks and played ball in the street, and neighbors visited over back fences. We knew everyone there, and everyone knew us. My mother had shared recipes with the other moms and baby-sat for half their children; she could tell you their birthdays from memory. Whatever doubts the neighbors had about my father's profession, they kept to themselves. To them, my parents were just Gina and Roy.

In the new neighborhood, however, we became the DeMeo family in a neighborhood where wealthy Italians were assumed to have Mafia connections. We might as well have had "Mob family" on a bronze plaque hung next to the front door. What had gone unspoken in the old neighborhood was whispered in the new one, though not yet to our faces. I think my mother would have been just as happy to stay where we were, but she was philosophical about the change. As the theme song for *The Jeffersons* claimed that year, the DeMeos were moving on up.

For the first time we had a maid as well, an Irish woman recommended by a friend of my father's. My mother could not take care of the new house alone. The maid came several times a week to help my mother with the cleaning. She was a strange woman with dark interests, whose favorite hobby during her time off was attending strangers' funerals. She read the obituaries daily and took notes on times and locations of memorial services. She was odd but kind-hearted.

The house my father built for us was beautiful, thousands of square feet, with marble floors and arching ceilings. In addition to the million dollars spent on its construction, my father hired an interior decorator to furnish it from basement to ceiling with the most expensive, state-of-the-art technology and custom-made furniture. He ended up with even more than he ordered, though: After we waited for months to have the furniture made, the furnituremaker went bankrupt. The bank locked up the warehouse and prepared to sell the contents at auction, including our furniture. When the decorator told my father what had happened, my dad hit the roof. All that time and money, and now there would be no furnishings. Dad insisted on knowing where the warehouse was, and that night after the decorator left, Dad called Freddy. Freddy made a couple of calls of his own, and about four the next morning, Freddy arrived with a large white truck and backed it into our garage. Inside we found not only our furniture but much of the other furniture in the warehouse. By the time they unloaded it all, it was nearly sunup. When the decorator saw it the next day, he didn't say a word. I don't think he wanted to know how it got there.

In our old house the only security system had been Major, our German shepherd, and though Major made the move with us, he was no longer the only thing protecting our house. My father had the house wired with a sophisticated burglar alarm and mounted surveillance cameras in the trees out front. Security cameras were fairly common in the new neighborhood, where many people kept valuables and cash in their homes. Dad had a shooting range and a full gym built in the basement, complete with weights and training machines, so he could work out every day. He was trying to keep his weight down; and though he never succeeded, he did manage to build more muscle than fat onto his stocky frame. He was incredibly strong, able to lift over three hundred pounds like it was nothing. The gym was for both of us since I was trying to fill out my skinny biceps as well.

The house backed directly onto the water, where the canal led out into the Atlantic Ocean a mile away. My father had a large wooden dock built adjacent to the property, with a slip where we could keep a boat. I could dive off the dock directly into the canal from my own backyard. There was a large patio area for entertaining, as well as a pool and a slide. Installing the pool turned into an unexpected adventure, at least for the builder.

Early in the construction, my mother noticed that the men digging the hole for the pool were digging it backward. She spoke to the foreman herself, but he refused to make the correction. My mother is no pushover, so she drew up her full four feet nine inches and repeated more forcibly, "I want the hole dug correctly."

The man retorted, "Bafangul!" assuming my mother wouldn't know he had just used an obscenity. He was wrong. Mom called my father at the Gemini and told him what had happened. He was not pleased.

When my father got home, we walked out to the building area together. My father looked unusually calm, always a bad sign. Unfortunately, when my father told the foreman he would have to redig the pool, the foreman replied, "Fuck you! I not doing no hole again."

I saw the veins pop out in my father's neck. Before the foreman knew what was happening, my dad had picked him up by his hair and belt and thrown him into the deep end of the pit. Then Dad climbed onto the bulldozer and started filling in the hole himself. As he did so, he shouted down to the guy, "Are you going to redig this fucking hole, or do you want to be buried in the deep end, where I'll think of you every time I swim over your bones?"

As the other workers dug the foreman out, he screamed at my father, "I gonna send you to jail!" My father chased him all the way back to the truck, wielding a shovel overhead. The workers piled into the back of the truck and roared away.

The next day the owner of the pool company showed up to apologize to my father, saying his cousin the foreman was from "the other side" (Italy) and didn't understand how things were done. Clearly, the owner had made a few phone calls and was more than a little anxious not to offend my father further. The pool was redug correctly, and when it was completed, the owner refused to give my father a bill. My father paid him the agreed-upon amount anyway, but the owner never cashed the check.

Just as we had in the old house, my dad and I spent time together making modifications to the new one. My father hired a contractor to put in a wide stone driveway, but when the man graded the area, he did it incorrectly. Dad told him from the beginning that the way he was doing it, there would be a dip in the middle of the driveway, but the man paid no attention. Sure enough, when he started laying the foundation, there was a dip. My father fired the guy and told me we would have to do it ourselves if we wanted it done right. Dad had his crew get him a load of cobblestones for the driveway, expecting them to go to a quarry and buy it. Instead, they contacted one of my father's guys in Manhattan, who was doing some roadwork for the city at the time. This guy had his crew dig up a cobblestone street in the middle of the night and bring the whole truckload to Massapequa. My father couldn't believe it; they had literally stolen an entire block of a Manhattan street and transported it to our front yard. The city never even noticed. The cobblestone apparently got lost in red tape.

Always overly careful about everything he built, Dad then asked a friend of his, who worked on bridges in the city, what the strongest form of concrete was. He didn't want the driveway crumbling after a few years of use. The friend gave us a bag of reinforced magnesium and told us to mix it with the concrete. My father had me pour the magnesium into the concrete mixture, and the result was a bond for the cobblestones that could probably survive a nuclear blast. It took us several Saturdays to finish the driveway, but it was beautiful when it was done. I drove by the old house recently, and twenty years later that driveway looks like the day we laid it, not a dip or a nick anywhere.

We tried to continue some of the old traditions in the new neighborhood. Our first summer there we held a Fourth of July party for our new neighbors. Just as in the old neighborhood, we invited everyone for blocks around, and many of them accepted. This was no neighborhood barbecue, however, with burgers sizzling on the grill. This celebration was a lavish affair befitting our new status. Instead of redwood picnic tables by a home-built pool, we held a catered event overlooking the water. Tables were laid out on the large deck one level above our pool, draped with white linen cloths and groaning with every kind of food imaginable. Steaks were cooked to order on the barbecue, and instead of beer and soda, there was Perrier and buckets of Dom Perignon champagne. Kids lined up to go down the slide into the pool, and their parents took turns cruising in our new yacht, docked behind our house. My father hired a small band with a singer to croon Sinatra tunes for the evening. Space was set aside for a dance floor under the open sky, and as the afternoon turned to dusk, couples swayed in the cool evening air. Once again there was a truckload of fireworks, but this time they exploded in the skies above the water. They looked like magic.

A few things did remain the same. Barbara and Jim came with two or three families from the old neighborhood. I think they felt a little out of place at first in the sophisticated new environment, but we were so glad to see them that they relaxed after a while and began to enjoy themselves. Some of my father's crew came as well, Freddy and Chris with their families, and Joey and Anthony. The mobsters in the group mingled freely with the stockbrokers, attorneys, and judge who were our guests. I wondered if the judge realized who he was talking to, who was hosting the party. My mother seemed glad to see Chris and Freddy, but she spoke to Anthony and Joey as little as possible. I could tell she didn't like them. Later that night I heard her tell my father that she didn't like having them around. She didn't trust them.

Once we settled into the new neighborhood, my father adopted a more sophisticated personal image. He also decided he needed a full-time driver. Freddy was the natural choice for the job: a combination race-car driver, mechanic, and bodyguard. The only problem was that Freddy was a little rough around the edges, so my father gave Freddy a makeover. Freddy's teeth had been bad since he was a kid, so my father paid a fortune in dental work, got him a good haircut and manicure, and had him fitted for a whole new wardrobe. Somewhere along the line Freddy even got most of the grease out of his pores. Outwardly, Freddy was a new man, but inwardly, he was still just Freddy, as doggedly loyal as ever.

Some vestiges of the old life remained. Uncle Joe still pulled up in his old Cadillac limo, as bluff and unpretentious as ever, and the Sunday dinners continued. Grandma DeMeo continued to show up for holidays and special occasions, to sit in her chair and wait for attention. If anyone understood the nature of power, my grandmother did. Grandma wielded guilt and disappointment like twin revolvers. She was still living with Aunt Marie, making her life a living hell. Aunt Marie had to listen to my grandmother's daily insistence that Grandma was going to wake up dead the next morning. She also had to endure being called a whore if my grandmother suspected my aunt was dating. As it was, Grandma DeMeo's visits were like the monthly inventory at a department store; the main reason she seemed to come was to go through the house and take mental notes on our new possessions. She had spent most of her adulthood envying Mrs. Profaci; now she fingered my mother's new mink coat in stiff-faced silence. In spite of the fact that my father had supported her generously since he was sixteen, Grandma bitterly envied her daughter-in-law's new acquisitions. My mother was living in the style to which my grandmother had always thought she was entitled. Ironically, though my mother enjoyed the things my father bought, they were never that important to her. She continued as before, focusing most of her time and money on her children.

When I entered the sixth grade, my father had begun educating me about the family finances. My father maneuvered his money expertly from enterprise to enterprise, being careful to make regular payments to the IRS. There was never a time when my father did not own and operate many businesses legally, for he was a shrewd investor who wanted to protect his capital. A sizable amount of his income was invested in stocks, bonds, and other traditional depositories, and he made certain I understood the importance of guarding my assets.

He also explained the ins and outs of the monetary system within the Mob, a system that simultaneously benefits and enslaves its members. Once a member begins paying a certain amount of money to the boss each week, he is expected not only to maintain but also to increase that amount. My father had long been kicking up twenty, thirty, even fifty thousand dollars a week, and there was continual pressure from above to increase the amount. If the tribute payments leveled off or lessened, the assumption would either be that he had outlived his usefulness or that he was pocketing part of the profits. Either was dangerous. He knew that Paul Castellano kept him in the family purely because my father was a big earner for the Gambinos. Castellano didn't like my father any more than my father liked him.

My father's loan-sharking business continued to bring in sizable profits, and by the time I was twelve, my father's auto theft ring had grown into the largest, most lucrative automobile theft operation in the Northeast. The enterprise had started out legitimately. My father's car dealerships on Long Island were providing luxury cars for the Arab market. The Arab requirements were very specific; none of the cars could have leather seats, for the Muslim religion forbade them from using leather. The demand was tremendous, and when the dealers couldn't get enough of the cars legally, they began stealing them. One stolen car brought fifteen thousand dollars in the Arab market, so the profit margin was huge.

When my father learned what was going on and saw the potential, he studied the problem. He was scientific about his operations. He hired a tool and die maker to create the special ratchet tool he had shown me. The tool made it possible to steal a car within seconds. The risk of getting caught in that amount of time was very small. Then my father did a little nosing around and found a man at General Motors who was willing to join the operation. He provided my father with the actual stamps and blanks used to print ID tags at the factory. With an inside man at the Department of Motor Vehicles, the scheme became virtually foolproof. The cars were taken off the street, re-tagged with factory equipment, issued new DMV registration, and made ready to ship within twenty-four hours. Transportation was simple, as the retagged cars looked all legal and thus could be shipped openly on cargo vessels. It was an astonishingly effective system that soon brought in hundreds of thousands of dollars a week. And since my father was meticulous about security, insisting that everyone wear gloves at all times, from thief to tagger, the cars could not be traced if intercepted.

My father was a criminal genius in the most literal sense. He was always refining his schemes. When he learned that the Arabs would also pay top dollar for American cigarettes, he hid cases of cigarettes in the trunks of the cars. Pornography was even more popular with the fundamentalist Muslims, so soon the cigarette cartons were packed with porn magazines as well. Once, when a new car dealer in Brooklyn who owed my father a large sum of money couldn't pay up, my father confiscated the keys to twenty luxury automobiles and told the dealer not to report the cars missing for a week. When the dealer finally did make the report, my father collected the insurance money as well. The dealer was out of debt, and my father had doubled his profit margin on the transaction.

The abortion clinic scheme my father created during those years was especially clever in exploiting human frailties—lust for money

and religious hypocrisy. When abortion clinics first began to prolif-
erate legally in the Northeast, many of the doctors involved became
the targets of threats and harassment. Picketers sealed off the
perimeters of many clinics, sometimes with threats of violence. My
father knew people in the medical community, and it wasn't long before they put him in touch with clinics that would pay my father for
protection. The protection was effective, but my father realized that
he would soon put himself out of business if he scared off the protestors permanently. So he decided to try an alternate approach.

He met with a group of the most outspoken zealots and offered to
make a deal. He would provide them with transportation, lunch, and
a hundred dollars a day if they would picket and threaten clinics in
New York and New Jersey. My father would pick the clinics. They had
to agree to go when he asked them to and to stay away when they were
told. The idea was to target a few clinics, scare the personnel, offer
them protection, and then move the protestors elsewhere once the
clinic started making payments to my father. That way my father
would make money coming and going, so to speak. As it turned out,
my father had no trouble finding takers among the religious. On the
contrary, they were only too happy to take money from the Mob and
go through the motions of staging protests on cue. I have no idea how
they rationalized their decision. Maybe they convinced themselves
that they were still making a statement.

One of his most intelligent schemes was largely legal. From a man
who owed him money, my father had acquired a lab that made pornographic films. The price of silver was very high at the time, and one
day it dawned on my father that the film they processed was covered
with silver nitrate. They were literally washing money down the drain
every time they processed the film. So he talked to a dentist friend
and found out that the dentist was aware of the problem, because he
used X-ray film in his practice. The dentist had purchased a special
filter that caught the silver nitrate when he processed the X rays. My

father purchased the same filters and installed them in his photo lab in New Jersey. They caught the silver crossover, which my father collected and sold for fifty dollars an ounce. Ultimately, the silver brought in tens of thousands of dollars. Soon he was treasure hunting for dentists who threw out the waste from X-ray processing and was "recycling" that, too.

He did get a bit carried away by the whole thing, however. Dad heard about an old dental building that had been torn down a few miles from our house, and he found out that the dentists had the medical waste buried on the property. Excited by the prospect of a treasure hunt, he went downtown and found a map of the property, complete with the location of a dry well. Late one night he took me down to the abandoned property with a couple of shovels and told me to start digging. The property was on the main highway in Massapequa, and though no one was interested in an abandoned dry well, my father didn't want to have to explain what he was up to. We started digging after midnight, and three hours later we were still digging. It was exhausting work, and all I wanted to do was go home, but my dad kept saying, "Keep digging, Al! I know there's silver down there!"

What my father didn't know was that in the same building, there was a proctologist who routinely gave barium enemas to his patients. At 4:00 A.M., after hours of digging, all we got for our effort was four feet of shit—literally. There we were, in the dark hours before sunrise, standing up to our knees in excrement. So much for the glamour of life in the Mafia. We never did find any silver down there.

As his income increased, the pressure to up the ante, to earn more, was continual. If you don't measure up financially in the Mob, they don't fire you. The only way you can leave is on a slab, and that is exactly what happens when you no longer pull your weight. My father had begun doing hits for money as well, though I knew nothing about that sideline at the time. I suspected by then that my father had killed people, but I felt certain that my dad used a gun only when absolutely necessary, to protect himself or somebody else. After all, that was the lesson he had schooled me in. Never use a gun unless you absolutely have to; but if you must, use it efficiently, for you may not get a second chance. Two in the head, make sure they're dead. I knew what that meant now.

Outwardly, I remained the same schoolboy I had always appeared to be, studying for exams and swimming in the canal on sunny days. But the fear that had haunted me in the old house grew even stronger in the new one. I knew that our glamorous life came with a price, and that with every step up, the risk of disaster was increasing. The price of our lifestyle would eventually be my father's life. It was a debt he would inevitably have to pay one day. I continued to kiss him good-bye every morning, and I still lay awake until I heard his car in the driveway at night. Increasingly, I asked to go with him, as though my presence could magically protect him.

I wondered sometimes what my sisters thought, for they seemed utterly oblivious to death's dark presence in our home. One Sunday, when my father made a rare visit to church with us, Lisa asked him why he didn't come forward with the rest of us to receive communion. My father's face darkened as he said matter of factly, "Because I'm not a hypocrite. I know who I am, and I know where I'm going in the end." Lisa seemed puzzled. I envied her confusion. I knew exactly what my father meant.

My father had finally achieved the power and affluence he had always dreamed of, but it brought him little pleasure. The cheerful, relaxed father of my early years was growing tense, brooding, silent. In *Paradise Lost*, Milton's Satan says that hell is wherever he is, for he cannot escape his own mind. I think it was so for my father. I watched my father, surrounded by every trapping of prosperity and achievement, slip further and further into the darkness. Increasingly, he would come home in the wee hours of the morning and hole up in his den, sometimes staying there for days. My mother would bring him food, which he largely left untouched. The only sound would be the television, which he sometimes let run twenty-four hours a day to fill the emptiness. He would stare at it in silence, almost in a trance. The pain he exuded in those moments was palpable. When I came home from school on those bleak afternoons, I would slip quietly into the den to be with him. I knew instinctively that he didn't want to talk. He did not want me to know about the violence that was becoming the center of his criminal life.

Our family was rapidly being drawn into a vortex of violence that was spinning out of control. With more and more money at stake, and an increasingly complex criminal enterprise, my father's operation began to draw the scrutiny of the authorities. Cars were disappearing off Manhattan streets in record numbers, and the hunt for the power behind the thefts was on. My father himself remained largely invisible to the police, who were looking higher up in the New York Mob families to find out who was involved and how it was being done. Yet with each month that passed, the investigation spread its tentacles wider, and my father knew it was only a matter of time before it caught up with him. Then when my father came home one dawn visibly upset, I knew something had gone wrong. He said nothing to me, but at the Gemini a few days later, I overheard him talking to the crew in Cousin Joe's apartment. Uncle Nino had been arrested. My father was working on a plan that would get him off, but meanwhile the attorneys had to be paid, and Nino's family had to be cared for. I heard my father say something about going through backyards, and I realized he had been cutting through yards and climbing fences to get cash to Nino's wife without being seen. When I asked my father about it later, he shrugged and said, "That's just what you do, Son. One of your guys goes down, you take care of things for him till he gets out."

We had been in the new house for two years when disaster struck. The truly fatal misstep occurred not long after my thirteenth birthday. My father's crew was becoming increasingly ambitious. With my father's rise in the Gambino family, a great deal of money was changing hands, and the crew was part of the operation that was making the money. They wanted a bigger share, and they wanted to prove that they could run an operation on their own. They were becoming reckless in their ambition. In the winter of 1979, Chris decided to run a game without telling my father. He had access to information about a large amount of money two Colombian drug couriers were bringing from Florida to New York, and Chris was supposed to broker the deal. Instead he saw easy money, so he killed the couriers and stole the money. Worse yet, he used my father's name in dealing with the Colombians. They knew him as "Chris DeMeo."

It didn't take much effort for the Colombians to trace the name back to New York, and from there to my father. Neither did it take long for word to reach Paul Castellano that the DeMeo crew had murdered one of the Colombian Mafia's own, endangering the entire Gambino crime family in the process. At about the same time as Castellano, my father found out what had happened from Nino Gaggi, who was out on bail.

For the first time, I saw my father out of control. He came home late one night white with rage and locked himself in his study. When I asked him what was wrong, he said only that Chris had done something colossally stupid, endangering Dad's entire operation in the process. What he didn't tell me that night was that Chris's blunder had put my father in imminent danger of being hit from within. Worst by far, however, was what it meant for our family. Unlike the Italian Mafia, the Colombians do not respect family boundaries. Decades before, the Commission—the "legislature" of the five New York crime families—had declared the wives and children of their members off limits. That rule had been carefully adhered to. Any member of the organization was subject to the most severe sanctions, but you were not allowed to harm an innocent relative. The Colombians had no such rule. On the contrary, they routinely murdered both immediate families and more distant relatives as a way of making their point. Terrorism was a standard part of their mode of operation.

Never in our lives had my father intentionally done something that would put anyone other than himself and his crew at risk. Suddenly our family was in imminent danger of being slaughtered. The changes in our home life were immediate and all-encompassing. The beautiful new house that my father had been so proud of became a fortress overnight. Dad moved Cousin Joe into the basement to keep an eye on us, making up a story for my sisters' benefit about Joe needing someplace to stay for a while. He cut down any foliage that interfered with the view from the surveillance cameras around our house and mounted spotlights everywhere outside, keeping it bright as noon twenty-four hours a day. When he couldn't see the stop where Lisa and I waited for the school bus in front of our neighbor's house, he offered the neighbor several thousand dollars if he'd cut down the tree that blocked the camera's view. When the neighbor said no, he even offered to have a crew come out and move the tree. When the neighbor still refused, a garbage truck "accidentally" crashed into the tree, knocking it down. He wanted us watched on closed circuit television every time we went outside the house. Dad told my mother as little as possible and said nothing to my sisters, but for the first time, he broke one of the cardinal rules of his life. He brought me into the danger.

Sitting down across from me, he explained what had happened. "People are going to come and try to kill me. They may try to hurt your sisters, too. From now on, I don't want any of you in the car with me. Freddy will take you wherever you need to go in a different car. I don't want you walking around on the public streets. I've done every-thing I can, but I can't be with you all the time. I need you to carry your gun whenever you leave the house, and you can't let your sisters go anywhere alone. I don't want your sisters to be scared, and you've all got to go to school. You've got to watch out for Lisa during lunch and breaks. Try not to let her notice, just keep an eye out." He paused, cleared his throat, and continued. "If anybody tries to hurt her, shoot to kill. You won't get a second chance."

I swallowed hard and nodded.

My father rubbed his face with his hands and then looked at me again. "I'm sorry, Al, I'm so sorry. I never wanted you to have to do this. But there's no one else I can trust. I'm counting on you." His face sagged with despair.

An unexpected calm came over me, an odd sensation, almost as if I had left my body. Feeling like someone else as I spoke the words, I reassured my father. "Don't worry, Dad. You can count on me. I won't let you down."

He stood up and hugged me, not the way a father hugs a child, but the way one man hugs another. I was a man now. At thirteen years old, I had become an adult.

And so it began. Each morning afterward, I slipped a gun into my pocket as routinely as I brushed my teeth and loaded my backpack before leaving for school. While other boys played PacMan or flirted with girls during breaks, I scanned the perimeter of the quad where my little sister stood chatting with her friends, oblivious to my watchfulness. At home I remained on alert, nervously roaming the house with Major when my father was gone. My father called several times a day to make certain everything was secure, and Freddy cruised the house regularly. For a while everything remained routine—a mailman or a newspaper delivery our only interruptions—but then one day a young Hispanic man came to our front door.

I was at school when he rang our doorbell. He told my mother he was a salesman. She told him she wasn't interested. He thanked her and said good-bye, but she noticed him driving by the house when I got home from school later that day. When my father returned home with Freddy in the late afternoon, the young man was still parked across the street from our house. As he did every time he returned now, Dad asked my mother if she had seen anything suspicious that

day. She told him that a dark, Hispanic-looking man had been hanging around our house. In fact, she told my father, he was still there.
She pointed through a window to an older model car across the
street.

My father whirled to look through the window, shouted down to
the basement for Cousin Joe to follow, then drew his gun and rushed
across the street, shouting at the man in the parked car. Freddy was
already running to get Dad's car. Seeing my father rush at him, the
young man immediately started his car and floored it out of there, the
sound of screeching tires violating the quiet of our neighborhood.
Dad and Joe ran back to the Cadillac and jumped in as Freddy rock-
eted down the street. The last thing I saw as I watched from the front
porch was my father and Cousin Joe leaning out the windows of the
car, guns drawn, as they careened around the corner and out of sight.

My mother went straight into the kitchen and started dinner as
soon as they left, trying to resume our regular routine as if it were any
other day. The only sign that she knew anything was wrong was the
banging of pans as she slammed them into place. A short while later
my sisters came home and went upstairs to their rooms, unaware that
anything had happened. I went to get my gun from its compartment
by my bed, checked the load, and shoved it in my pants. Then I came
back down and sat in a chair in the foyer facing the door, waiting, listening for the slightest sound. I felt strangely calm, detached, every
cell of my body poised to do whatever might be required of me.

It seemed like forever before my father returned. An hour later I
heard the engine roar as he pulled to a stop in our driveway. I was already on my feet as he rushed through the front door. Glancing
around the foyer, he asked, "Where's your mother?"

"Kitchen."

"Your sisters?"

"Upstairs."

Reaching into his pants, he pulled out a revolver. I could smell the
gunpowder, and as he passed it to me, I could feel the heat from the

metal. I had never seen such intensity on his face, but he was utterly focused. "Wipe it down and wrap it in a garbage bag. Be ready to get rid of it when I tell you." He disappeared upstairs.

Hiding the gun under my shirt, I went into the kitchen and ripped several paper towels off the roll, then pulled a garbage bag from the drawer. My mother said, "Did your father come in?" I nodded and disappeared up the stairs after my father.

In my room I wiped the gun carefully, then put it in the garbage bag. I slipped on my leather jacket and shoved the garbage bag in the inside pocket, then left my room in time to see my father emerge from his study with a small bag. He was calling my sisters' names as he went back downstairs. Hearing the urgency in his voice, they hurried down after him, where my mother waited at the foot of the stairs. His instructions were terse.

"Pack a bag, now. Take whatever you need, but hurry. You have five minutes."

My mother's face was a mask of anger and fear, but my sisters looked bewildered. My father's voice hardened as he ordered, "Do it! Now! Be in the car in five minutes." All four of us scattered upstairs; my father was behind us in seconds, tossing each one of us a large garbage bag. "Put your stuff in there."

Within five minutes we were all outside, where my father tossed the heavy garbage bags into the trunk and slid behind the driver's seat. The car was still running. My sisters were pale with terror, utterly confused by what was happening.

As he started to pull away, I realized what we'd forgotten. "Dad! The dogs!"

Without a word Dad stopped the car and went back inside. A minute later he was back, shoving Major into the backseat and putting Benji into Debra's arms. We pulled out of the drive and into the darkness.

Within minutes we were speeding through the quiet streets of

Massapequa at more than eighty miles an hour. My mother, thin-lipped and white-faced, said, "When are we coming back, Roy?"

"Never," my father replied. "We're never coming back." My mother and sisters started sobbing, my mother turning her face away from my father as she began to cry. Only my father and I didn't weep. I patted my gun for reassurance as I looked down at the floor. There were bullet holes in the matting.

My father was silent until we were out of the city, but as the hours passed, he began to talk to us. I kept waiting for one of my sisters to say, "Why, Daddy?" but they didn't. I didn't know whether they already knew the answer, or whether they didn't want to know. I only know that they didn't ask, then or ever. My father began talking more calmly, trying to soothe us.

"It'll be nice, you'll see. We'll wait a few weeks until things calm down and I can get some money together. Then we'll move on north, buy some land, maybe do some farming. I'll be home a lot more. You can go to school there. You'll like it. I hear it's really pretty." My mother just stared straight ahead, without saying a word.

We drove well into the night, out of the city, north to upstate New York. Finally, in a rural area I had never seen before, we stopped at a small motel. While my father checked us in, we unloaded the Cadillac as fast as we could. Once we were in the room, my father told us to stay there until he returned. He had some business to take care of, but he would be back as soon as he could. Once he'd done what he needed to, he told us, we would be going north, across the border into Canada. And with that, he was gone. My mother comforted my sisters and told us all to go to bed. I went into the bathroom to change clothes and hide the gun in my pajamas, then climbed into bed and lay there in the darkness and listened to my sisters' breathing as they slowly drifted into exhausted sleep. I don't think my mother slept at all that night. Neither did I.

We remained at the motel for nearly two weeks. My father came back the next day to make sure we were safe and give my mother some cash and then left again. He was driving a new car. My mother did her best to keep us fed and entertained, but there was no way she could camouflage the grimness of the situation. There was anger in her face, a mixture of rage and sadness that I had never seen before. We passed the time as best we could. Debra had brought her camera, and she went outside in the mornings to take pictures around the cabin. I wandered along behind, keeping her in view, my gun hidden. Lisa buried herself in a book the way she always did, and my mother alternately watched television and paced around the cabin. I made grocery runs and patrolled the perimeter, pretending to take hikes. The time crawled by. My father came by twice more to check on us but then left again immediately. He did not tell me where he was going.

At the end of the second week, my father returned and abruptly announced that we were going home. No one asked any questions. We simply piled into the car and drove back to Long Island. When we finally pulled into the driveway, I remember thinking that the house looked different now. Maybe it was because I'd never expected to see it again. My sisters and I picked up our garbage bags of belongings and went inside to unpack.

The man who returned to the house with us that evening was different, too. He was not the father I remembered. We didn't have access to newspapers while we were in hiding, but now I watched as my father sat in the kitchen that night, reading through the papers we'd found piled on our front porch. Debra helped my mother start dinner. Suddenly I saw him stiffen and stare at the paper. He put it down, then picked it up and read it again. He must have read it a hundred times. It was as though he simply couldn't take in what it said.

The article described a gangland hit two week earlier, a dramatic daylight chase through the streets of Long Island culminating in a shoot-out. Or more accurately, a shooting, for the victim had never returned fire. A speeding car had pulled up next to a young Hispanic man, the occupants emptying nearly three hundred rounds of ammunition into his car. The victim's body was riddled with bullets. Witnesses gave conflicting descriptions of the assailants, and so far the police had no leads. The motive for the shooting remained a mystery. The victim, a young Long Island man who was selling vacuums door to door to pay his way through college, had no criminal ties. No guns were found in his car.

All the color drained out of my father's face. The kid who had come to our front door hadn't been part of a hit squad. He was just an innocent bystander who had stumbled into a lethal situation. Over and over, my father read the articles, unable to take in what he was learning. He had killed an innocent kid. Somebody's son. As Debra and I watched in stunned silence, my father started to cry. He sat there, staring down at the paper, tears running down his face. Then he stood up and, without saying a word, went up to his study and shut the door.

My father continued to go through the motions of doing what was necessary, but the light was gone from his eyes. I learned that he had been able to dispose of the car and other evidence. Cousin Joe, who couldn't even shoot straight, had shot several holes in our own car in the excitement of the chase. Our car contained damning ballistic evidence, but my father had gotten rid of the Cadillac that first night. He and my mother spoke to each other less and less. My sisters gradually returned to normal, and I began going through the summertime motions, swimming every day in the canal behind our house. Everything resumed its normal course. Everything, that is, but my father.

The harsh reality of what he had done opened a fissure in my father that widened with every passing day. He was a broken man. I watched in silence as he began to disintegrate. It was weeks before he could eat normally, days before he could eat at all. During the day he sat in the darkness of his den; at night he went out and then returned to pace until sunup. As I lay in bed listening to him walk back and forth, back and forth, the silence was occasionally broken by the sound of retching in the bathroom. After all the years of shutting his eyes to what he was doing, of hiding behind the rationalization that killing was just an unpleasant but necessary part of doing business, he was suddenly confronted with the reality of who he had become. This was no gangster he had killed; this was somebody's innocent son. He knew that in destroying the college student's family, he had also destroyed ours.

There was one final piece of business that would have to be taken care of if he were to survive. Paul Castellano was livid about the killing of the college student. To kill an innocent kid in broad daylight, in front of witnesses, was insanely stupid and risky. Castellano still suspected that my father had been involved in the hit on the Colombians, and because of the hit, the Gambino family now stood trapped between twin dangers: reprisals from the Colombians and investigation by the federal task force. Castellano knew that Chris had done it, and there was little doubt he would order Chris hit as soon as possible. They had to find a way to appease Big Paul, or he would have them all killed.

A few nights later, my father did not come home. Swallowing my fear, I walked the house all night with Major, guarding my family in his absence. When he finally came home the next day, I was weak with relief. He was pale and drawn, saying nothing as he went into his office and closed the door. That evening we ate dinner in the kitchen, and when my sisters went upstairs afterward, I sat in the kitchen with my father while my mother put the plates in the dishwasher. There was a small television in the kitchen, and we were playing cards and staring at it in silence when the evening news came on. I was looking down at my cards when I heard the newscaster say, "The body of a young man identified as Christopher Rosenberg was found early this morning on a deserted street in Brooklyn. Rosenberg had been shot several times, and his car was riddled with bullets from an automatic weapon. Police say it appears to be a gangland hit." As I looked up at the screen, my father rose from his chair and snapped off the TV. My mother stopped rinsing the dish she was holding and stood unmoving. My mouth went dry, but my mind felt unnaturally focused, even calm. No one said a word. My father left the room, went upstairs to his office, and closed the door. He did not come out for nearly two days.

A couple of weeks later I went to the Gemini with my father for the first time since Chris was murdered. Freddy was there, and Joey and Anthony. As my father took his customary place at the table, I saw Anthony move with a hint of swagger to Chris's chair and sit down at my father's right hand. Joey slid into Anthony's old place. There was no grief in their faces, only a greater air of arrogance. I could smell it. I felt my father stiffen, but his face was impassive.

Prison officials use the expression "dead man walking" to describe a man on his way to be executed. My father was now a dead man walking. His own execution was just a matter of time, and he knew it. The life he had once gloried in as a great adventure had turned into a horrible dream from which there would be no waking. The life force he had once exuded was gone.

At thirteen, I knew my father was already dead.

six

SOLDIER

POSING WITH A BEAR ON A HUNTING TRIP WITH THE CREW

Men at some time are masters of their fates:
The fault, dear Brutus, is not in our stars,
But in ourselves, that we are underlings.

—SHAKESPEARE, *Julius Caesar*

When I was five years old, I chased off several twelve-year-olds who were trying to steal my sister's bike. I was half their size, but I made up for it with protective rage. That passion returned years later when I saw my father's life threatened. In the summer of my thirteenth year, I became a soldier in my father's army.

In the uproar following my father's murder of the college student, the crew went into hiding. Anthony and Joey disappeared, and for a while even my father didn't know where they were. Word eventually trickled back that they were in California. Cousin Joe went into hiding in a safe house near Times Square, and my father told my mother that he might have to leave unexpectedly for a couple of months. Only Freddy carried on normally for the time being, keeping an eye on the Gemini when no one else was there. My father was afraid to go near the place. There had been dozens of witnesses to the college student's shooting, and though my father had gotten rid of our car immediately, he lived in daily fear that someone would identify him.

The strain on my parents' marriage was obvious. They never fought, at least in front of us kids, but my mother was increasingly silent and tense. The relaxed affection I had always seen between them seemed to dissolve. My mother had always kept out of my father's business, being told nothing about his criminal pursuits, turning a blind eye to what she didn't want to know. Until I was thirteen, there was no reason for her to know. Now, however, she could no longer ignore my father's life outside our house. Our flight into hiding had changed all that. She had dedicated her life to creating a safe, happy home for us, and now she was living with the knowledge that her children's lives might be in danger.

Official-looking cars were parked down the street from our house almost twenty-four hours a day now. The black sidewall tires, silver half-moon hubcaps, and unusually large antennas marked them as government issue. It didn't take lettering on the doors to tell me they were surveillance vehicles. The men who sat in them, reading the newspaper or chatting as they watched the house, made little effort to hide their purpose. When either of my parents left the house, an un-marked car would pull out behind them and trail them wherever they went. Local police also began to appear in the area. The stop sign down the block suddenly required a patrol officer to monitor the in-tersection. The neighbors were well aware of the influx of cops roam-ing our normally quiet neighborhood. Cars would slow down when they passed our driveway, and I would see people leaning over to point at our house through the car windows. Some of them were neighbors, pointing us out to their passengers like a tourist attrac-tion. If they noticed me watching, they drove away. Word spread rap-idly in the wealthy little enclave, and at times it got so bad that there was a traffic jam in front of our house, with people anxious to see where "the mobster's family" lived. The days in the old neighbor-hood, when we were just Roy and Gina and the kids, were gone.

With his world crumbling around him, my father began turning to me in ways he had never done before. One night not long after we came back from hiding upstate, my father asked me to come to his study. He sat in his desk chair, his head in his hands, his body sag-ging with fatigue. I knew he hadn't slept in nights. When he looked up at me, his face was pale, his eyes haunted. He had to keep clearing his throat as he spoke to keep his emotions under control.

"Al, I need your help. I have to bring you into this. I'm so sorry, Son. I don't want you to do any of this, but I can't think of another way. I can't trust anybody else." His voice was shaking.

Instead of being frightened by his words, I felt myself growing stronger. My father needed me.

"It's all right, Dad, don't worry. What do you need?"

"It's like this. Big Paul's pretty upset about what's been going on. There's a lot of pressure on him. Rats are coming out of the wood-work with this witness-protection program. It's not like the old days. The FBI's got him under surveillance for this RICO law. The Colombians are okay for now, but I don't know if it'll last. There are people looking to kill me. I don't know where Anthony and Joey are, and that worries me. They should have told me if they were going on the lam. Your uncle Nino's worried that Dominick will turn, thinks we ought to take him out, but I don't want to do it. He's got his kids and all, and his wife's a real nice girl. Freddy will do anything I ask him, but Freddy's just . . . well, you know Freddy. I need your help to get away."

"Whatever you need, Dad."

"It's like this. I may have to leave in a hurry, and I may not be able to come back. I need to be able to get word to you, make sure the family's all right, have you take care of things for me. Can you do that, Son?"

"Sure, Dad, it's not a problem."

"Okay." He got out of his chair. I stood up, too, and followed him to the large cabinet on the far wall of his study. It was a beautiful piece, hand-carved and made to order for the new house. "Let me show you something."

He reached up above the carved panel to twist the knob that crowned the piece. I heard a click, and he put his hands on the top panel and lifted it off. Reaching inside, he took out a bundle of hundred-dollar bills.

"I keep extra cash in here. There's enough for a couple of months if you need it. I'll give you the bank account numbers. There's plenty there, and it's legit. Your mother and sisters will be all right if anything happens."

I nodded. "I got it."

"Okay. Tomorrow we'll go for a little drive, and I'll show you how I'll contact you. We can't use the phones at home anymore, not for anything important. They may be bugged. You'll have to check the house for bugs, too. Freddy's getting me something for that."

"Whatever you need."

My father nodded. "Okay, then." He looked exhausted.

It was past midnight. "You want me to stay up with you, Dad?"

"No, Al, you get some sleep. You got school tomorrow. I don't want you missing school."

"Sure." I moved to hug him. "Good night, Dad."

"Good night, Son." I felt his arms tighten around me as he held me close for a moment. He kissed me on the head and in a voice tight with emotion said, "I love you, Allie."

"I love you, too, Dad. Don't worry about me. Everything's going to be all right."

The next day after school, Dad and I went for a drive. As he pulled into traffic on the main drag near our house, he handed me a list. "You need to memorize this, Al, and then you need to get rid of it." I looked down at what he'd written. "#1 pay phone by men's room in pizza parlor. Sundays at 1. #2 pay phone on sidewalk by Burger King. Mondays at 3:30. #3 pay phone on second floor of May's, by electronics section. Tuesdays at 4. #4 pay phone in parking lot of grocery store. Wednesdays at 6." The list went on and on.

"If I need to go away in a hurry, I'll give you one of these numbers, so you'll know where and when I'll contact you. If I can't make the phone appointment, go to the next number up. Got it?"

"Got it." He slowed down as we approached the first location, a pizza parlor about a mile from our house. "That's the first one. I'm going to drop you off and go around the block. You go pretend you need to use the phone and meet me back outside." I got out of the car and went inside. The hostess directed me to the phone. No one paid the slightest attention to a polite thirteen-year-old kid looking to make a call.

A couple of minutes later Dad picked me up at the curb, and we continued on our route. It seemed normal, like learning the houses for a paper route. Dad continued, "Now this is very important, Al. You have to make sure you're not being followed. There's cars watching the house more and more these days. You need to practice taking as many different routes as possible, and you never go directly there. Make some stops on the way, pick up a burger, you know, normal stuff, so they won't get suspicious. Just make sure you lose them before you get to the destination."

"No problem, Dad. I'll start practicing on my bike tomorrow."

"Good." He paused a moment, then said, "Oh, and Al?"

"Yeah, Dad?"

"If I disappear and you don't hear from me, just go to number four. Keep going there every day until I call. It could take a couple of days."

"Sure, Dad, whatever you say." He seemed worried, but I told myself there was nothing to worry about. This was simple. Dad and I were going to take care of things. Everything would still be all right.

A few days later my father disappeared, leaving me the most cryptic of messages: the number of a phone booth. I was to be there at the end of the week to receive his call. I told my sisters Daddy was away on business. They seemed to assume that Dad was having money problems that he was trying to resolve. School was out by then, and I was glad I didn't have to leave the house every morning for the time being.

I continued to carry a concealed gun when I was with my mom or my sisters, and at night I patrolled the house with Major, armed. I moved quietly, and my sisters never heard me pass their bedroom doors. I knew that if someone broke in and I had to shoot, I would not miss. My father had shown me how the burglar alarm worked, and I checked the electrical contacts regularly. It took nearly an hour to check the windows in all three stories. He'd also showed me how to short circuit the system with a metal clip if I needed to get out unde-tected at night. I knew how to use the electronic scanning device, and I checked the house for bugs at least twice a day. The device was tiny, like a keyless entry system for a car, and I could sit down in the living room with my mother or sisters and scan the room without their ever seeing what I was doing.

I was worried about my mother. For the first time, as I wandered the house sleepless in the long nights, I saw my mother sitting alone in the darkness of our elegant living room. She would sit staring, her face filled with vacant sorrow, a drink in her hand. I had never known her to drink much alcohol, but in the suffocating fear of those end-less nights, I watched in silence as she sipped the liquid like medica-tion. Guilty for spying on her privacy, I would creep quietly back up the stairs into the darkness. As far as I know, she never noticed I was there.

Only months into puberty, I found myself with all the rights—and all the responsibilities—of a man and a soldier. As the world around me altered irrevocably, my psyche began to alter with it. From the time I was eight years old, fear had been the dominating principle of my ex-istence. At the center of that fear was the knowledge that one day my dad would not come home. Yet when confronted with the possibility of that nightmare finally coming true, the terror mysteriously seemed to disappear. I was no longer conscious of anxiety, only of fierce, focused determination to keep my father alive. Like boys who go to war and are forced into manhood overnight, I no longer had the luxury of being afraid. Our lives were rapidly being reduced to simple survival. I felt very little emotion of any kind anymore. Instead I lived somewhere outside my body, my consciousness hovering nearby but never quite connecting, waiting for Friday when the phone would ring.

The call finally came. I had been extra careful on my trip to the phone booth, making three stops on the way and spending over two hours in side routes for a trip that usually took twenty minutes on my bike. My father was fine, he told me, holed up in a safe house with Cousin Joe in Manhattan. He needed a little more time to let his beard grow and make a few arrangements, but then we'd be leaving the country together for a little while. Meanwhile, he'd keep in touch once a week. How were my mother and sisters? They were fine, I told him. I had everything under control. He told me I'd better get home and told me the number for the next contact.

Things went on like this for over six weeks before I finally got the call I'd been waiting for. I was to tell my mother I'd be away with Dad for a couple of weeks. Then I was to pack some things in a garbage bag, sneak out the back of the house in the middle of the night, and swim across to meet him on the other side of the canal, near a cul de sac. "And Al?"

"Yeah, Dad?"

"Be careful, Son, you hear me?"

"Sure, Dad, I'll be careful."

I wasn't frightened the night I swam the canal; I was relieved to finally be doing something. I missed my father desperately, and I was happier in hiding with him than at home without him. My father drove me to a safe house near Forty-Second Street in the city, where Cousin Joe was still hiding out. I almost laughed when I saw Joe. In an attempt to disguise himself, he had tried to dye his white hair red, but instead it had turned clown orange. He looked absolutely ridiculous. My father sent me to the drugstore with a list of hair-care products, and when I got back, Dad and I redyed Joe's hair ourselves. It didn't come out great, but at least people wouldn't point and laugh if they saw him. For the first few days we stayed inside most of the time, talking and watching TV while Joe cooked. A couple of mornings Dad and I walked down to the corner deli for breakfast, just to get out of the house for a while. My father wore dark glasses and a baseball cap, and with the new beard, even I barely recognized him. One afternoon we went to a matinee and saw *Poltergeist*, which had just come out that summer. Mostly, though, we just talked as Dad filled me in on the plan he was formulating.

If it became too dangerous for him to remain in the United States, he needed a place he could escape to permanently. He didn't want to go any place that required a passport, because a false passport meant federal prison if he got caught. The most practical choice was the Bahamas. He had already gotten a false Italian birth certificate and three American ID's in different names to travel with; he would establish another identity in the islands. I would need false identities as well, for I would not be able to travel back and forth to see him under my own name. He laid out three sets of identification for me on the coffee table in the safe house, each consisting of a driver's license, a birth certificate, and a credit card. If the travel reservations were made with cash instead of a credit card, he pointed out, it would look suspicious. The cover had to be as complete as possible. The birthdays on all three of mine were my real birthday, but the year was different. I had to seem old enough to travel alone. It seemed funny that I had three driver's licenses, but I couldn't use any of them to drive. I didn't even know how. Dad told me to memorize the information for all three identities until I could use them flawlessly, without appearing to think about what I was saying. We would be leaving for the islands in just a few days.

He also told me what to pack. I was to bring all the things any kid would bring on a vacation in the Bahamas, including my swim gear and a couple of books that looked like assigned summer reading. He had also gotten me a copy of *Penthouse* to put in my carry-on where the customs officials would be certain to find it. That way they would be so distracted by the photos that they wouldn't pay much attention to me.

Dad had booked us on separate flights to make certain no one connected us. His left eight hours before mine; a few hours after he took off, I checked my baggage and then sat around La Guardia, reading magazines and eating junk food like a typical teenager on vacation. I wondered if Uncle Vinny still worked there. Those trips there with Dad seemed like several lifetimes ago.

My flight was uneventful, and when I landed a few hours later, I took a cab to the hotel as my father had instructed me. I already knew what room he was booked in. The hotel was on the beach. The scenery was breathtaking, turquoise waves rolling onto a crystal beach, and the luxury hotel had every amenity, but we weren't there to enjoy ourselves. This was serious business. Dad made a couple of calls, and early the next morning we rented a car and drove to the department of vital statistics downtown. A man was waiting for us in an office there. We went inside, and I watched my father count one thousand dollars into his hand. Ten minutes later we left with a new Bahamian identity for my father, complete with a genuine birth certificate. It was that simple.

The next few days were spent driving around, acquainting ourselves with the area, looking at houses to rent. I needed to be able to find my father without asking around too much if he moved there. We also needed a cover in case anyone wondered what we were doing there, so my father signed me up for scuba lessons. I was already an accomplished swimmer, but after several days of diving, I earned my scuba diving certification. If anyone asked me how I had spent my time, I would have an answer for them.

Our last night there, we went down to the beach at sunset. I would be leaving for home early the next morning, since school started in a week; my father would take a later flight. If word on the street indicated it was safe enough, my father would come home. If not, I knew what to do. We sat on the sand side by side, gazing out to sea. The ocean turned from gold to bloodred, painting a path of liquid sunlight to the glowing orb sinking beneath the horizon. It was so beautiful, it made my throat catch. I looked over at my father, who sat in silence next to me, blind to the overpowering beauty all around us. I wondered if we would ever be there together again. The next morning, I left for New York and the beginning of the eighth grade. My mother never knew where I had been.

A month later my father came home. Anthony and Joey came back from California. I never did find out what they were doing there. Cousin Joe moved from the safe house back into his apartment in Brooklyn, though Dad never took me to the Gemini anymore. He didn't think it was safe. For a while, life seemed to resume its normal rhythm. As I settled into the eighth grade, I continued to behave in public like any other Long Island teenager, doing my homework and going to the movies. My real life remained private, a secret only my father and I shared. I was rapidly becoming a skilled, effortless liar. All the secrets I had to hide from the world, all the strategies I needed to mask with my schoolboy appearance, all the things I couldn't tell my mother—these things formed a disguise as effective as anything my father kept in the trunk of his car. The most frightening thing about this elaborate double life was that it was beginning to seem normal to me. I was coming to understand my father's ability to keep his worlds separate. Unlike criminals, however, I was deeply uncomfortable with the continual need for duplicity. I carried an ever-present load of anxiety like other kids carried their backpacks.

By the time I graduated from the eighth grade at the end of the year, my transformation into a junior wiseguy was nearly complete.

As a graduation gift, my father gave me a platinum watch ringed with diamonds exactly like his own. It was a symbolic gesture as much as a gift. The watch was totally inappropriate for a boy of fourteen; it was a rich man's watch, a symbol of success and of power.

The saving grace of that year, and of all the years since then, came in the form of two guys named Tommy and Nick.

Nick came into my life one afternoon as I crossed the school grounds on my way home. Nick was a tall, burly kid with a big heart and a tendency to get into fights, and that day he was hopelessly outnumbered. Five kids had jumped him, and seeing him swinging gallantly at the ring of boys around him, I jumped in to help. I barely knew him, but I knew an unfair fight when I saw one, and I came to his defense. I was still short for my age but strong and skilled; and between the two of us, Nick and I sent the others running. From that day on, we remained fast friends. Nick was kind, loyal, and warm hearted. He didn't care what my father did for a living, and he didn't ask. I was just his friend Al. For the first time, in and out of school, I knew someone had my back. It felt good.

Tommy became part of my life the summer before the ninth grade. Tommy's family lived down the street from us. I knew Tommy's younger sister from school, and one afternoon she invited me over to swim. I walked with her out to the pool, and there was this tousle-haired blond guy sitting in a pool of blood on the deck. He had cut his foot working on their boat. Tommy was older than I was, but we hit it off immediately. We talked and joked for a while and ended up taking the boat out into the canal. Tommy knew who my father was; everyone in the neighborhood knew. He just didn't care. He was more interested in swimming and girls and sneaking some beer down to the dock on a hot summer evening. Tommy told me he'd hang out with the Wop if I'd hang out with the Kraut. It sounded like a deal to me. I took him home to dinner one night, and once he'd tasted my mother's cooking, he practically moved in. Between my pretty sisters and my mother's food, he was at our house more than I was. When I had to go away with my father, Tommy volunteered to "hang out and keep an eye on things." That meant flirting with Debra and making sure my mother never had to wrap up any leftovers.

When most people say they would never have survived without their friends, they don't mean it literally. I do. I would never have survived, physically or psychologically, without Tommy and Nick. They became the brothers I never had, and I knew they would die for me if necessary, just as I would for them. They made my life survivable.

My father knew that. The first time he met Tommy, he said that Tommy would be my friend for life. In an atmosphere of continual fear and betrayal, my father told me I could trust Tommy. Tommy was one of the few people my father allowed into the family on a regular basis during those years. He never talked business in front of Tommy, of course, and Tommy never asked me a single question about my father's business or my occasional disappearing act. When my father's crew came over on business, Tommy would vanish up the stairs or head home. On sunny days my father would sometimes take Tommy and Nick with us out on the boat. We would dive and fish or just lie in the warm sun. On the boat with Tommy and Nick, life seemed almost normal.

I knew some of the kids at school whispered about where my family's money really came from, but no one ever said anything to me. I did well in my classes because my father remained a stickler about homework and school participation. Even when he needed my help, he would wait for a weekend or vacation before involving me. I was never allowed to cut class. It was a strict family rule. My little sister never missed a day of school, ever, from kindergarten to college. I enrolled in Regents' classes in ninth grade, the college-track classes on Long Island. My father talked to me constantly about the importance of going to college. He'd never had the opportunity, for he'd had to start supporting his mother and Uncle Joe when he was still in high school, but he didn't want that kind of life for me. As soon as the family was safe and he could find a way out, I was to have nothing more to do with the Mob. I was going to be a doctor or maybe a stockbroker, whatever I wanted, just so it was something I could be proud of. He made me promise that, whatever happened to him, I would finish college. I promised.

My father tried hard to keep my daily life as normal as possible. For the most part, he seemed to be succeeding. At school I was a model student, always on time and prepared. I spent breaks and lunch times with Tommy and Nick. Tommy had a car, so we went off campus at lunch breaks to Burger King or Taco Bell, sometimes bringing a carload of classmates with us. When I was in town, I went to Saturday afternoon football games in the fall and to pool parties in warm weather. I had plenty of friends, from all groups, but there was one difference. Except for Tommy and Nick, I never brought them home. All of my socializing took place at school or at someone else's house. People thought of me as the comedian of the group. I still cracked jokes like I had when I was in elementary school. I couldn't have looked more carefree or well adjusted, but even in the middle of a party, I felt like I wasn't really there. One night I found myself standing by a friend's pool, laughing and joking about his idiot history teacher, yet all the time my mind a million miles away. I was always wondering if my father was safe, if there would be a message for me when I got home, if something bad had happened. No matter how many people surrounded me, I felt separate from them, like a spotlight isolating a singer on a stage. It was like pretending to be a teenager, for how could I take the outcome of a football game seriously when our family's life was at stake—literally. Being a high school student was my cover, not my reality.

My father still took me camping when he could, but even these father–son outings were being steadily transformed into survival lessons. Dad gave me his old copy of the Boy Scout handbook and told me to study it carefully. If we had to hide out in the woods, he told me, knowing how to survive outdoors without supplies would be essential. Trips upstate together became opportunities to put what I read into practice. The key lesson in these outings was "use what you have and make use of what you find." On one trip we ran out of both food and water, and it took longer than my father expected to reach a source of fresh water. We had been walking nearly all day when we came across a well near a cabin deep in the woods. The well's cover had a padlock to keep animals from getting into it. After several futile attempts to open it, my father pulled out his handgun and shot the lock off. "Use what you have, Al," he told me. If that meant using a revolver instead of a bucket to get water, then you used the revolver.

By the end of freshman year, with my father gone more and more of the time, it became my responsibility to do cash collections in his absence. For the most part, it was little different from a paper route after school. My father simply took me around, introduced me to his loan customers, and said, "This is my son, Albert. He'll be picking up your payments when I'm out of town." And I would. The customers weren't underworld types; they were salesmen, shop owners, and mechanics. I would stop by their places of business on a Friday afternoon, pick up a paper bag or an envelope, thank them, and take the money home. I never even counted it. Customers observed a certain honor system based on a mixture of intimidation and respect. Nobody wanted to cheat the Mob.

Since I was still too young for a real driver's license, Tommy drove me on these errands. He had a pretty good idea what was going on, and eventually I confided bits and pieces to him. I even gave him a nickname befitting his new status: "Tommy Wheels," my driver, just as Freddy was my father's driver. I don't know what Tommy's parents would have said if they'd known what he was doing, but we were teenagers, and to Tommy it was all a lark. What was the big deal about dropping me off at the drugstore and circling the block to pick me up a few minutes later? The only danger he saw was boredom. One afternoon he got a bright idea to liven things up a bit, and against my better judgment, I went along with him.

I was due to make the weekly collection from Joe the barber, and I knew it would be a challenge. Joe was a deadbeat in every sense of the word. A chronic gambler, Joe had gambled away the money his family needed for his daughter's surgery. Sitting in the barber's chair one day, my father overheard Joe's wife crying as she told her husband he'd just lost the money for an operation their daughter needed. Joe knew my father only as a customer in those days, but overhearing the conversation, my father asked Joe how much the surgery would cost. Joe told him, and my father handed the money over on the spot. Joe thanked him profusely and solemnly promised to keep to the payment schedule they agreed on. His daughter had the surgery, and for a while Joe stuck to the bargain. As his daughter improved, however, Joe gradually slipped back into his old ways and began gambling away the payments he'd promised my father. My father disliked Joe and had contempt for him because of the way he treated his wife and kids. He told Joe he'd better not catch him gambling again. In spite of warnings, Joe continued to shortchange my dad week after week.

Tommy had heard most of this story, and one week he came up with a way to collect the cash. We'd already been there twice that week, and each time we were told that Joe had just left, and could we come back another time? I wasn't about to beat him up to make the collection, but I did want to get the payment. We knew that Joe was sneaking out the back door every time we arrived, so Tommy got the bright idea of trapping him. I was doubtful, but Tommy kept saying, "Come on, Al, it'll be fun!" Tommy was older and considerably bigger than I was, and he wanted to flex his muscles. So we showed up at the barber shop unexpectedly one afternoon, and Tommy stationed himself at the back door while I went in the front. Tommy pushed a trash barrel directly behind the back door while he waited.

Sure enough, the minute I walked in the front door, I heard someone running and took off after him. Joe dashed straight out the back and into the trash can, tripping and falling into the alley. By the time I got there, Tommy had Joe by the collar, obviously having the time of his life. I looked at Joe and said, "Come on, Joe, nobody wants to hurt you, but you owe my father some money, and we all know you're gambling again. So for God's sake, just get it over with and pay up." Joe counted out the cash while I watched, and that was that. Tommy laughed all the way home. It was the most fun he'd ever had. I only hoped my father didn't find out. He didn't like my taking unnecessary risks.

Nothing was fun for me anymore. The price I had paid for losing my fear was that my capacity for joy went with it. I could and did experience pleasure at times, but happiness was beyond my reach. I went through the motions. I was always the glad hand and big spender in my small group of friends. Even by the standards of wealthy Massapequa, I had money to burn. My father, consumed with guilt for what he was exposing me to, tried to make it up to me by showering me with everything money could buy. And in his world, money could buy just about anything.

One weekend shortly after my fourteenth birthday, my father brought me along while he made a trip to the country, where a friend of his raised Thoroughbreds. I had been there many times; my father kept several horses of his own there, for himself and for Debra, who was an expert rider. On that particular afternoon, he casually suggested I go to the barn while he talked with his friend and see a fine new Thoroughbred he'd brought in. I walked to the barn and made my way down the row of stalls to the area my father had mentioned. When I got there, I was baffled to find that the stall was empty, but a beautiful young Italian girl was standing there. I thought she must be a stable hand or a rider, so I asked her if she knew where the new Thoroughbred was. She laughed and said, "Right here."

I still didn't get it. Looking around, I said, "Where?"

As I stared in amazement, she pulled her shirt over her head, unfastened her bra, and drew me forward to fondle her breasts, murmuring, "Happy birthday, Al." I felt my body go white hot. Seconds later she began removing my clothing and drew me down into the straw. At fourteen years old, I lost my virginity in a literal roll in the hay.

Afterward I returned to my father and his friend in a daze. Dad laughed and slapped me on the back, asking, "How did you like your birthday present, Son?" I tried to play it off like it was no big deal, but I could feel my face growing hot. Both men laughed. From then on, my father told me, I could have any woman I wanted from the string of call girls my father's operation financed. I already knew he had prostitutes working for him; I had seen them hanging around his operations when I went to New Jersey with him. I had passed another of my father's rites of passage. Now, I was a man.

Tommy and Nick, when they heard about it, thought I was the luckiest kid on the face of the earth and wanted to know when they could get in on the action. I had begun picking up collections from an escort service when my father was out of town. Dad had ordered a limo to pick me up at the house and take me to the city to make the collections. It was a very expensive agency that catered to the wealthy and famous of Manhattan, and the first time I went in there, I thought the women who came and went were the most beautiful creatures I had ever seen. One afternoon, when the owner took me in the back to give me the payment, I looked him right in the eye and said, "Thanks. I'm taking three girls with me for the evening, too."

The man looked at me, startled. "What did you say?"

"I said I'll take three girls. On the house."

I could tell he was angry, but he didn't dare refuse me. For all he knew, my father had ordered the girls as part of the payment. Fifteen minutes later I was in the limo with three women who looked like supermodels, feeling like I had just scored the biggest coup any high school boy had ever made. I told the driver to take me to Little Italy; then I got Tommy on the phone and told him to get Nick and meet me at a restaurant on Mulberry Street. I had a surprise for them. When the guys got to the restaurant an hour later, their eyes nearly fell out of their heads. I played it cool, acting like they were just three women I had met at the restaurant. Afterward we got in the limo, and I ordered the chauffeur to keep driving around the city until I told him to stop. Then I put up the window and made a pass at one of the girls. Naturally, she didn't say no.

Nick was beginning to figure it out, but Tommy had actually bought my whole ridiculous story. He was in the process of talking earnestly to one of the call girls, telling her about his classes and plans for college. Finally he said, "Hey, if I called you sometime, would you maybe go to dinner or to the movies with me? I really like you."

The girl laughed at him and said, "Honey, you can't afford me."

Tommy looked confused and embarrassed, but Nick and I roared with laughter. Finally I said, "Tommy, you idiot, she's a hooker! She belongs to one of my father's associates."

"You can do whatever you want with me tonight, cutie," she said with a wink. "It's on the house." Tommy's face turned beet red beneath the freckles. Luckily for him, the girl knew what to do even if he didn't. Afterward he and Nick bragged to all the guys at school about the women they'd had. I don't think anyone believed them, but it didn't matter to them. They felt like the coolest guys in school.

With access to a limo whenever my father was out of town, I continued to pick up a few call girls every time I picked up cash at the escort service. After a few rounds of this, the owner was furious, for the girls were worth considerable money to him. When he finally mentioned it to my father, my dad hit the roof. He hadn't yelled at me like that since I was a little kid. That was the last of the call girls, but it wasn't the last of the women.

I wasn't even fifteen yet, but I felt like a man, and I was already playing the part. I began trying to fill my emotional void with pleasure. Whenever the fear set in again, I would pick up my friends, a couple of beautiful girls, and a bottle of champagne and drown my consciousness. Afterward I was left exhausted and empty, but while it lasted, I felt a rush of counterfeit power. In those moments I was strong, invulnerable. There were no more free call girls, but I soon found that plenty of women would go with me for free during these nights on the town. It was my first taste of the sexual allure the Mafia holds for many women. I played into that notion, and I learned to use it to my advantage in the secret life I was leading. In Massapequa I remained a shy, awkward adolescent. I had my first girlfriend at school, a sweet, traditional girl. I could perform like a man with a prostitute, but my hands still sweated at the thought of putting my arm around my girl.

By the time I entered my second year of high school, my father was disappearing regularly, and I took on more and more of the cash collections for his businesses. It bothered my father, and he repeatedly apologized for putting me in that position, but it continued to happen. One of my father's most lucrative businesses at that time, next to the car theft operation, was a string of sex shops and prostitution rings on Forty-Second Street in Manhattan. Forty-Second Street was the red light district of New York City in those days, and its sidewalks were lined with hookers leaning against storefronts that advertised sex malls and pornographic films. Many of those stores were my father's. It was another world that most teenagers never enter.

To authorize the money pickups, my father introduced me to the pimp that ran the prostitution ring. He knew the system well and ran the day-to-day operations. My father's only role was financial. The pimp had a girlfriend, a strikingly beautiful woman who lived with him but also worked as a call girl. I was shocked the first time I heard him set up the woman he claimed to love with a customer. I asked my father about it, and he said that to the pimp, the girlfriend was an expensive commodity that he couldn't afford to waste. She fetched top dollar, and it would be foolish to give up the revenue she could bring in. It was a practical matter. Besides, she did it willingly. All the women in the ring did. They made far more money than they could ever make doing traditional jobs; they had expensive clothing and jewelry, and some had nice apartments where they could raise their children in comfort. It was a good deal for everyone, my father reassured me.

I listened to what he was saying, and on one level, it made sense. Yet a distant voice in the back of my head echoed other words my father had taught me: Always treat a woman with respect, for she is somebody's daughter, mother, or sister. I thought of my own sisters. I knew there was something wrong with what I was hearing, but I couldn't figure out what it was. There was a fundamental contradiction in what I was experiencing.

My two sets of morality came close to colliding one afternoon as I was making a routine collection for my dad. The Roxy Theatre, once the pride of Broadway, had been converted into a sex mall that my father now owned. Once famous, it towered over Forty-Second Street like some grand old lady of years gone by. I had never been inside, but in my imagination, the glory of former years still lingered. I was excited at the prospect of entering the old building. It would be like walking into the past.

Nothing I'd seen so far prepared me for what I met inside. I had made many collections on Forty-Second Street by then. An associate of my father called Tony Cigars would pick me up at the house in a black Cadillac limo and drive me into the city after I finished my homework. The collections themselves were simple; most of them involved walking into some shabby office and picking up an envelope or a small package and slipping it into my jacket. Afterward I would take the money home and put it in the carved cabinet in my father's office or take it to Cousin Joe to place in the safe. The collections were usually depressing more than disturbing. But what I saw inside the once dignified walls of the Roxy was far beyond anything I could have imagined.

The arched ceiling still bore the elaborate gilded carvings of the early part of the century, when vaudeville ruled. Even the neglected paint and the loose plaster couldn't obscure the remnants of the Roxy's former beauty. As I followed the manager through the lobby, however, I noticed a row of what appeared to be small stalls or cages lining the walls. Someone had erected a cheap wall with flashy paint on the entrances and peep holes on the sides with sliding panels. A Hasidic Jew was emerging from one of them, dusting off his black coat as he did so. Hasidic Jews, the manager explained, were some of their best customers. Their religion forbade certain sex acts with women of their own faith, including their wives, so they frequented the shops on Forty-Second Street instead. Besides, he snickered, it was easy to hide any number of things under those long, loose coats.

As we passed the stall the man was emerging from, I couldn't resist glancing aside. In a small, filthy space, hardly big enough to lie down in, a naked woman sat staring blankly in the corner. She seemed indifferent to the body fluids pooled on the floor around her. The stench that emerged from the space nearly made me retch. "Jesus Christ," I thought, "an animal wouldn't mate in that place." I stared at the man walking by me, but he was indifferent to my reaction. With no apparent sense of shame, he calmly walked toward the exit. As we neared the end of the row of cubicles, I saw a Hispanic man working in one of the spaces. He had a bucket and a mop, and he was swamping body fluids out of the cubicle the way you would muck out a stall. Once again, a wave of nausea swept over me. Turning to the manager, I said, "Jesus! Nobody should have to do that job."

The manager just shrugged and said, "He's paid well."

As we passed the last stall and headed toward the main theater, we passed the former concession stand. An old-fashioned popcorn machine still sat there, a relic of the days when kids bought intermission treats between films.

We rounded the corner into the main auditorium, and the manager led me down the aisle toward the wings, where the small office was situated. As I walked toward the front of the auditorium, I looked around in the vast space. The place was surprisingly crowded for the middle of the afternoon. Large, dusty velvet curtains framed a stage with old-fashioned footlights lining the apron. Music was playing on a bad loudspeaker, and as I looked up at the stage, I was stunned to see a very pregnant woman parading around, completely naked. She was walking up and down with several other women, all of them nude, displaying herself for customers. The manager told me that the women were competing for the highest spenders. The pregnant one always got the best offers, he told me. The crowd loved the pregnant ones, the bigger the better.

As I watched in sickened fascination, the women made their deals and the lights dimmed as they began to dance. I visibly flinched when, as though on cue, men all over the auditorium unzipped their flies and began masturbating. The sound was so loud, it actually echoed. A chorus of groaning began. I looked away, longing to cover my ears, and hurried toward the office in the wings. The smell was becoming overpowering. As I began walking faster, I noticed the soles of my shoes sticking to the floor. Looking down, expecting to see the residue of chewing gum or candy, I realized that the floor was coated with a mixture of semen and urine. My gorge rose. Taking the package that was offered to me and shoving it inside my coat, I nearly ran from the premises.

That evening, when I got home, I peeled off every stitch of my clothing and threw it all in the garbage. Doubled over the toilet, I vomited until my stomach ached. Then I turned on the water as hot as

I could stand it and climbed in the shower. I lathered myself over and over, scrubbing until my skin was raw, drenching my scalp with shampoo. But nothing seemed to get rid of the smell, of the film of filth that still clung to my body. Finally I got out of the shower and rummaged through the medicine cabinet for the box of Q-Tips. Soaking them in alcohol, I began scrubbing the inside of my nostrils, anything to remove the stench that seemed to linger there. My hands were shaking, and I could barely keep a grip on the cotton swabs. Finally I gave up and crawled into bed, where I lay sleepless in the darkness, trying to will the obscene images out of my memory. I didn't dare close my eyes.

Later, in the small hours of the morning, I heard movement downstairs. Trying to quiet my breathing, I slipped from under the sheets and picked up the .38 I always kept loaded and ready in the compartment by my bed. Moving down the darkened hall as silently as a shadow, I crept toward the stairway. "Shit!" I murmured as I realized that Major was in the run out back. Why hadn't he barked? In the silence that was nearly absolute, I discerned a movement. Leaping forward in one instinctive motion, I lifted my gun to fire. At the same moment, another figure leapt toward me, into the faint reflection of the security lights outside the window, gun pointed directly at me. Finger on the trigger, I felt my body go rigid. The face looking back at me was my father's. We both froze, our faces masks of fear as we realized what had nearly happened. Neither of us said a word. Turning silently, my father went back down the stairs, and I followed him, gun still drawn. We cautiously checked every door and window as we had practiced so many times before. Outside the kitchen window, a branch was scraping against the glass. Satisfied at last that the house was safe, we climbed the stairs together, still in silence, and went to our rooms. I lay down on top of the bedspread and waited once again for sleep to come and release me. That night, like so many others, it never came.

seven

REDEMPTION

SUMMER 1993. WITH CARDBOARD CUTOUTS OF
CROCKETT AND TUBBS

I am in blood
Stepp'd in so far that, should I wade no more,
Returning were as tedious as go o'er.

—SHAKESPEARE, *Macbeth*

My father died for his own sins, not for the sins of others. Those sins were many and serious, and by the end, he knew it. My father knew that his own damnation was certain, and he told me so in the most direct terms, but the last wish of his heart was that my sisters and I would not suffer the same fate. So he did the only thing he knew how to do that might make things right. He gave his own life in hopes of saving ours. The pain that I felt on his passing was like a sword run into my heart, and there were times I thought I would surely bleed to death. In Christ's hours on the Cross, scripture tells us that mankind's sin shut God temporarily from his son's view. At the end, my father's sins shut him away from me. I had never felt so utterly forsaken.

The events of the year before had set a complicated chain of events in motion, all leading to the same conclusion: the disintegration of my father's criminal career. For the first time, my father was arrested. In his twenty-five years in the Mob, that had never happened before. He was in the process of opening a Plato's Retreat—a sex mall like the one on Forty-Second Street—across state lines in New Jersey. The rumor going around was that the mall was actually a cover for a prostitution ring, and my father got called into FBI headquarters in

Jersey and booked on charges of soliciting prostitution. At that time the feds had strong suspicions about my father's business, but they did not yet have evidence to indict him. The arrest in Jersey was an opportunity to get him on the books and possibly hold him on something that would stick until they were ready to prosecute him for more serious offenses. They still weren't certain where he fit into the Castellano investigation, but they knew he was a player of some kind. They never charged him, and he spent only one night in jail. But the arrest destroyed any illusions he was still nurturing about anonymity. He was fingerprinted, voice printed, and photographed. He now had a record that was public knowledge. The Gemini Twins were booked with him, along with Cousin Joe. It seemed a minor incident in the scheme of things, but it unnerved my father. It brought him one step closer to being terminated by Paul Castellano as a bad risk. And the implied exposure and scrutiny threatened his auto theft ring, whose income was the only thing keeping Castellano from killing him. We had embarked on desperate times.

By 1982 Big Paul was being squeezed so tightly by the FBI that he had begun eliminating anyone who posed a risk. My father knew he was next. He spent hours talking to me about it in his study at night. One night at Freddy's house, as I sat in the living room watching television, I heard Freddy and Dad talking in the kitchen.

"Paul's greedy, and he's not giving respect to the guys who do the work for him. He wants all the money, but he doesn't want to do any of the dirty work himself. He keeps putting us out there, he's going to get us killed even if he doesn't order the hit himself. I don't trust him."

"You think we should try to take him out?" Freddy asked.

"I don't know. That's some serious shit. And what if we did? Nino doesn't want his job, and neither do I. I don't know. Maybe we ought to have a plan just in case."

They tossed around several ideas, but the hard part would be getting away without being identified. Paul Castellano was always surrounded by bodyguards. Finally Freddy made a suggestion.

"Tell you what, I could supercharge one of my bikes, and we could use that. If you ride on the back with a Mac Ten, you could take him out easy no matter how fast we were going. And we'd be out of there before his guys got near a car. They'd never catch us, and we could ditch the bike in the river and be home before anybody knew the difference."

My father said he'd think about it, maybe talk to Nino. They'd put the plan on the back burner for now, but if things got bad enough, he'd think about trying it.

My father's fears were well founded. The first blow that struck close to home was Freddy's arrest. After operating for so many years without attracting suspicion, the crew had become careless. The cardinal rule of all my father's operations was precision and caution. The crew was instructed to dispose of anything in the car that could tie it to its legal owner. My father exploded when he arrived at Freddy's garage one afternoon to find the crew parading around in the clothing of a Hasidic Jew. Many of the cars they stole belonged to the Hasids, whose religious restrictions were nearly identical to the Middle Eastern Arabs that made up my father's primary market. Like Muslims, Hasidic Jews could not sit on leather, so their preferred car was a luxury automobile with velour upholstery. The crew couldn't resist dressing up in the coat and hat they had found in the back seat.

They had also become careless in other areas. They didn't always bother to put on gloves when working on the cars, the first thing my father had taught me when he talked about stolen merchandise. It was awkward to handle the VIN tags with gloves on, so Freddy had swapped a few tags without wearing gloves, thinking he had successfully wiped the prints off. He was wrong. The authorities had figured out that large numbers of stolen cars were being shipped to the Middle East, and they were so determined to catch the thieves that federal agents actually went to Kuwait and dusted luxury cars for prints as they came off the ships. They found Freddy's thumbprint on a falsified VIN tag, ran the prints, and arrested him. They had him dead to rights, for Freddy was incapable of telling a credible story to cover up what he'd done. My father knew that Freddy would never turn on him, but he also knew that Freddy was the equivalent of a neon arrow pointing directly at him.

For a while my father nursed the illusion that even with Freddy in jail, the government still didn't have enough information to stop the theft ring, or enough evidence to indict him. Freddy was old school Mafia, and he kept his mouth shut and took the fall for my father. My father kept his part of the bargain as well, providing generous financial support for Freddy's wife and kids. They came for holidays with our family. The December after Freddy was arrested, I went with my dad to buy them all Christmas gifts.

Only months after Freddy's arrest, there was another blow to my father's operation. One of the stolen cars had Torahs and other holy objects in the back seat, and my father felt it would be sacrilegious to keep them. He told the crew to wrap the things up and drop them off secretly at the local synagogue. They did what he asked, but they couldn't resist touching the objects first—without gloves. The result was another set of prints, and another arrest, this one with devastating consequences.

Vito Arena turned out to be the key the government needed to finally indict my father. My father had taken Vito into his crew a couple of years earlier, as a favor to another Mob family. Vito was a hit man for another *capo*, and both the *capo* and another member of the crew wanted Vito brought into the stolen car operation. Vito was unusual, and most of the crew didn't much care for him. At over 350 pounds, Vito was morbidly obese. He was also openly gay in a time when it was totally unacceptable to be out. Anthony and Joey objected strenuously, insisting a "fat fag" hanging around was bad for their image. But my father told them it didn't matter what Vito did in his off time as long as he followed orders.

Ironically, it was his sexual life that helped turn Vito. When Vito was first arrested, my father arranged to get him out on bail, but Vito fled and went into hiding. My father was nervous, knowing Vito would probably turn. He knew that Vito's only real loyalty was to his boyfriend, not to the Mob. When the government couldn't find Vito, they decided to use his boyfriend as bait. They arrested his boyfriend on some charge or other and put the word out that if Vito wanted his boyfriend back, he would have to come and get him. So Vito negotiated a deal. If the government put him and his boyfriend in the same cell and met a list of random demands, including a barber's chair for Vito's cell, Vito would not only return but would turn informant. The government couldn't write up the plea bargain fast enough. They finally had a key figure in the auto theft ring who was willing to tell what he knew. And Vito knew a lot, more than enough to cripple the theft ring and convict my father. In a futile attempt to intimidate Vito, my father raided Vito's apartment and confiscated a large collection of photographs showing Vito engaged in sex acts with other men. He hoped the photos would give him some control over Vito, or at least discredit Vito with the authorities.

My father was growing desperate. He knew it was only a matter of time before he was arrested, and this time it would stick. Far worse from my father's point of view was his fear that by involving me in the escape plans, he was risking my life along with his. Vito's arrest further upped the ante with Paul Castellano. The theft operation was already crippled, and if the pressure got much worse, he might have to shut it down altogether. It was a given that a member who couldn't produce would be eliminated. If the money dried up, Castellano would certainly have my father killed.

The trips to the Bahamas, which had been less frequent for a while, resumed. My father became increasingly careful with cash, putting as much aside in legitimate accounts as he dared. The house was already in my mother's name, and he had an attorney make sure that as many of our assets as possible were protected. He took out additional insurance policies and supplemented the college funds he kept for me and my sisters.

We had long planned and practiced my father's disappearance. Those plans were no longer adequate, though, for as long as they believed he was alive, the FBI would pursue him. Machiavelli advises that if all else fails, it is best to fake one's own death and disappear into permanent exile. The time had come to plan my father's "death," and it had to be utterly convincing. There was only one person my father could trust to carry out this desperate scenario. At sixteen, I would be my father's assassin.

We talked about it one night in his study. It was increasingly clear that he would probably need to disappear, and soon, before the FBI had him arrested or Paul Castellano had him killed. We had been meeting every night after dinner for weeks, tossing out ideas, reviewing options.

"The problem is the death certificate. Without it, your mother can't collect my insurance, and the government won't believe I'm really dead. If I just disappear, we'll never get one and someone will be after you forever. Everyone has to believe I'm dead. Otherwise it will never work. It's the only way we'll be safe."

"Can't we just get some blood? We could smear it on the car. If it's the same blood type, they might not know the difference."

"They'll never buy it. No bullet hole, no flesh, no blood trail. It has to be convincing. There's only one way. You'll have to shoot me."

I knew he was right. I quieted the turmoil in my mind and focused on what he was saying. I had to get this right. "What about Mom? What am I going to tell her?"

"You're not going to tell her anything. Everyone will have to believe I'm dead. In a couple of years, when everything settles down, you can tell her and your sisters what happened. Not till I tell you, though. Not till it's safe. It could be quite a while."

"How do you want to do it?"

"I'll have to take our car so they'll run the plates for an ID. I'll take it out somewhere, the warehouse district probably, someplace in the middle of nowhere. We'll need another car, too. I'll need you to steal one for me, else they might trace it to me. I'll show you how. I'm sorry, Son. I don't like asking you to steal something. You won't ever have to do it again."

"It's okay, Dad."

"You'll have to wear gloves, of course. You can use your Walther-PP K-S. It should leave a big enough hole for the blood and flesh evidence." The Walther was exactly like the gun James Bond carried in the movies. I kept it in a secret compartment my father had built into my bedside table so I could reach it easily if anyone broke in during the night. "You'll need to break it up after and get rid of the pieces when you dump the car. And you'll have to bring bandages and something to disinfect the wound. The bullet will go all the way through, so you won't need to worry about that. After you drag me to the other car, I'll need you to patch me up good enough to get me on a plane. If anybody sees the blood, they might call the cops."

I managed to keep my voice steady as I asked, "What if I hurt you, Dad? Hurt you bad, I mean?"

"You'll be careful. It'll be all right. Let me show you something." My father took a medical book down from the bookshelf behind his desk and opened it to a chart of the human body in the front. "Come around here, son," he told me.

His fingers on the chart, he began pointing out the location of the main arteries and vital organs in the middle of the torso. "You'll have to aim very carefully, but we'll be all right." He lifted his shirt and pulled a piece of fat out from the side of his body. "See? Right here. There'll be plenty of flesh this way, and you'll be a good two inches from anything vital. It shouldn't be any problem." Closing the book, he took a ruler out of the desk and told me to get my gun and come downstairs to the garage.

As my father walked around the car, thinking, we considered two possible scenarios. The first was for him to stop the car and open the door, as if someone else had pulled the door open. I would crouch inside the front door near the floor, point the gun up at him, and shoot him in the left side so that the bullet would go through his body and into the back seat. The angle was awkward, though, and he was afraid it might not leave enough flesh evidence.

The second scenario was better because it would look like a real inside job. I would get in the back seat right behind him and shoot through the seat back so the bullet would go into the dashboard. The seat back would be soaked with blood, and the bullet with the flesh evidence would be easy to find in the dashboard.

Once we decided on the trajectory, we needed to make sure I didn't miss. My father began measuring the front and back seats of the car. He sat down in the driver's seat, pulled out a piece of skin, and had me measure the exact distance from the outer edge of the seat back to the place the bullet needed to pierce his skin. I measured it three times to make certain I had it right. Then I measured the same distance on the back of the upholstery. The seam on the brown leather upholstery was in almost exactly the right position. With a little adjustment, the alignment was perfect. We practiced several times, my father climbing into the front seat and adjusting his body to the correct position, then me climbing in the back and placing the gun barrel against the seam at the correct height. When we both felt confident we had it right, we turned out the garage light and went back upstairs.

Years later, I was asked if I could have actually pulled the trigger. Without hesitation, I answered yes. If the only way to save my father was to put bullets into him, I would have done it. I rehearsed the plan in my mind a hundred times as I lay in bed that night. I was not going to let my father down. I would pull that trigger, and I wouldn't miss.

Before we could put the plan into action, however, another blow descended. Cousin Joe got himself in trouble once again. All of the crew had been told to lie low and be careful, but Joe got tired of staying home. Late one night the phone rang, and Joe's voice said, "Roy, I'm in a jam." Joe had gotten into a brawl with some guy at a bar, and Joe had pulled a knife and stabbed him. The guy was expected to recover, but the wounds were pretty bad, and Joe knew he would be arrested and probably never get out this time. Still the idiot he had been when he robbed the bank, Joe was actually calling from a pay phone at the bar. My father told him to pack a bag; he'd have someone pick him up immediately.

It wasn't difficult to get the victim's name and address. It was in the papers the next day that an unidentified man in his sixties had stabbed a patron at a local bar. My father put out a few feelers and found out that the guy was determined to press charges. My father couldn't afford to have one more associate implicated in a felony, particularly one who was a relative. That evening my dad said we had to make a little trip. As soon as I got in the car, he handed me a gun and a pair of gloves. The gun wasn't loaded, he told me as I checked the clip. I wouldn't actually have to hurt anybody; he just needed me to help scare the guy Joe had stabbed. Once we were in the guy's apartment, I was to stand behind the victim and hold a gun to his head so he wouldn't move until my father finished talking to him.

It was dark when we arrived. When a man's voice responded to my father's knock, my father held a phony police ID up to the peephole in the door. As soon as the man opened the door, my father shut it and backed him onto the couch. I moved swiftly to my place behind the chair and put the revolver to the man's temple.

Speaking rapidly, my father said, "I'm not here to hurt you. I'm here to resolve a problem." As the man watched in silence, my father counted out twenty-five thousand dollars in large bills onto the coffee table in front of him. "There's twenty-five thousand here. If you drop the investigation against the man who stabbed you, you can keep the money, and you'll never see us again. If you press charges, I'll have to ask my son here to put a bullet through your head. Is that clear?"

The man nodded quickly. "Sure, sure, whatever."

My father released the man and nodded at me. I pocketed the gun, and Dad signaled me to go to the door. Within seconds we were driving away. I looked back up at the window. The lights were still out, and no one was watching. The street was quiet.

For a while nobody said a word. Finally my father reached over and rubbed me roughly on the shoulder. "Sorry you had to do that, Son."

"It's okay, Dad. It's not a problem."

I knew it gave many people a rush to pull a gun on someone. I'd felt no rush, only a sickened pain deep in my stomach. It was the closest I ever came to harming another human being.

The next day we met Cousin Joe at the safe house where he'd taken refuge, stuck him in the back seat of the car, and drove him to La Guardia. The last act of Cousin Joe's tragic little farce took place there. My father had lectured him all the way there on behaving himself; it was essential, my father repeated, that he not attract any unnecessary attention. Joe was subdued, even docile as we passed through the security scans on our way to the gates. Obviously, we had all left our guns locked up in the car. But as Joe put his carry-on bag onto the conveyor belt to pass through the x-ray machine, I noticed the security attendant doing a double take. She peered into the screen in puzzlement, then said to the attendant next to her, "You need to take a look at this bag." My father and I glanced at each other as the attendants began removing the contents of Joe's bag and laying them out on the table. What on earth? Surely Joe hadn't been stupid enough to put his gun through the security check.

He hadn't. Instead he had packed a couple dozen of his favorite things, to get him happily through his weeks in exile. Among his other bizarre qualities, Cousin Joe was more than a little perverted. He had a fascination with sex toys, and his large collection of unusual devices took up quite a bit of space in his apartment behind the Gemini. While other attendants and passengers gathered around in fascination, the security personnel systematically unpacked a truly astonishing collection of sexual aids. To say that they attracted considerable attention is an understatement. A small crowd of onlookers was soon juggling for position to get a better view. My father couldn't believe it. "Jesus Christ!" he exclaimed and walked away, shaking his head in disgust. Joe seemed puzzled by all the attention he was attracting. Eventually the security personnel decided that the objects might be unusual, but as the toys were neither dangerous nor illegal, they soon packed everything back in the bag and sent Joe on his way.

The crowd began to disperse, but I could feel their eyes follow us as Joe made his way sheepishly to the departure gate. My father was too angry to speak. I gave Joe a hug and watched as my hapless cousin made his way down the ramp toward the plane. What a piece of work he was. Years later, as the Gemini myths multiplied, Cousin Joe would become legendary as Dracula, a ghoulish creature of nightmare proportions. He could be a nightmare, all right, just not in the sense his reputation later implied. In my eyes, he was always more pathetic than sinister.

As the summer wore on, my father sank further and further into depression. For the first time in my life, we didn't even go through the motions of a Fourth of July celebration. My father lay in bed in the dark all that day, and my sisters went over to a friend's house. When the sun set over the water that evening, Tommy and I sat on the dock and halfheartedly set off a few small rockets. There would be no barbecue, no neighbors coming to celebrate. The only sound came from the distant celebration of other families across the water.

I knew my father was deeply depressed. I attributed his sadness to his decision to go into permanent hiding, leaving the family behind forever. So often that last summer, we went out on the ocean together. I had my own speedboat, a gift for my sixteenth birthday, but we usually took my father's small yacht. Sometimes we went alone; other times Tommy or Nick went with us. While I drove, my father would sit in a deck chair near the stern, staring silently out into the distance. When we finally dropped anchor, I would fish or dive into the chilly Atlantic for a swim. My father would just sit there, often for hours, unmoving and unspeaking, gazing at the horizon. I wanted to believe that he was at peace in those moments, but I knew he wasn't. As the sun sank lower on the horizon, I would sit down next to him, the only sound the gentle lapping of the waves and the cry of gulls overhead. Finally, as the sky changed from blue to gold, I would turn the boat around and head back to Massapequa and the world he would soon leave behind permanently.

That fall I returned for my junior year of high school. Despite the chaos in my personal life, my grades remained good, and I tried to go through the motions of being a typical teenage boy. I had a steady girlfriend at last, a beautiful young girl with glossy black hair and a stunning smile, the prettiest girl in my class. She was kind, sweet, the sort of girl every high school boy dreams about, and she really cared about me. With all the rumors in the neighborhood, she must have known what my father did for a living, but she never alluded to it directly. One day she asked me why I was so sad sometimes. She wanted to understand, she said. I asked her if she had ever seen *The Godfather*. She said yes, though she didn't remember it that well. I told her she should read the book, read about the son, about Michael Corleone. That was the closest she could come to understanding my life.

My father was gone more than ever as fall darkened to winter, and when he did come home, he isolated himself. I developed the habit of picking up copies of the New York papers every day after school and bringing them home to my father. He would sit in his office for hours, scanning the obituaries, reading and rereading the articles.

The federal task force was closing in on the New York crime families with a vengeance. Each day brought news of a new arrest or of someone else turning informant. The crime pages and the obituaries were filled with names my father recognized. His friends were dying faster than his enemies. As I'd done as a young boy, I read the papers in private, too. Only this time, I reacted not with terror but with resolve. We'd pull this off, my father and I. We'd get him out of there before anything happened to him. I was just waiting for his signal.

I watched as our million-dollar mansion gradually became my father's prison. He was increasingly afraid to leave it, increasingly afraid that if he did, he would never return. The man who had once seemed invulnerable to me now lived in continual fear. I thought often of how meaningless our wealth had become. "Vanity of vanities," said the prophet from my Sunday school lessons, "vanity of vanities." We had everything money could buy—marble floors and yachts and expensive jewelry—and we could enjoy none of it. I wonder if he thought sometimes of that first house in Massapequa, where I'd learned to ride my bike and Jim the policeman dropped by for barbecues. I would have given anything to go back to that place and time.

Sensing the end would come soon, my father seemed intent on passing along every bit of knowledge he could think of. Some of it was advice: Be aware of your surroundings, sniff out the betrayer, always keep your cool, let others do the talking. Other times it was information. So-and-so was the person to go to if I needed a particular thing. He made sure I recognized the faces of anyone I might need to deal with, and that they recognized mine. He went over the bank accounts with me, the mortgage papers, the life insurance policies. I knew the names and numbers of our attorneys, our banker, our broker. I could manage the family's finances by myself if I had to. And he was always testing me, putting me in high-stress situations that required me to rely on my own skills and wit.

That winter a neighbor of ours had a long talk with my father.

Years later, the neighbor told me about that conversation. The man was a stockbroker—a very successful one—and though law-abiding himself, he liked my father and considered him a friend. It no longer took much guesswork for the neighbors to realize how deeply my father was in trouble, and the friend was worried. He knew how gifted my father was in managing and developing his legitimate assets. Our neighbor broached the forbidden topic with a courage I admired. "Why don't you quit this career you've made for yourself and come work with me? You're a natural for the financial markets. This life of yours is no good, for you or Gina or the children. You need to put it behind you."

"There is no way out for me. There hasn't been for a long time. I made my choices, and I have to live by them. Please just promise me one thing. Don't let Al follow in my footsteps. Get him a job on Wall Street when he's old enough. I'm not going to be around much longer. If you'd keep an eye on Gina and the kids, help them out every now and then, it'd mean everything to me."

The neighbor promised and returned home sober and reflective. He kept his promise to my father. He gave me a job on Wall Street the following summer, and every summer after that until I graduated from college and became a broker on my own. I will always wonder what my father's life would have been like if the interested neighbor down the block from him when he was a teenager had been a stockbroker instead of Joseph Profaci's brother.

Holidays had always been a major event at our house, but that winter, we seemed to be a house in mourning. My mother did her best with food and presents, but we were just going through the motions. Grandma and Uncle Joe came for Christmas as always, and even Cousin Joe returned from hiding to join us for Christmas dinner. That year, though, my father didn't even come down to eat. As we opened presents and pretended to have a good time, he remained locked upstairs in his study. Christmas came and went, but he never emerged.

A week later, New Year's of 1983, he still hadn't come out. The darkness in our home was palpable. As the days crept by, I told myself he was planning his escape. The weather was very cold, the roads icy, but no snow had fallen. It had not been a white Christmas. The next day was Debra's twenty-second birthday. Debra had graduated from high school and was attending art school in the city, but she still lived at home. My mother was already busy cooking for the celebration. Delicious aromas wafted through the house.

My final conversation with my father took place on the evening of January 9, 1983. That evening I went into my father's office to talk to him after dinner. I shut the door quietly behind me and took my accustomed place on the leather couch that faced his desk. My father sat in his chair behind the desk, looking out the window at the slate-gray canal. A single lamp glowed in the half-light of the office. For some reason my senses were heightened that evening. I noticed the intricate carving on the familiar wooden desk, the feel of the leather through the wool fabric under my thighs. It was very quiet. I watched my father in silence, memorizing his face as I had every night since the long ago evening I had first discovered what my father really did for a living. He looked tired, his skin sallow from fatigue or ill health, but he also seemed more relaxed than he had in weeks. He had made a decision.

After a few moments' silence, he turned to look at me and said flatly, "Al, I'm not going to be around much longer."

I said, "I know, Dad." All the plans, the years of rehearsing his escape flashed through my mind. "I'm ready. I know what to do."

He sighed, laid his hands flat on the desk, and leaned forward to look directly into my eyes. "Al, what are you going to do if I get killed?"

I felt like someone had punched me in the stomach. "I don't know, Dad. Well, I mean, I'll find out who did it, and I'll kill them. I just don't know exactly how."

Coming around the desk, my father grabbed me and pulled me to my feet. It was the first time in my life he had touched me in anger. "You will do no such thing. You will put me in a garbage bag and throw me away and pretend it never happened. And you will go to college, and you will have a good life. Do you understand me?"

My heart flooded with foreboding, but I nodded my head and said, "Sure, Dad, sure, whatever you want. But that's not going to happen. You're going away. Everything will be all right."

Abruptly, my father pulled me into his arms and hugged me as tight as he could, crushing my head against his chest. His voice was choked with emotion as he spoke. "Al, this is the life I chose, and this is just part of that life. I can't be a rat, and if I stay, they'll ruin all your lives. I'm going on my own terms. It's the only thing I can still do for you." He must have held me for five minutes before he finally released me. Then he said, "Take care of your mother and sisters for me" and turned away.

I told myself he was going to the Bahamas again, and this time he wasn't coming back. I almost believed it.

As I turned to go, I said the words I always said to him at parting. "I love you, Dad." And I left the room. A few minutes later I heard him get into the car and drive away. I never saw him alive again.

That night I lay in my bed as I had for years, staring at my bedroom window, waiting to see the headlights of my father's car as he turned into the driveway. Our conversation played and replayed continuously in my mind. My father would escape, I kept telling myself. He would get away. They would never find him; he was too clever, we had planned everything too well. They wouldn't kill him because they'd never find him. He'd come home tonight or the next night or the night after that. And if he didn't, one of the pay phones would ring, and I would be there to get it. I ran the route through my mind, repeating the times and places like a litany. I wouldn't let him down.

The next evening a beautiful dinner was laid out for my sister's birthday, the presents wrapped and ready for her to open, but still my father didn't come. My mother called around, but no one had seen him. This wasn't like my father; he never missed one of our birthdays. Finally I told my mother we should go ahead and eat, that Daddy had some business to take care of. An hour later, my sister blew out twenty-two candles. Afterward she went out to celebrate with her friends.

My father didn't come home that night, or the night after that. Hoping to get rid of the stone in the pit of my stomach, I called Uncle Nino. Nino was brusque. No one had seen him. My mother sensed my anxiety and asked if we should call the police to report him missing. I told her no, I was sure Dad was all right. She should wait a while longer, I told her. Five days after he disappeared, I told my mother to go to the police station and file a missing person report. I went with her. It was part of the plan my father had taught me; if he disappeared without telling me and didn't come home in five days, I should have my mother file a report. It would seem suspicious if she didn't and make his disappearing act seem less authentic.

I kept telling myself that everything was fine, that he had just executed one of our long-rehearsed plans, but inside I was filled with dread. I had stopped eating and sleeping, counting the hours until I could go to the designated phone booth and wait for a message. The plan for his sudden disappearance was for me to go to the phone across from the Massapequa diner at 8:00 P.M. one week after he left, to wait for his call. By the time the day came, I was frantic. The diner was only a few miles from our house, an easy twenty-minute bike ride, but I left long before it was time. I was so afraid of being followed that I wound through the streets for hours, indifferent to the cold winter air. When I finally reached the pay phone, I was shaking with nerves. For three hours I stood staring at that phone, sick with fear, waiting for a ring that never came. It was the longest night of my life.

The next day, more than a week after my father had told me good-bye, I went into his office to get some cash out of his desk for my mother to go grocery shopping. When I slid open the top drawer to take out the bills, I froze. There, lined up neatly in a perfect row, were all my father's personal possessions: his pinky ring, his diamond watch, his wallet with the pictures of us children, his wedding ring—and his gun. Lying next to the gun was a small pamphlet. I picked it up. It was from the local Catholic church. My father had gone to confession. Every pore in my body went numb, and my vision began to blur. My father would never leave the house without those things, unless . . . and it came to me. "If I stay, I'll ruin your lives, Al," he had told me. I thought he had meant stay in New York. He had meant stay. Period. He had known what was being planned. And he had put his gun in the drawer and driven himself to his own death. It was his final act of atonement, the only gift he could still give his family.

I took out the cash and shut the drawer. Then I went back in the kitchen and gave it to my mother. My eyes were dry and tearless, my hands steady. I had promised my father I would do whatever was needed. I intended to keep that promise. Then I walked upstairs, sat on the edge of my bed, and stared unseeing out my bedroom window. I would not see my father's headlights as he pulled into the driveway that night. The nightmare that had haunted me since I was seven years old had finally come true.

The next few days were almost unendurable. I kept my silence, and I waited. My mother was convinced that my father had gone into hiding once again, and I said nothing to change her mind. During the day I went to school; at night I paced the hallways, gun at the ready, checking and rechecking every door and window. I was the man of the house now. I could neither eat nor sleep. A sword was suspended over all of our heads, and I was waiting for it to descend. I steeled my-self for the blow.

It came on the night of January 18—my seventeenth birthday. My mother had baked a cake, and I was at the table with her and my sisters, trying to act as if nothing were wrong. Just as I blew out the candles, the doorbell rang. I went to answer it. My mother followed a short distance behind.

A crowd of police officers stood on the porch. There were at least a dozen of them; it seemed more like twenty, streaming across the porch and down the steps behind. Bracing myself, I asked them what they wanted. They said they had some news about my father and asked if my mother was home. Catching sight of her behind me, they shoved me aside and pushed through the door before I realized what was happening. Six of them streamed through the door with the icy January wind, fanning out through the foyer and into the living room and dining room before I was able to block the entrance. The lead detective's face was impassive, but the others glanced at each other as they took in the marble and crystal of the entryway, their faces masks of contempt. The mobster's house. It was like being invaded by enemy troops. This wasn't a standard unit; this was a small army. I tried to get closer to my mother, longing to protect her, but two officers stepped between us, blocking my way.

"Roy's dead, Gina," one of the detectives said. I flinched at the familiarity with which they spoke to my mother. "We found his body in the trunk of his car." There was no attempt to soften the blow. I had the sense they were hitting as hard as they could in hopes of shocking my mother into revealing something.

The lead detective herded her to the nearest chair, encircling her so that I could not get close. My mother sat there, pale and silent, her eyes straight ahead as they began reeling off the facts of the case.

"Your husband's maroon Cadillac was found abandoned on a street in Brooklyn. We received a complaint from a local businessman who said it had been parked there for days. After running the plates, we towed the car to our impound lot and dusted for prints. Afterward one of our officers popped the trunk. Your husband's body was inside." He paused for a reaction, and when he didn't get one, he continued.

"Your husband was shot seven times in the face and hands. The freezing weather kept his body from decomposing, or we might have located it sooner. We're waiting for the body to thaw before removing him from the trunk, but somebody from the family will have to come down to the morgue tomorrow to give us a positive ID. We're certain it's your husband; several of our officers recognized him. But we need a family ID to make it official." Handing her a piece of paper, "This is the address of the morgue. You'll need to have someone there early tomorrow. Also, do you know anything about a crystal chandelier? We found one on top of the body."

The room had gone slightly blurry as I listened to this rendition. All I could think about was getting to my mother, but the officers wouldn't let me. The men on either side of me watched my face the entire time. One of them was smiling. Everything seemed to have gone into slow motion, and I couldn't get it to resume normal speed. Somewhere in the background, far away, I heard Debra scream.

The sound of my sister's cry galvanized my mother into action. Looking defiantly into the detective's eyes, she rose to her feet and began backing him toward the front door, her four-foot-nine-inch frame pulled to its full height. "Get out of my house!"

"You have any idea who did this, Gina?" the detective asked as my mother continued backing him toward the door.

"You gotta have some ideas," another officer interrupted. He watched her eagerly, avariciously, like a circling vulture, his contempt for my father palpable. I had moved next to my mother when she rose, and the two of us herded them back out the door.

Relegated once more to the front porch, the lead detective handed my mother his business card and said they'd be in touch. "Give me a call if you think of anything."

There was movement on the walkway as the small army started back toward their patrol cars. The neighbors from next door had come onto their front lawn to see what was going on, but all I could hear was the sound of my sisters sobbing. As the lead detective turned to go, he handed me a card and said, "Get in touch with us, Albert. You cooperate, we'll find out who killed your father." I shut the door behind him and threw the lock. My sisters ran to my mother, crying. My mother had gone deathly pale, but she didn't shed a tear. She put her arms around them mechanically, murmuring words of comfort. I don't think she had any idea what she was saying. I went directly upstairs, to my father's study, and called the only person I knew who might help me. My uncle Nino.

Nino refused to take my call.

For a brief moment, I felt like I was going to pass out. Then pulling myself together once again, I went downstairs to where my mother and sisters huddled in the living room.

Later that evening the doorbell rang again. Debra answered the door. It was Tommy, come to share my birthday cake and watch a little television. I heard my sister murmur something and Tommy say, "What? Oh, my God. Oh, God. I don't know what to say. Where's Al?"

"Go home, Tommy," my sister told him and shut the door.

I spent the evening making phone calls, to my uncle Joe, my great-uncle Albert, Uncle Louis, Aunt Marie, and my grandmother. I called the morgue and got directions for the next morning. I didn't want my mother to see my father's body. He would look pretty bad. I was going to call for a driver to take me, but Uncle Louis said he'd take me.

My sisters took my mother upstairs later that evening. I heard her say to Lisa, "Did you eat, honey? You want some dinner?" as they led her to her bedroom. I found her there later, sitting silently on the bed. She looked up at me. "He's not dead, Albert. You know that. He's gone away somewhere again. He wouldn't let himself get killed. He's too smart for that." I let her talk. What good would it do to argue with her? She would find out the truth soon enough.

Later that night, after my mother had finally gone to bed, I sat at the desk in my father's office. There would be a great deal to arrange, a great deal to do in the next few days. I began making lists of all the people to call, all the arrangements to be made. Somewhere nearby a dark void of pain hovered, beckoning. I ignored it and continued writing.

eight

VENGEANCE IS MINE

MY SEVENTEENTH BIRTHDAY

I have supp'd full with horrors.

—SHAKESPEARE, *Macbeth*

It was the nightmare again. Somewhere before dawn I had slipped into a fitful slumber, the room filled with ghostly images as I turned and twisted in my sheets, sweat drenching the bed. I was back in my room as a seven-year-old, leaning against the window that overlooked our driveway, the glass cold against my cheek. The street outside was eerily silent, the only movement a faint scratching of tree branches on the side of the house. Major lay next to me, his head on my lap. I muttered to myself, random promises to a God who didn't seem particularly interested as I searched through the darkness for the headlights of my father's car. Down the block and across the street, our neighbors slept, undisturbed by the specters of gunshots, by the phantom plunge of a knife into a human torso. Where had my father gone that night, his trunk again filled with guns and knives and mysterious disguises? I held a coin in my sweaty palm and began to flip it. Heads he was safe, tails he was . . . tails. I flipped it again. Heads he was safe, tails he was . . . tails. Fear loomed from the darkness of the driveway and circled around me. I flipped it again. Tails. Tails. Tails. Tails. . . .

I awoke with a start, managing just in time to stifle the scream rising in my throat. For a moment all was confusion, the terror of the night lost in the white noise of sunlight streaming through my window. Then it came back to me. This was not a dream. The police, the FBI agents, the cars, and the phone calls. All those things were real. I forced my aching body from the bed. Eight o'clock. My uncle Louis would be here soon. We were going to the morgue to identify my father's body.

I showered quickly and pulled on some clothes. The door to my mother's room was closed as I made my way down the hall. My sisters' rooms were quiet. I hoped that they were still asleep. On the dining room table I could see the remnants of my birthday cake, seventeen candles half-burned and covered with clumps of pale icing. A few minutes later I heard a car pull into the driveway, and I went outside to climb in next to Uncle Louis before he rang the bell and disturbed my mother. I had told my mother that I would take care of the funeral arrangements, that Dad and I had discussed what to do. She'd simply nodded at me, her face blank. She seemed stunned, moving around the house like a sleepwalker.

Neither of us said a word as Uncle Louis backed into the street. His face was ashen in the morning light. My father's body had been found in Canarsie and taken to the morgue in Brooklyn for identification and autopsy. The bare branches of trees were stiff and frozen, and Uncle Louis's car slipped slightly as the tires hit the ice. As we drove through the gray January morning, a song came on the radio. It was Frank Sinatra's "Summer Wind." I felt a stab of pain, and for a moment I nearly lost control. My mind flashed back five months, to last summer. My father and I had been driving down this same highway together, the windows rolled down, warm wind blowing in our faces. Dad had thrown his head back to laugh as I reminded him of the time I was nine and put an explosive from the joke store in my mother's cigarettes to stop her from smoking. After all, the Surgeon General hadn't said anything about gunpowder being harmful. She'd lit up at Barbara's house and scared both of them half to death. It didn't stop her from smoking, but even she thought it was funny. Gina DeMeo's exploding cigarette became legendary in the neighborhood. I remembered how good it had felt to hear my father laugh again. He laughed so seldom by then.

There was no summer wind that morning, only pale January light and frozen yellow grass on the roadside. The song came to an end, and the news started. "Local authorities report that the body of reputed mobster Roy DeMeo. . . ." My uncle abruptly snapped the radio off. We drove north, then turned along the coast again toward Brooklyn. It was beautiful along this stretch of highway. On my right was a golf course, farther along the stables where my father used to take my sisters and me riding. To my left was the ocean. I remembered my father telling me that he would sometimes "borrow" the riding horses when he was a kid and go for a gallop along the beach as the sun rose. It was the only time, he'd told me, that he ever felt really free.

My body was cold as I stared out the window of my uncle's car that morning. Somewhere in the distance I was acutely aware of pain, the sensation I felt when the dentist blew air on an exposed nerve, but this pain burned throughout my body. I knew the pain was mine, but somehow I couldn't connect with it. It was odd to be riding with my uncle Louis. I couldn't remember the last time I had been in his car. It was nice of him to go, but it made little difference to me. My father's final charge to me ran through my head: "Take care of the family, Al. Take care of your mother and sisters." It was the only thing left I could do for him. I was not going to fail him.

I looked at the clock on the dashboard. A little before nine. It seemed strange that the clock was still moving, still alive, while my father was gone. I forced myself not to think ahead. One step at a time.

It was still early when we pulled up to the morgue. A security officer in the lobby of the building directed us around to the back. As I descended the stairs to the horror that awaited me below, I mentally rehearsed every moment that lay ahead, trying to anticipate each possibility so that nothing would catch me off guard. How bad was he going to look? Would he still even look like my father? Somewhere in the back of my mind, I could hear the litany of my father's voice: "Stay strong, act like a man, don't let them see what you're feeling." Something icy slipped through my veins and into my muscles, stiffening my legs, slowing my progress. There was little danger of my betraying any emotion. I felt nothing at all, only the coldness that was making my limbs unmanageable. My heart, like my body, had gone into hibernation.

At some point during my descent of the stairs, everything went into slow motion. When we reached the bottom landing, I paused for a moment before reaching for the doorknob. As my fingers closed over the knob, I recoiled from its coldness. I motioned my uncle through ahead of me, then followed a few feet behind. The room that opened before us was filled with men, far more than the staff I'd expected. My eyes went automatically to their shoes. Federal issue. Thick-soled, heavy cop shoes, not like the comfortable white ones some of the lab workers were wearing. *Always look at their shoes*, my father had taught me. And the hair. Cheap regulation haircuts. All of them were dressed in white lab coats like something out of a bad horror movie, but I knew who they were. Feds. They were waiting for me, their eyes on my face as I walked by. The stage had been set before we even got there.

The walls around us were a drab hospital green, and the air smelled like the chemicals that preserved frogs in my lab class at school. Nausea swept over me. I identified myself to the attendant, and he led us toward a small cubicle with a glass viewing window. The curtain was closed. I felt the "morgue attendants" gather behind me as I approached the glass. They were watching me intently, waiting to see what I would do.

A moment later someone inside opened the curtain. I heard my uncle Louis cry out and begin sobbing. He turned in front of me, trying to shield me from the sight on the other side, but I pushed past him and up to the window. I pressed my face against the glass and gazed inside. I could feel a dozen pairs of eyes boring into me as I looked.

There on a metal slab lay something that barely resembled a human being. The limbs were contorted from lying frozen in the trunk of a car for ten days. Blood had congealed and frozen under his skin, dark blue and red and purple in deep splotches. One hand was clutched against his chest, and there was a bullet hole in it. Part of my mind registered it as a defensive gesture. He must have thrown his hands up instinctively when he heard the gunfire. There were holes in his chest also, and three in his head. One bullet had blown his eye out of the socket; two others had passed through his skull behind each ear, execution style. There were seven bullet holes altogether. Seven bullet holes in my father. Yet as I continued to stare at the grotesque corpse that lay before me, I could make no connection to the man who had wrapped me in his arms so tightly ten days before. No tears came. Those eager faces would not see me cry.

I said, "That's him, that's my father," and started to turn away. A dark-haired officer in a suit and tie stepped closer and told me to look again. Detective, NYPD probably.

"You see the bullet holes, Albert? They shot him seven times. Did you notice that? Do you know who did it? Don't you want to help us find the guys who did this? Look at him, Albert. Look at your father."

The officer wore a look of concern, but somewhere behind his eyes I could see a gleam that was almost greedy. He wanted something he thought I had, and he wanted it badly. I held my body upright and replied, "I have no idea," then turned away and started for the exit. Uncle Louis followed, still crying. Two officers caught up to me.

"We need to ask you a few questions, Albert. Do you mind coming down to the station?" It was clearly a rhetorical question.

Half an hour later I sat alone in the squad room at the police station with two officers.

"Don't you care who killed your father?"

"Nope."

"The only thing we care about is finding your father's killer. You understand that, don't you?"

"Bullshit."

That ended it. Within minutes they released me, and I was back in the car with my uncle, driving through the gray afternoon toward Massapequa.

My uncle was hungry, so we stopped at a Jewish deli in Brooklyn where I used to go with my father. They had the best corned beef in town. We sat down inside and ordered a couple of hot dogs. While we waited for them to arrive, my uncle kept crying and saying, "Did you see what they did to him? I remember when he was a baby." He looked around the deli, saying, "I used to bring him here when we were kids." I couldn't eat, but when it was time to leave, I noticed the bill still lying on the table. Uncle Louis nodded at it and said, "You going to get that, Albert?"

"Sure, Uncle Louis. Whatever you want." A lousy two-dollar hot dog, and he waited for me to get the bill. It had always been that way. The family expected my father to pay for everything. Now, apparently, it was my job.

I asked my uncle to stop by the shopping center on the way back to Massapequa. He was going to drop me off at the funeral home before he headed back to the city. I wanted to finish all the funeral arrangements that afternoon and get my father buried as quickly as possible, before anything got in the newspapers and the memorial turned into a circus. I didn't want my mother to have to go through his things, so I brought his best suit to the funeral home. Even if nobody saw him,

I wanted him to be buried in something nice. I thought back to a few years before, when Louis's son had been killed in an accident. My father had made the funeral arrangements and paid all the expenses to spare Uncle Louis the pain. I wondered why Uncle Louis didn't try to spare me. The money didn't bother me. I had plenty of it. I wanted my father's brother to care how I felt.

Uncle Louis dropped me off at the funeral home shortly before noon. The morgue was transferring my father's body that afternoon, and I had to make certain my mother and sisters never saw it. The next day was Saturday, and I wanted to have him waked and buried by Sunday night. Dragging things out would only make it worse.

The funeral home was on the main highway through Massapequa, about a mile from the old neighborhood. It was family owned and run. The director was very kind. He had already been notified that my father's body was on the way. We discussed the arrangements and agreed to have everything ready for a service in the slumber room the next evening. He showed me photographs of caskets, and I chose a wooden one, a beautiful dark mahogany. I remember thinking that my father would have liked it. He'd spent hours teaching me about wood in his workshop when I was a child. The funeral director asked me whether I wanted an open coffin. I said no, that my father had been shot, and no one had found him for several days, so the body looked very bad. If the director was shocked, he didn't show it. He assured me that he could make my father look fairly presentable before the rest of the family saw him if I wanted, but I said no. We agreed on a closed coffin. I left the clothes I'd brought for my father and walked down the block to the local Catholic church to arrange for the wake.

The church was a beautiful building, well endowed by wealthy parishioners. Towering stained glass crowned gleaming brass doors. My father hadn't attended church in years, but he was still nominally Catholic, and I wanted a Catholic service for him. I didn't know the priest there, but he knew who I was. This had been Carlo Gambino's church. I introduced myself, and a barely concealed sneer flitted across his face. As I began to explain that I needed him to officiate at a mass for my father's wake, he immediately began to object. "I don't think it would be appropriate to wake your father here. Besides, it's impossible to schedule on such short notice." The implication was clear. A lowlife like my father was not welcome there, even in death.

If I hadn't known that the large circular stained-glass window and brass doors to the sanctuary had been donated a few years earlier by Carlo Gambino himself, I might have felt less enraged. The neighborhood called this the godfather's church. I reached into my pocket and began to peel hundred-dollar bills off a roll into the priest's hand. After the first few bills, I looked up at him and said, "Would it be possible now?"

The priest smiled at me. "Certainly, Mr. DeMeo. What time did you want the mass to begin?" I counted out a few more bills, answered his question, and left in disgust. Another man of God with his hand out.

Afterward I took a cab home, but when I got there, my mother told me there was an urgent message from the funeral director. I called another cab and went straight back.

The funeral director was pacing up and down when I got there. He ushered me into his office and shut the door.

"Mr. DeMeo, I've just had a visit from the FBI. They told me they were going to set up hidden microphones and cameras in the slumber room and the lobby, even inside your father's casket. I flatly refused, but they got pretty ugly. One of them threatened to shut me down if I didn't cooperate." I could see that his hands were shaking, but his voice was earnest. "I told them no, Mr. DeMeo, that this was a sanctified place. It's none of my business what your father did for a living. Your family deserves to grieve in private." Then he went on to warn me that they had pulled their vans across the street afterward and set up surveillance in the buildings across the street. "I'm sorry," he told me. "I just thought you should know."

For the first time that day, I felt tears sting my eyes. "Thank you, sir, thank you very much," I said, gripping his hand. "You don't know how much your kindness means to me and my family." I thanked him again and left.

When I got home a little while later, Debra took me quietly aside and asked, "Is it really Daddy, Al?"

"Yeah, it really is."

"Are you sure? Because Mommy thinks maybe . . ."

"It's him. I'm sure."

She nodded her head soberly. I continued, "I don't want Mommy to see him. It would be . . . very bad for her. You know?" She understood. A few minutes later I saw her talking to my younger sister. Lisa was nodding through her tears.

To this day, my mother believes it was somebody else in that casket, that my father tricked everyone and got away. She knew that dead or alive, he was never coming back. But a part of her clings to the notion that somewhere, he is alive and well, that someone else's loved one was slaughtered and stuffed in a trunk. Some truths are too painful to accept. If it comforts her to believe a lie, so be it. She survived twenty-five years of lies by believing one truth: My father loved us. Whatever outsiders believed, we knew that my father loved us all.

If anything symbolizes the bitter futility of life in the Mafia, it is a mobster's funeral. Movies still show the funeral processions of the old guard among the godfathers, trains of cars filled with flowers, elaborate masses with crowds of mourners. Carlo Gambino went out that way, but he was the last one who did. With surveillance everywhere and rampant distrust within the organization, mob funerals in recent decades are barren affairs. No one comes except the immediate family and a ragtag collection of civilian friends. The swarms of people who had surrounded my father in his heyday, who had rushed to bring me presents and show him respect, had vanished. In their place were vans filled with cameras and microphones across from an empty church. Even the curiosity seekers stayed away. My father was being realistic when he told me to put him in a garbage bag and pretend he had never lived. As far as his associates were concerned, his existence was already forgotten. Only one of his associates came, a minor player who had known my father since they were kids. He showed up at the funeral home after dark wearing a hat and sunglasses, jumpy as a rabbit but determined to pay his respects. None of the Gemini crew came to the funeral.

The next two days survive in my memory as fragments, sharp-edged pieces of a mosaic I cannot reconstruct. I remember my uncle Joe, his face a mask of sorrow beneath his Grizzly Adams beard. Scrupulously honest himself, he had nevertheless loved my father devotedly, and in losing him, he lost not so much a big brother as a father. He stood silent and stricken in the shadow of my father's coffin. Jim and Barbara were there with their children, along with five other families from the old neighborhood. From the new neighborhood, only our next-door neighbors and Dad's stockbroker friend showed up. No one else so much as called. Tommy and Nick were there with their families, looking uncomfortable in their dark suits. Tommy had really loved my father, and his freckled face was riddled with sadness. Nick, always the protector, watched me with a brow furrowed with worry. I was touched to see Mrs. Profaci enter the viewing room, her face still beautiful in age. I understood enough by then to know that it couldn't have been pleasant for her. The stigma from her former brother-in-law still clung to her as my father's did to us. No one stayed long. There was nothing to say in the face of the circumstances.

My grandmother held court, first at the funeral home and later at mass, her erect form draped in black widow's weeds. This was her moment. She had lost a second son, and she considered it fitting and proper that she be the center of attention in the family drama. She received condolences with a sorrowful countenance, but I wondered what she was really feeling. Aunt Marie was silent and sad, but my cousin Benny watched the proceedings like we were exotic animals at the zoo. Uncle Louis had called that morning, on my grandmother's behalf, to make certain my father's death wouldn't lessen her support check and to find out how much money Grandma had been bequeathed in my father's will. Even in death, my father remained my grandmother's meal ticket more than her son. He was also interested in knowing whether my father had left him anything, and if so, did I know how much? I suggested he call my father's lawyer.

And most of all, I remember my mother and my sisters, deathly white and silent beside the coffin. Tears slid quietly down my sisters' faces, but like me, my mother didn't cry.

I was the man of the house now. It was my responsibility to take my father's place, to care for my mother and sisters in his absence. I moved about the funeral parlor in my best suit, greeting visitors, thanking them for coming. I comforted my sisters, checked on my mother, checked and rechecked final details with the funeral director. I stood tall by my father's coffin, my face impassive, my form erect. My voice never trembled as I spoke with the mourners, and I resolutely detached myself from the discolored figure lying inside the mahogany container, covered with flowers. I was seventeen years and two days old, and I had already lived a lifetime.

I've been told the mass was lovely. I don't remember. I do remember standing in the chapel at St. John's Cemetery in Queens the next day, again greeting the straggle of mourners who found their way there. Another priest said a few words, and it was over. My mother laid a rose on my father's coffin, and when it was my turn, I placed my own rose on the casket and leaned to kiss it one last time. Later that day the family grave would be opened and my father buried with his ancestors under a simple stone marked "DeMeo." Carlo Gambino and Joseph Profaci were buried only a few hundred yards away. As the limousine bearing my mother and sisters and I wound slowly toward the gates, I gazed out the window at the crypts that lined the drive of the old cemetery. They were hauntingly beautiful, dozens, perhaps hundreds of white marble angels, their wings arched protectively over the loved ones below. I wanted to believe that somehow, somewhere, my father rested in peace.

Wherever we went in the days that followed, I knew we were watched, for the eyes of the government were everywhere. Our very private grief was being recorded, down to the most minute detail, by an army of public servants. Plain white vans sat across the street twenty-four hours a day, and a government car followed me every time I left the house. Among the four of us, the government seemed primarily interested in me. My mother was indifferent to the surveillance, rarely appearing to notice the presence of those prying eyes. I did what I could to keep my sisters from noticing the unwanted attention, bringing movies home to keep them away from the television, allowing no newspapers in the house. "Reputed mobster Roy DeMeo found murdered. . . ." No, they didn't need to hear that. They never needed to hear that. Nor did they need to see the photograph in the paper of my father's frozen body in the trunk of our car, a crystal chandelier resting on top of him like a bizarre monument. We had lost our father. That was all they ever needed to know. Meanwhile Nick and Tommy worried, constantly asking me if I was all right. Of course, I was all right. I didn't feel a thing. I couldn't understand why they seemed so worried about me. My father was counting on me. I would be fine.

On Monday I returned to school and tried to appear as if everything were normal. I showered and dressed and strode onto campus as if nothing had happened. But something had happened, and every student in my high school knew it. The weekend news reports had torn the veil of secrecy that had covered my home life for years. For the first time at school, people actually backed away from me as I approached, turning their backs, averting their eyes. I could hear the whispers as I passed. "That's the mobster's son . . . yeah, his name's Al . . . murdered his father . . . blew his head off . . . heard the body was already decomposed . . . heard Al is in the Mafia, too . . . think he's ever killed anybody?" I ignored them and went from class to class, grateful for the two classes I had with Nick that day. He sat silently beside me, his glare daring anyone to say something while he was around. I sat quietly, intent on my books, listening politely as my teachers droned on about history and English and geometry. The fact that I couldn't understand a word they were saying was irrelevant. I was there, and I was strong. Yet my teachers avoided my gaze, as unable as my peers to speak openly to the mobster's son about his father.

Only my Italian teacher had the courage to speak to me with compassion about my father. As my last period of that interminable day ended and my classmates crowded out the door, he asked me to stay behind a minute and speak to him. Shutting the door behind the stragglers, he sat down at a desk and motioned for me to sit down across from him. His words were straightforward and unaffected. "Al, I heard about your father's death. I'm so very sorry. I just wanted to tell you that if you need anything, someone to talk to, anything at all, you come to me. I know how rough this must be, and I'm here for you." For the first time since the funeral, tears welled up in the face of his simple kindness. I mumbled a few words in thanks and shook his hand. He stood up, put his hand briefly on my shoulder, and returned to the front of the room to collect the papers on his desk. I wonder if he ever knew what his thoughtfulness meant to me.

One other person also treated me with caring, though in his case it remained unspoken. Determined to prove to myself and the rest of the world that I was still strong, I went to the athletic field after school and told the coach I wanted to join the football team. He looked at me a moment, then told me to change and meet him back on the field. We never talked about it, but somehow I knew he understood. I wasn't much of a player, but he allowed me to work out with the team every day and to sit on the bench at games.

The following Sunday I made the first of countless journeys to my father's grave. Across the street from the cemetery, I asked the cabbie to drop me off by a flower vendor's shop and went inside to make my purchase. Overhead hung dozens of wreaths dedicated in loving memory to mothers, husbands, beloved friends. Carnation crosses proclaimed the hope of resurrection. I chose my father's favorite, a dozen long-stemmed roses, deep red like Italian burgundy. I asked the woman to put them in a vase for me, and I added a small ribbon that read "In loving memory of my father." But when it came time to pay, I discovered to my confused embarrassment that I had given all my cash to the cab driver. In the emotion of the moment, I had gone out without enough cash. I felt my face grow hot, and tears of disappointment stung my eyes as I shamefacedly admitted that I couldn't pay for the flowers, that I had given all my money to the cabbie. To my surprise, the woman behind the counter simply picked up the vase and put the flowers in my hands.

Stammering in confusion, I said, "You don't understand. I made a mistake. I can't pay for these."

Her kind face smiled back at me. "I understand. You take these flowers, you go visit with your father. You don't worry about anything. You bring me the money when you can."

Unable to speak, I nodded my thanks and carried the flowers out to the sidewalk. As I kneeled by my father's grave a few minutes later, her face remained with me, softening ever so slightly the raw pain that was now a permanent part of my existence. The next Sunday I brought her the money, and the Sunday after that I returned for another dozen roses. Eighteen years and hundreds of journeys to the cemetery later, I still buy my flowers from the same woman, at the same shop.

Financially, life went on as it always had. The house and all our principal possessions were in my mother's name. There were life insurance policies for my mother and grandmother, savings accounts, college funds, all legal and carefully thought out. My father had planned well. We were set for the remainder of our lives. The hundreds of thousands of dollars owed by my father's loan-shark customers would go unclaimed, the loans forgiven in my father's death. I could have tried to collect them if I'd wanted. I knew where he kept his records, and many of his customers knew me—but those debts would die with my father. I had no heart for any of his criminal enterprises. And I knew my father wouldn't want me to.

There was one final bit of business that remained for me to do. My father's car remained in the impound lot, where it had been towed the afternoon they found his body. It was a maroon 1983 Cadillac Coupe DeVille, worth a fair amount of money, and it had to be claimed and sold at auction. I did not want my mother to see it, so I arranged with my uncle Joe to go pick it up at the impound yard. We were treated with contempt by the police officers there, but I was used to that. To them I wasn't a teenager or even a human being; I was just the mobster's son, and I was treated accordingly. After days of filling out paperwork and making endless phone calls, I went to the impound lot with Uncle Joe to get the car.

Standing there in the lot with Uncle Joe, I stared at my father's Cadillac in disbelief. I had never seen anything like it, even on television. The forensic team had dusted every inch of it, inside and out, and the maroon of the exterior was completely submerged under a thick coating of powder. We walked gingerly around it, and when I opened the door to peer inside, I could see that the seat cushions and dashboard had the same heavy coating. I remembered all the Sunday afternoons of my childhood spent cleaning my father's car. He had always been so particular about his cars, keeping them shiny and spotless inside and out. Uncle Joe looked over at me and shook his head incredulously. Then, using his sleeve to wipe a small clear space in the windshield, he slid behind the wheel. I climbed in next to him. In spite of the cold, we rolled down the power windows so Joe could see to drive. The engine turned over as smoothly as ever, and Joe pulled carefully out of the lot and onto the expressway. Neither of us spoke a single word all the way home.

When we reached Uncle Joe's house, he pulled the car onto the front lawn and turned off the ignition. Both of us climbed out and just stood there quietly a little longer, staring at the car. After a few minutes Uncle Joe said he was going in the house to clean up for dinner and told me to do the same. Joe disappeared into the house, but I couldn't bring myself to leave. That Cadillac was the last link I still had to my father. I had made countless trips with him in that car. He had spent his final days on earth imprisoned in it. I needed to say good-bye. I needed to spend a few last minutes in the same space he had so recently inhabited. I needed to understand how it had felt for him, even in death.

I slid inside, behind the wheel, and leaned my head back with my eyes closed. Beneath the musty smell of the chemical dust, the scent of my father's aftershave still lingered. The leather upholstery cradled my head. I tried to imagine my father's last journey in that car, tried to reach back through the last two weeks to his final moments in that same seat, but search as I might, I could not find him. I could not sense him. Finally I gave up and decided to join my uncle in the house. But as I turned to open the car door, a sudden impulse made me reach inside the glove compartment and pop open the trunk. There was a soft click as I felt it open. Sliding across the seat, I stepped onto the grass and went around to the back of the car.

I had already been to the morgue, already identified my father's twisted remains, already seen the worst there was to see. I did not think it would do me any more harm to look in the trunk, to see the space that had become his tomb. It was a morbid impulse; it was also my last chance to feel close to my father. Whatever the source of the need, I knew I had to look into that trunk.

I took my time circling the car, edging slowly toward the rear. The first thing that hit me was the smell of congealed blood; the second was the sight of white paper, contrasting starkly with the frozen sea of dark red in which it was suspended. For a moment my mind went blank. What was it? I moved closer to look.

The trunk itself was a shallow pool of blood, frozen into immobility in the winter light. I reached a tentative finger out to touch one of the papers that lay scattered beneath me. It stuck to the trunk mat. Finding a spot on the mat that appeared to be clean, I held the mat down with one hand and gingerly pulled one of the papers loose with the other. It was a white wrapper, the kind that surgical gloves come in. The trunk was littered with them, like a polluted pond. I lifted my other hand and realized that it was sticky. I looked down at it. It was coated with blood. My father's blood.

Suddenly, after so many days of numbness, I felt a shock pulse through my body, and I began to shake. Looking down at the soiled pile in front of me, I suddenly could see it all. A cold, lonely street in Brooklyn, a group of police officers popping the trunk open. My father's body, contorted inside, on top of him the chandelier he was taking to Goodwill for my mother. The morgue workers gathering around the back of the car to hoist my father's body from the trunk like garbage. After all, they did this kind of thing every day, and besides, he was just another mobster, the victim of just another gangland hit. The swarm of forensic officers snapping their rubber gloves into place, dropping the wrappers where my father's body had lain, peeling the gloves off when they finished and tossing them in the trunk of our family car like it was a garbage bin.

And then I went further back, and I was seven years old again, finding the knife and disguises in the trunk of our Cadillac, wondering what my father did with those things in the middle of the night. I clenched my fist to keep from crying out in pain. The heat from my body dissolved the sticky mass in my left hand, and as I looked down in sickened disbelief, I saw my father's blood running down my wrist. For the first time in my life, I felt my body consumed with rage, blind, overpowering rage. My father's words came back to me: "No, Al, you will not take revenge. You will forget I ever lived." But I knew that I could not, would not, let it end this way.

Into the silence of that terrible moment, I heard my uncle shouting from the front porch. "Al!" he called sharply. "Al, stop it! Let it go! Enough!" I could hear the mixture of anger and fear in his voice. I closed the trunk and walked into his house.

As I stood in his small, warm bathroom, I could feel the winter cold seeping from my body. My limbs began to thaw, and I could feel the blood pumping through my chest. Yet as my body warmed, my heart grew colder, and though I scrubbed my father's blood from my skin, I knew that the stain would never leave me. The rage still pulsing through my veins settled into a steady course, and I made my resolve. Vengeance would be mine, I promised my father. I would find his killers, and I would kill them myself.

nine

DOUBLE JEOPARDY

ME AND DAD ON MY FIFTEENTH BIRTHDAY

This is most brave,
That I, the son of a dear father murder'd,
Prompted to my revenge by heaven and hell,
Must, like a whore, unpack my heart with words.

—SHAKESPEARE, *Hamlet*

I had been in training for my father's death since I was twelve years old. I thought I was prepared for it, and from a practical point of view, I was. What I was not prepared for was the abyss of pain that opened beneath me with his passing. My father's final advice to me had been to forget him and to have a good life. The problem was that I didn't have the faintest idea how to do that. So instead I did what most people do in the aftermath of sudden loss: I carried on in the way I was accustomed to. And that meant taking care of business for my father. Not his Mob business. My father had started down that path at the same age I was, seventeen, and I knew where the journey ended. It was a journey I did not want to take. It was the other business of his life that I shouldered.

I bought my first car that spring, a black Corvette, after getting my first legal driver's license. My father and I had planned to pick the car out together. My family occupied most of my attention. I made it a point to be home as much as possible. Like a protective father, I brought home videos to keep my sisters occupied, took them and my mother out to dinner and to the movies. I even stopped by my mother's favorite diner now and then, to pick up a hamburger and fries for her as my father had once done. She patted me sadly, unable to eat what I'd brought her, but I knew she appreciated the gesture.

I also tried to take responsibility for people who had depended on my father. I had watched my dad take care of people all his life. It was clear that Cousin Joe could not survive on his own; it was equally clear that he would never be able to stay out of trouble. I knew my father would want Joe to be cared for in his old age, so I told him to pack his things and get ready to leave New York permanently. Then I put a sizable bundle of cash in a paper bag and told Joe I was taking him to the airport for a final good-bye. I told him that I didn't want to know where he was going, but that I wished him well. I also told him that I never wanted to hear from him again. To my surprise, when I started to tell him good-bye at the airport, his eyes filled with tears, and he told me he wanted me to have something to remember him by. It was the only thing he had to give me in the way of a legacy, he said. Then he handed me a battered copy of an old journal, filled with notes and handwritten copies of his special recipes. He knew I liked his cooking and hoped that I would use the recipes and remember him. Along with the recipes were little anecdotes, funny stories and comments about the men he had cooked for. It was the last I ever saw of Cousin Joe.

I also felt a sense of responsibility for Freddy, who was still inside. Freddy was devastated by my father's death. Unable to read and capable of writing only his name, Freddy was like a lost child in the wake of my father's murder. Things got even worse for Freddy when his brother Richie was murdered shortly after my father was killed. Richie had worked for my father on and off for several years as part of Dad's auto theft ring. Richie DiNome was an upscale version of Freddy—dark, handsome, smarter, younger. He was a talented thief who could steal twenty cars in a single night. The FBI was pushing Richie hard to turn informant, offering to make a deal for Freddy if Richie turned. One night Richie disappeared, his body turning up a week later with bullets through the back of his head. Someone in the Mob had gotten nervous. Richie knew too much.

Several weeks after our father's funeral, Debra and I went to visit Freddy in jail to see how he was doing. It was a strange visit, for I knew immediately that something was wrong. In all the years I had known Freddy, I had never seen him behave so oddly. He kept asking me, as though he had memorized the questions, "So Albert, who do you think murdered your father? Do you think it might have been one of his associates?" Freddy never talked like that; it was clear he had been coached. It didn't take a genius to realize that Freddy had made some kind of deal to turn informant, but he wasn't bright enough to carry it off believably. Freddy would have gone to the grave for my father, but with Richie dead and his family in need, I knew it would be simple to turn Freddy if he thought he was helping to catch my father's killer. I told him I had no idea who had performed the hit and cut the visit short. Debra asked me why Freddy was acting so strange. I told her I didn't know. The change in Freddy made me very uncomfortable. If I couldn't trust him, whom could I trust?

From the night I saw my father's blood on my hands, I became obsessed with finding his killer's identity. No ounce of common sense, no pang of conscience, no dying warning from my father's mouth had changed my resolution. I needed a cause, and avenging my father's death gave me one.

Despite my unwillingness to discuss it with Freddy, I knew as well as he did that my father's murderer was probably one of his associates. Everything about the murder pointed to an inside job. The question was, who? In the weeks following my father's death, that question had haunted my every waking moment and often followed me into sleep. Paul Castellano was the obvious choice for sending the order, but who had carried it out? Experience told me someone in my father's crew had been involved, though I didn't want to believe it. The afternoon I went by the Gemini to pick up Cousin Joe for the ride to the airport, Anthony and Joey were sitting around the table with some of the minor players. Anthony was sitting in my father's chair, with Joey on his right in my old spot. I felt my stomach tighten, but the Twins just smiled lazily and said, "How ya doin', Albert?"

While I debated which of my father's old crew, if any, I could trust, they made the first overtures and got in touch with me. They needed to tie up some loose ends, they told me, and they needed some of my father's things to do that. They wanted his "Shylock book," a leather ledger where he kept the information on his loan-shark collections. They told me they were going to collect the additional money owed to my father for "us," but they couldn't do that without the book. I knew they were lying. They had no intention of sharing anything they collected; their primary motive was lining their own pockets. Among them all, my father's crew owed him hundreds of thousands of dollars, which they certainly weren't going to pay my family. The crew always spent more than they made, borrowing against the next big score. And finally, they wanted my father's tagging tools, worth a potential fortune if they continued stealing cars. I knew that none of them had either the brains or the discipline to run the operation without my father, but they hadn't figured that out yet. I agreed to meet with them and discuss the details, hoping it would give me a chance to size them up in person.

I suggested we meet at the diner where they used to meet my father. The diner was a nice, family-style restaurant on the main road through Massapequa. It seemed like a safe enough place for such a meeting. I had no idea where Freddy had kept the tagging tools. The ledger was hidden in the cabinet at home. I'd used it to make collections when Dad was in hiding, but I had no intention of turning it over to the crew.

They were all waiting for me in the parking lot when I drove up that afternoon. The Gemini Twins were there, along with a couple of other guys I barely knew. When they motioned me into the car so we could drive while we talked, I climbed in between Joey and Anthony without a second thought. I assumed they were worried about eavesdroppers in the diner. It wasn't until we pulled out of the parking lot that I realized my mistake. As the driver merged onto the highway, Anthony and Joey pulled their coats back so I could see. Both of them had guns sticking out of their belts. I looked at the back of the driver's head and the man riding shotgun up front, and my heart stopped. I had walked into an ambush. "Holy shit," I thought, "this is a hit, and I walked right into it."

As we drove through the fading Long Island afternoon, Joey and Anthony began questioning me about the tagging tools. I told them I didn't know where they were. They seemed to believe me. But when they asked about the loan shark book, I denied knowing anything about it. "I don't know anything about any book," I insisted. "Dad kept all the accounts in his head as far as I know. He told me who to collect from when he needed me to do a pickup, but that's all I know. I don't know anything about a book." They knew I was lying. I guess it was stupid, but I was trying to buy some time. And if they killed me anyway, I certainly wasn't going to hand over something worth that much money first.

"We're trying to help you, Albert," Anthony kept saying. He tried to look sad, but he couldn't quite pull it off.

It was nearly an hour later when I realized, with an indescribable sense of relief, that they had decided to take me back to the diner. I'm still not certain why they did it. I think they were testing me, hoping I would come up with what they wanted if they played me right. They reminded me of the police with their good cop, bad cop tactics. As they pulled into the parking lot and stopped to let me out, Anthony looked me right in the eye and said, "Oh, Albert—our deep condolences on your father's tragic death. You need anything, you call us." I felt a chill go through me. I knew I was talking to my father's murderers.

Stepping into the parking lot, I replied, "Sure, guys, take care of yourselves. I'll be in touch."

And with that I strode back to my car as my father had taught me to—confident, fearless, arrogant. It was only when I had pulled out of

the parking lot and headed for the relative safety of home that I allowed the relief to wash over me. I knew how close I had just come to
being killed.

So began the cat-and-mouse game I played with my father's old
crew for weeks to come. We each wanted something the other had:
They wanted any money-making tools my father had left in my pos-
session, and I wanted a clearer understanding of who had been involved in my father's murder and how. Trying to stay one step ahead
of them, I agreed to continued meetings at the diner, but not in the
car. I sometimes met them inside for a meal; usually, though, I stood
in the parking lot to speak with them. Only yards away from where we
stood, a steady stream of suburban traffic flowed by and women took
their toddlers for walks in strollers, blissfully unaware of the negoti-
ations taking place within their view.

I had some extra insurance the next time. I knew that a public setting wasn't enough to guarantee my safety. I'd told my friend Nick
what had happened, and he'd insisted on coming with me the next
time. Nick was no wiseguy; he was just my friend, and he had been
backing me up since junior high school, no questions asked. I didn't
try to talk him out of it. I'd have done the same thing for him. I told
him to arrive in the parking lot a few minutes before I did, where he
could keep an eye on me from a distance. I also gave him a loaded
rifle to keep trained on all of us—just in case. I was in completely over
my head, but I hadn't realized it yet.

The Mob wasn't the only game I was playing. I was also targeted in
an FBI investigation. Someone—probably Freddy—had told them
how close I'd been to my father. At this crucial point in their investigation of Paul Castellano and Nino Gaggi, they saw me as a potential
gold mine of information about my father's criminal enterprises,
someone who could put most of his associates behind bars. And they
assumed that, because my father's associates were implicated in his
murder, I would be willing to cooperate. They were wrong.

It is difficult to explain to an outsider why I was so reluctant to turn informant. After all, I was infinitely more intent on identifying my father's killers than the government could ever be. But the reality was that my options were limited. To begin with, I did not have much of the information they believed I had. I knew quite a bit about the loan-shark operations, as well as bits and pieces of his auto theft and pornography enterprises. But, except for the murder of the college student and some uncomfortable intuitions that he might have been involved in hits on other mobsters, I knew nothing about the violence they hinted at. The most obvious drawback to cooperating with the authorities, though, was fear for my own safety. If I became involved in their investigation in any way, I knew that the Mafia would murder me long before any case went to trial, and my father's killers would go free.

My refusal to cooperate with the authorities did not sit well with them. In the weeks following my father's murder, they did everything they could to force me to work with them. They couldn't subpoena me, since I was still under age. But they could call me in for "just a few more questions" about my father's death. When I left the house, they followed me, and when veiled threats didn't work, they tried sympathizing with me about my "poor murdered father." They couldn't have cared less about my father. They loathed him. They were glad he was dead, and I knew it. So they continued to question, and I continued to deny knowing anything, always in the politest possible terms. Finally I called a lawyer who'd been on my father's payroll, and the harassment stopped. Until I turned eighteen, there was little else they could do.

As the gray winter days melted away, the internal pressure gradually became intolerable. I continued going through the motions of living, but I couldn't hold anything in my mind but my father's dead face. I considered my options. I had a local mechanic build a hidden compartment into my new car where I could keep a gun and had him supercharge my car in case I had to make a fast escape. If I was going to act, I needed to do it soon, but the one-man army I had formed

lacked the firepower to do the job. My entire stock of weaponry con-
sisted of a sawed-off shotgun, a Browning 9mm., two .38s, and a pile
of ammunition. It would not be enough, I reasoned, not nearly
enough. I considered the vague plan I had formed a suicide mission.
If I had asked Tommy and Nick, they would probably have helped me,
but I was not willing to take my friends with me to certain death. My
only hope of taking out my father's betrayers lay in greater firepower.
I had heard my father refer to hidden arsenals that included not only
stores of automatic weapons but also C-4 grenades and bulletproof
vests. I needed access to those arsenals now, but I didn't know where
he'd kept them. After weeks of agonizing, I decided to make a call to
the one person I believed I could still trust: Nino Gaggi. Uncle Nino
had been avoiding me for weeks, but I told myself that was for his
own safety. After several attempts, I finally got through to him. I told
him that I thought I knew who had killed my father, and I needed my
dad's old weapon supply to take care of business. Did he know where
it was? He told me he'd look into it and get back to me.

   Two days after I made the call, I went out on a date with my steady
girlfriend. We had become more serious after my father's death,
when I needed comfort. I knew it might be our last date, for I was
planning to do the hit as soon as Nino got back to me. Somehow that
knowledge gave me peace, for I believed I was doing the right thing at
last. I had nothing more to lose. I savored every moment with my girl.
She was so beautiful, so gentle. We had a wonderful evening: dinner
in my favorite Long Island restaurant followed by a long walk on the
beach, holding hands and sinking our bare toes into the sand.
Moonlight shone on the water, and for the first time since my father's death, I felt like I could breathe. There was a glorious sense of
seclusion as we walked together that night, her fingers twined in
mine and the taste of salt on my tongue. Afterward I drove her home
through the dark, silent streets and shared a lingering kiss on the
front porch of her parents' home, breathing her into my heart.

Driving down the deserted highway afterward, the lights of suburbia asleep for the night, I rolled down the car windows and let the warm wind blow through my hair. My whole body sighed in the relief of that moment.

I never saw it coming. One minute I was cruising down the darkened highway listening to Frank Sinatra on the tape player; the next, four cars came out of nowhere, surrounding me and forcing me off the road. I saw only a blur of green as my Corvette careened off the highway and down an embankment, coming to rest with a loud splintering sound as it hit the trees. My head hit the windshield, shattering the glass, and in the chaos I instinctively popped the catch and grabbed my gun, rolling out of the car on the passenger side. Hitting the ground shoulder first, I managed to fire two shots blindly into the darkness, in the general direction of my pursuers. I couldn't see anything. Someone stepped on my wrist, pinning it against the ground, and I felt my gun pulled from my hand. Hands reached down to grab me from two different directions, and someone slammed me up against the side of my car. Dark figures were on either side of me, pinning my wrists back against the roof, my arms splayed in a mock crucifixion. Blood ran into my eyes, and I struggled to make out shapes in the darkness.

I think there were four of them. All wore dark clothing and black ski masks pulled over their heads. I could barely make out their eyes, but I knew who they were. The Gemini Twins. A familiar voice said, "We're not going to kill you this time, Al, out of respect for your father. But you make any more threats, we'll do what we have to do." He hit me with the butt of his gun, hard, in my left eye socket. I heard a splintering sound, then felt a blow from the other side. The last thing I remember is confusion and pain as I slipped into unconsciousness.

Several hours later I gradually became aware of someone shouting my name. Hands shook my shoulder, gently but urgently. I tried to blink through the blood caking my eyes. "Dad?" I whispered. I knew that voice. "Nick?" I murmured from a red cave of pain. There was something horribly wrong with my body. I was ice cold, and I couldn't seem to move.

I could hear the panic in Nick's voice, and I knew he was crying. "Al? Al? Are you all right? Al?" Incredibly, Nick had spotted my smoking car on the side of the road on the way home from work, glimmering through the trees. Slowing down to look, he thought he could make out the shape of a familiar vehicle. Slamming on the brakes, he had leapt from his own car and slid down the shallow embankment toward the lights. It was there that he found me, motionless in a pool of blood. My body was stiff and cold from shock and from hours in the night air, and at first he thought I was dead. Dizzy with relief to hear me answer him, he gathered me in his arms and laid me gently in the back seat of his car.

I only wanted to go home, but he insisted on taking me to the hospital. He went by my house to get my mother, and minutes later he carried me into the emergency room, my mother weeping a few feet behind. The last thing I remember is whispering urgently to him, "Don't tell her anything." He had nothing to tell, for I was in no shape to give any information, but he nodded nonetheless. Then I slid into the blessed relief of unconsciousness.

The surgery took over eight hours. My cheekbone, eye socket, and most of the left side of my face had been shattered. The surgeon inserted a small wire cage to replace my eye socket and did his best to rebuild my face. Miraculously, my eye had been spared permanent damage. I would not lose my sight. I was going to need several more operations to restore my face cosmetically, the doctors told my mother, but I would be all right. When I regained consciousness late the next day, the doctors informed me that I had been incredibly lucky. If Nick had come along even thirty minutes later, I would have died from shock and loss of blood. Nick was there when I came out of the anesthesia and for part of every day afterward, until I was finally able to leave the hospital.

So were the feds. Federal agents had showed up within hours of my admission and stayed in the operating room for most of the surgery, ready to take notes in case I said something under anesthesia. They came and went regularly from my room, sometimes questioning me openly, other times posing as attendants or orderlies. Their faces swam in and out of my view. I had told no one what really happened that night; as far as anyone knew, I'd had a bad car accident and smashed my face on the windshield. Yet the officers were suspicious and used the opportunity to try once again to secure my cooperation. It was easy enough to evade their questions, in spite of my being a captive audience in the hospital bed. Between the pain, the pain medicine, and the weakness, I slipped in and out of consciousness for days. It was simple enough to pretend unconsciousness when I wanted to be left alone. Besides, it was difficult for me to speak with the extensive damage to my face, so they didn't press the issue.

I had not been in the hospital since I was four years old, for the surgery that helped correct my vision. I thought about that first surgery as I lay there with bandages covering one eye. This time, though, my father wouldn't be there when the bandages came off. The long weeks of recovery in the hospital gradually began to bring a clarity I hadn't had since my father's murder. Pain and immobility served as a kind of truth serum, producing not the truths the government wanted, but the truths I needed. I'd told myself that I owed it to my father to take revenge, but I had been deluding myself. My father's "friends" had murdered him and nearly killed me on behalf of an organization that glorified loyalty. My friend Nick, on the other hand, with nothing to gain but at genuine personal risk, had put himself on the line once again to save my life. When the room swam back into focus following my surgery, his face had been there next to my mother's and sisters', anxiously peering down at me. I owed it to all of them never to put myself in that kind of danger again. They had already suffered enough.

When I finally got out of the hospital, I did my best to leave the past behind. Searing headaches hit me sometimes, but each time one did, I used it to remind myself how useless vengeance was. The crew, their warning delivered, left me alone, and I never contacted any of them again. I even stopped visiting Freddy. It was time to bury the past.

The school year ended while I was hospitalized, and summer came to Long Island. I did my best to return to the business of being seventeen years old, swimming in the backyard pool and boating on the canal with Tommy and my girlfriend. College was only a year away, and I began filling out applications. I did not want to spend the rest of my life as the mobster's son.

Unfortunately, the government had other ideas. The federal task force that had been pursuing the New York Mob under the RICO statute for so many years had reached a crucial point in the Castellano investigation. With convictions multiplying and top mobsters turning informant, they scented victory. District Attorney Rudolph Giuliani and his prosecutors were waging a holy war, and as in all wars, personal rights were expendable in the conflict. I became collateral damage in the all-out assault on the crime families of New York.

With my father gone, I thought the surveillance on our family would fade away. Instead it shifted focus, from my father to me. Every time I left the house, someone followed me. I assumed that once the officers saw I had no further contact with my father's associates or enterprises, they would leave me alone. I was wrong. They followed me everywhere: to school, to the movies, even on dates. Like my face, my car had been restored after the wreck and was almost as good as new. It became a beacon for local police. Cops repeatedly pulled me over for imaginary traffic violations, searching my car for God knows what. It was humiliating. I found myself standing on the side of the highway next to my girlfriend while agents rummaged through my car and passing motorists slowed down to stare. My girlfriend was supportive and patient, but it was deeply embarrassing. The only illegal item I was transporting remained untouched, hidden in its compartment under the dashboard. I still didn't feel safe leaving the house without my gun. The superchargers I'd installed on my car enabled me to escape the surveillance vehicles at times, but they also led to a long string of speeding tickets and a suspended license. As summer turned into fall and I returned for my senior year of high school, I became increasingly angry and frustrated. Why wouldn't they just leave me alone? I wasn't doing anything wrong.

Driving with a suspended license eventually landed me in court. Angry and unrepentant, I faced the judge ready to do battle. I knew I was guilty only of driving with a suspended license. When I was told to approach the bench for a plea, however, I realized that I knew the court officer sitting in front of me. He had been on my father's payroll for years, making cases disappear. About the same time I recognized him, he recognized me. Telling my lawyer I wanted a private conference with the officer, I went aside and said to him, "Now we both know these charges are going to be dropped. Don't we?" The unspoken threat was clear. He would be prosecuted if the authorities knew about the favors he'd done my father.

Shifting uneasily, he nodded and said, "Certainly, Mr. DeMeo." The charges were dropped, and my mother was furious. She thought that I was spinning out of control and deserved to be punished. She was right, of course. For me, though, it wasn't that simple. I'd watched the legal system talk out of both sides of its mouth all my life. Many of my father's associates were judges or cops. If the government persisted in treating me as the mobster's son, I thought, so be it. They couldn't have it both ways. They were bending all the rules to get to me. Why shouldn't I bend a few of my own?

As the months went by and the harassment continued, I became angrier and angrier. Any hope of a normal life was long gone. The government would never let me shed my father's identity. I felt like Exhibit A in the court of public opinion. One afternoon I was pulled over again and told that I was wanted for several outstanding traffic warrants; I was handcuffed and put into a police car for the ride down to central booking. They had cuffed me tightly, but the physical pain in my wrists was secondary to the psychological misery I felt during the ride.

"Well, well, well, if it isn't the mobster's son," the officer said as he shoved me in the car. "Don't hit your head!" he cautioned as he cracked my skull against the cruiser's roof.

His partner chuckled as he took his place up front. "What do you say we take a little ride down to the station, you arrogant little piece of shit?"

All the way down to the station, they taunted me about my father as I sat trapped behind the steel mesh of the patrol car. When they jerked me out of the car to go inside, I started demanding my lawyer, shouting, "You can't do this to me! I want my attorney!"

"Can't do this? Who the fuck do you think you are? We're cops. We can do anything we want."

Something burst inside, and blind with rage, I lost control completely. I tried to head butt the officer, kicking wildly as they subdued me. One of them pepper sprayed my face while they shackled me, and I collapsed to the ground, blind and writhing in pain. I felt like a trapped animal.

A few minutes later I was thrust into a jail cell where I was shackled to the wall, still cuffed. The struggle had aggravated my skull injuries, and the pain in my bad eye was agonizing. The rank smell of the man they chained me next to nearly gagged me. There were nearly twenty men crammed in the cell with me, most of them ranting and raving, spitting, and urinating on the floor. It was like being plunged into a nightmare. When a police officer walked by the cell a short while later, a tall black man a few feet from me unzipped his pants and began urinating on the officer. Within seconds a barrage of officers descended on the cell, and all hell broke loose. The man they were after squatted and filled his hands with his own excrement, then began throwing it at the officers. Other prisoners followed suit. I sat against the wall, sickened. How had I ended up in this madhouse? Eventually officers restrained the men they were after, but no one attempted to clean up the pool of urine and bowel movements that littered the floor. The stench was overpowering.

With the troublemakers quieted, I became the main attraction for passersby. Officers and jail workers lined up on the other side of the bars to point me out like I was some bizarre species of animal. "Hey, wiseguy!" they called out. "Having fun, little gangster?" The hours dragged on, and I kept asking for a lawyer, asking why I wasn't being booked or taken in front of a judge. Eventually I started talking to the other men in my cell and found out that some of them were pretty good guys, just frustrated with the way they were being treated. They advised me to be patient, said making a scene would only make things worse for me. I knew they were right, and I settled down to wait as best I could.

I remained shackled all day and most of the night. The arresting officers "forgot" about me for more than twelve hours, finally rediscovering my paperwork shortly before dawn the next day. When I was taken before a judge at last, he informed me that the original arrest was for failing to appear in response to a series of traffic tickets. The odd thing about this was that I had never seen any of the tickets they showed me. God knows, I had been guilty of speeding, but I always paid my tickets. But the pile of citations they put in front of me— these, I had never seen before, and I didn't recognize any of the cars I had supposedly been driving. When I pointed this out to the judge, he sarcastically inquired if someone else had been driving other cars while using my name. I was finally released to my lawyer, but I was very disturbed by what had happened in that courtroom. What was going on here? Who was making up charges against me?

A psychological war was being waged against me, and I was losing.

I wasn't yet eighteen, but I had already developed bleeding ulcers. Home once again, I spent over an hour in the steam room and shower trying to feel clean. Afterward, as I lay in bed, I mentally listed every crime I had ever committed. Speeding and carrying a concealed weapon, yes. Collecting packages for my father? Yes, probably a crime, for some of them had undoubtedly contained illicit cash or stolen property, though I never opened any of them. Aiding and abetting a felon? But my father hadn't been a felon at the time; he'd never even been charged. Failing to report crimes I had known about? Was that illegal? Did it make any difference that I was a minor during all of it? I didn't know. Drenched in fear, confusion, and guilt, I struggled to sort out the nature of my misdeeds. I had never thought of myself as a criminal; I had thought of myself as a son helping his father. Had I been wrong? And what if I had? I knew that if given the same choices tomorrow, I would help my father again. Did that make me a criminal, too? I didn't know. How long was this going to go on? How far would they go? Sometimes I wished they'd just sentence me and get it over with. Anything was better than this constant anxiety.

The real question that haunted me, however, was not what I had done, but why they hated me so much—and they obviously did. I knew that in their eyes, I was a junior wiseguy, an obnoxious adolescent with a chip on his shoulder. That much I understood, but it didn't explain the passionate contempt they treated me with. One night, sleepless as usual, I went into the bathroom to rinse my face with cold water and caught my own reflection in the mirror. It startled me. *Funny*, I thought, *I never realized how much I look like my father.* And that was when it hit me. It wasn't me they hated. They hated my father, and every time they looked at me, they saw my father's face. In their eyes, I wasn't just the mobster's son; I was the mobster. I had spent a lifetime trying to walk, talk, and dress exactly like my dad. In a moment of wrenching clarity, I realized I had succeeded.

ten

· ·

COLLATERAL DAMAGE

MY FATHER'S FAKE IDS

*The question is whether cruelty is used well or badly.
Cruelty badly used is that which, although infrequent
to begin with, as time goes on, rather
than disappearing, grows in intensity.*

—MACHIAVELLI, *The Prince*

As the year of my father's death drew to a close, I found myself trapped in a vicious circle. The attorney I'd hired had gotten the government to back off a little, citing my age, but with my eighteenth birthday on the horizon, I knew the respite was temporary. More menacing, my father's former associates were keeping an eye on me again. The Gemini Twins had been arrested and released on bail, under indictment with Nino Gaggi for a long list of charges. My testimony could have put them behind bars for many years, and they knew I had no reason to show them mercy. Even if I escaped government harassment, I could be right back where I started: at the business end of a gangster's gun. I had to get smarter, or I would never see eighteen.

With no one to advise me, I turned for help to my father's old counselor, that sixteenth-century wiseguy Niccolò Machiavelli. In the wake of my father's murder, I'd come roaring out of my cave of pain like Machiavelli's lion, teeth bared and thirsty for blood. So far, it had only served to make things worse. It was time to look to that other symbol of the Sicilian proverb, the fox. In Machiavelli's fable, the fox represents cunning, the ability to outwit an opponent through manipulation and misdirection. If I were going to escape the system that had me trapped, I would have to learn how to manipulate it. So I fired the legitimate attorney who had been representing me and hired a Mob lawyer, a guy by the name of Jay Silverstein. I picked a man who knew the legal system but had no compunctions about client privilege. I knew for certain that Jay was on the Gambino payroll. It was the perfect defense against the double jeopardy in which I found myself. With a smart and aggressive attorney in the courtroom, I could get immunity and some protection against the government. And since Jay would repeat every word of my legal transactions to the Mob behind my back, they could be sure I had not turned informant.

One year to the day after the authorities rang our doorbell to tell me my father was dead, the doorbell rang again. I was blowing out the candles on my eighteenth birthday cake, trying to smile for my mother when the chimes sounded. She was waging her own war of survival, and for her that included carrying on family traditions that we found hard to enjoy. On the front steps of our home stood a man in a suit, a process server who handed me a subpoena and said, "Happy birthday, Mr. DeMeo. You're served." I was ordered to report to the office of Walter Mack, prosecutor for the southern district of New York, at 9:00 Monday morning.

I drove into the city early on Monday and met Jay at his office, twenty blocks from the Manhattan courthouse that housed Mack's office. I was dressed in my best suit and tie, shoes polished, and hair slicked down against the winter wind. I tried to look adult and collected, but inside I felt like a frightened six-year-old. What were they going to do to me? Threaten me? Arrest me? Jay suggested we walk to the courthouse, and as we made our way down the crowded street, he coached me on what to expect. "Mack's heading up the Castellano investigation, trying to nail him under the RICO laws. I don't think he's after you; he just needs evidence to indict Castellano. He'll probably ask you a lot of questions about your father's business dealings. Be polite but don't give him any information. I'll handle it if there's a problem. I don't want you saying anything unless they offer you immunity."

I nodded my head mechanically as he talked, but I was finding it harder and harder to listen. Something strange was happening. The more we walked, the farther away the courthouse seemed. I could see it blocks ahead of us, a tall imposing building with Roman columns and marble steps, symbol of justice for the state of New York. Yet with every step it seemed to recede. The sidewalk had turned into a moving ribbon, growing longer as I walked. I had the curious sensation I was in a wind tunnel like the one I'd seen at a fair when I was a child. Manhattan streets are always windy in January, but this wind was an icy hand pushing me back. I leaned into it. It seemed impossible to make any headway. Jay's voice faded completely as I began talking to myself: "This is my lot, this is what's dealt me, I have to hold on, I have to be left standing at the end." For a moment I thought I'd said the words aloud; with a start I realized the voice was only in my head. I forced myself to concentrate again on what Jay was saying, but the sights and sounds around us made him difficult to hear. Everything seemed unnaturally bright, abnormally loud. Vendors shouted, "Hot dogs!" "Pretzels!" so sharply it hurt my ears. The smell of shoe polish burned my nostrils as a dark face called out, "Need a shine, buddy?" My eyes watered from the glare. I couldn't hear, couldn't think. What was wrong with me? Like a robot, I forced my body up the marble steps to the courthouse, fighting the G-forces one leg at a time. When we finally reached the top, I nearly fell into the lobby, soaked in sweat and weak with exhaustion.

The white morning glare disappeared abruptly as we entered a dim foyer. The place smelled of varnish, floor wax, and generations of human sweat. Jay gestured toward an elevator, and as we moved toward it, everything shifted into warp speed. The hall disappeared beneath my feet, the elevator seeming to shoot upward. When I got

off at the ninth floor and turned to follow Jay toward an office at the
end of the hall, I was overcome with vertigo. I fought the impulse to
reach out for the wall to balance myself as I walked. Long before I was
ready, I found myself in front of a glass door with gold lettering on it:
Walter Mack, New York State Attorney's Office. A light shone on the
other side. Jay rapped twice with his knuckles, someone shouted
"Come in," and we were behind the door. I expected a receptionist,
but instead I saw a man sitting at a desk, looking across at me. Walter
Mack. I held out my hand, but ignoring it, he gestured at us to sit
down.

I had come to do what was required of me, and I entered the room
expecting to find a man doing the same. Mack was doing his job, my
father would have told me; he had nothing personal against me. One
glimpse of his face dispelled that illusion. The man looking across at
me radiated animosity, the same animosity I had already encoun-
tered with investigators. He rose to his feet and walked around the
desk to look down at me. At six feet, five inches, Mack's skinny frame
towered over me, his face raw and reddened, topped by fair, thinning
hair. When he opened his mouth to speak to me, I saw that his teeth
were crooked and discolored and wondered briefly why he'd never
had them fixed. His clothes, too, were cheap and ill-fitting. *Don't
they pay this guy decently?* I thought. Suddenly I was painfully aware of
my own manicured nails and Italian suit. I cleared my throat nervously and waited for someone to say something.

Sitting back down behind his desk, Mack turned to Jay and
opened with, "We believe Al knows a great deal about his father's
business, a great deal more than he's telling us." Without pausing for
a reply, he turned to me and said, "We believe that he was, in fact, ac-
tively involved in all aspects of his father's business dealings." I
thought it was odd that he kept referring to me in third person as if I
weren't there.

Before my attorney had a chance to reply, Mack preempted him with, "We are, however, willing to discuss certain incentives if your client decides to cooperate." And with that he proceeded to explain the witness-protection program. If I would share everything I knew about my father, the government would give me a new identity and relocate me where my father's associates couldn't find me. *Funny*, I thought, *my father was going to try the same thing with his disappearing act.*

I listened politely as Mack outlined the government's offer in more detail. Accepting it was out of the question, but I didn't want to antagonize him further by refusing up front. The only thing I knew about the witness-protection program was my father's description: "The place where rats go after they sell out their friends." As for the government ensuring my safety, I considered that a joke. I knew that if the Mob really wanted to find me, they would. I would be a fish out of water in the Midwest, where he was talking about sending me. Besides, everyone has a price, and I had seen government employees on the Mob payroll all my life. Nobody could guarantee my safety. My father had realized the same thing about his own escape plans. Sometimes the only way out was to stay and face the consequences. Meanwhile, I would be abandoning the one role that still gave any meaning to my life: the protector of my mother and sisters. My father had died to keep them safe. Leaving them was out of the question.

Perhaps most important of all, in turning informant I would be abandoning the most deeply ingrained lesson of my life: Never rat on anyone. Even if it means you get blamed for something you didn't do, even if it means losing your own life, you don't tell. I believed in the traditional code of silence to the core of my being. I had tried to take revenge on my father's murderers myself, but I could never turn them over to the authorities. Even if I'd decided to finger them, I don't think I could have forced the words out of my mouth. I would have choked trying.

When Mack finally paused for a response, I didn't wait for my attorney to reply. "No thank you, Mr. Mack. I'm afraid I couldn't accept that offer, sir."

His eyes narrowed momentarily, and I saw a vein begin to bulge on the side of his thin neck. His raw skin turned a shade redder as he turned to Jay.

"I would advise your client to accept our offer if I were you," he went on as if I weren't there. "Without it he will become subject to prosecution himself."

"Are you charging my client with something at this time?" Jay asked rather belligerently.

"Not at this time," Mack replied after a moment's pause. Then, shifting tactics, "I do have to point out, however, that if Albert doesn't testify, I will feel compelled to subpoena his sisters." Sorting through some papers on his desk, he continued, "I believe Debra is his older sister's name, is it not? And Lisa, yes, Lisa will be eighteen next year, I believe." He knew perfectly well when she would be eighteen. Mack struck me as the kind of man who knew the content of every sheet of paper among the stacks on his desk. Anger welling within me, I struggled to maintain my composure. My fear was gone; I felt more focused than I had since my father's funeral. I knew what I was facing now. This was a war. I knew how to behave in a war. *Be calm, Al, and think*, I heard my father's voice say to me. *Stay aware of everything around you. That's how you survive.* No smart-mouthed civil servant was going to come after my family. I would play out this game to the end.

As my lawyer and the prosecutor talked on, I silently sized up my opponent. I think my politeness irritated him most of all. In his eyes I was an arrogant little punk, stone cold and defiant, and my careful courtesy seemed to him another form of disrespect. Every time he looked at me, the vein on the side of his neck bulged visibly.

After what felt like hours, Mack dismissed us with a final admonition to Jay for his client to think carefully about the consequences of refusing the government's generosity. As we walked back down the

courthouse steps, I breathed deeply of the cold winter air and said,
"What's next, Jay?"

"They'll probably subpoena you before a grand jury. Don't worry,
Al. I'll make sure they grant you immunity." *Immunity from what?* I
wondered.

I did not tell my mother or sisters what had happened in Walter
Mack's office. When Debra asked, I just said he wanted to ask me a
couple of questions about Dad's murder. I did not want her worrying.

The weather warmed toward spring, and each day I expected another process server to appear on my doorstep, but no one did. I had
actually begun to hope the ordeal was over, that the prosecutor knew
his threats were empty. I was graduating from high school in a couple
of months, and there were parties nearly every weekend. I went with
my girlfriend and tried to enjoy myself, but it was difficult to relax.
Tommy was already in college, but Nick would be graduating in my
class. Senior prom was the big social event of that semester, and my
girlfriend had spent weeks planning her dress and hair. I knew how
important the special night was to her. I ordered a limo and prepared
to go with Nick and Tommy and their dates. Even though he had
graduated, Tommy was taking a girl in my class. That evening we all
met at my house, and the last thing we did before getting in the limo
was to line up on the sidewalk so my mother could take pictures of us
all in our formal attire. We were all too busy smiling for the camera to
notice a stranger approaching on the sidewalk.

"Albert DeMeo?" he inquired.

Immediately wary, I replied, "Yeah. Why?"

He pulled an envelope out of his inside jacket pocket and threw it
at me. It glanced off my chest and landed on the sidewalk.

"You've just been served," he grinned and then walked off down
the street.

I felt myself flush deeply as my girlfriend looked at me and said,
"Al . . . ?"

Tommy and Nick had already taken their dates by the arm and

guided them into the limo, away from me and the humiliation of the moment.

Leaning over to pick up the envelope from the sidewalk, I tried to sound reassuring as I told my girlfriend, "Everything's fine. I just need to go in the house for a minute and make a phone call. Then we're out of here." Her face was sad, uncertain. I kissed her on the cheek. "It's fine. Don't worry about a thing. I'll make a call, we'll go have a good time."

I went quickly upstairs to my father's study and called Jay at home. He told me to meet him at his office in the morning. Then I went back down to the limo and climbed inside. As the driver pulled away, I asked, "Who wants a drink?" and everyone laughed with relief. We spent the next six hours dancing the night away at a country club with the class of 1984. Tommy says we had a good time. I don't remember a thing about it.

A date had been set for my first appearance before the grand jury investigating Nino Gaggi and the Gemini crew. Jay explained the process to me carefully. We would go to the courthouse, where I would be taken into a room filled with a jury composed of citizens from all walks of life. There would be no judge, and Mack would be there as prosecutor for the Southern District of New York. I would be interrogated, probably extensively, about my father's business dealings. Jay told me to take the Fifth Amendment on everything they asked me, except for verifying my identity. He had not yet been able to secure me immunity, but he was confident the government would offer it when it became clear I would not testify without it.

The psychological war with the government I had been drafted into escalated steadily. Surveillance vehicles reemerged in growing numbers from the night of the prom. As my grand jury date approached, a series of odd incidents began occurring. They began with my car radio, stolen from the parking lot while my girlfriend and I were in a movie theater. Since we had been tailed to the theater, I

went over to ask the surveillance team if they'd seen anyone tamper-
ing with my car. They told me they didn't know what I was talking
about. They hadn't seen anyone near my car. I didn't think too much
about the incident until the T-top was stolen off my car a couple of
nights later, while I was eating in a restaurant with Tommy and Nick.
Then a few days later, I went into the backyard one morning to dis-
cover that my speedboat cover had been taken while the boat was
moored to the floating dock out back. And finally, on the morning I
was scheduled to testify, I went out to the driveway to find all four
tires of my car flat. All of these incidents had taken place while government cars surveyed me continually. In spite of their ongoing
presence, the agents all claimed to have seen nothing. One suggested
some of my "Mob buddies" had done it. That was a ridiculous suggestion. I knew the Mob wasn't responsible for any of it. If they
wanted to influence my testimony, they would threaten me directly,
more likely kill me. Besides, I knew Jay had told them I was not going
to testify against them. That was why I'd hired him in the first place.

Everything about the grand jury system is designed to intimidate.
To begin with, attorneys are not allowed in the jury chamber, so each
participant, witness or accused, enters the jury chamber alone. I had
not been warned about this the first time I testified; Jay gave me this
information at the door of the jury chamber as I entered that morning. Horrified, I responded, "You're not coming with me?" No, he
replied, I could leave the chamber whenever I wanted talk to him, but
he would not be allowed in the room with me. I was unnerved by this
unexpected turn of events. Even the door the court clerk directed me
to enter was intimidating. Large and heavy, with the seal of New York
State on the outside, it radiated authority. I felt suddenly very small
as I pushed it open and walked through the portal.

Inside the chamber, on both sides of me, jurors sat on tiered
benches that looked like bleachers. As I walked toward a table
straight ahead, I was painfully aware of a hundred pairs of eyes star-

ing down at me, the mobster's son. The faces above me represented a cross-section of New York City: male and female, old and young, poor and middle class, black and brown and white—I had the eerie sensation that the entire city was there. *What did they see when they looked at me?* I wondered. I had dressed carefully for the occasion in a conservative suit and tie, shoes shined, and hair combed. Yet no amount of scrubbing and brushing could make me look like the frightened teenager I really was. I knew that the jury saw the same thing the government saw when they looked at me: the junior wiseguy, a miniature version of my father. The mask of bravado I put on to get me through the moment only made things worse, yet it was the only mask I had.

I was shown to a chair at the end of a long, heavy wooden table. Mack sat at the other end, seemingly miles away. After a lengthy pause, during which I could feel my hands shaking, he began to question me. His questions were slow, deliberate, repetitive. After verifying my name and address, I began taking the Fifth: "I respectfully decline to answer the question on the grounds that it might incriminate me." When a witness takes the Fifth four or five times in a row, the prosecutor usually stops the proceedings for a ruling from the judge. Mack did not stop. He kept on asking me questions.

"What did your father do for a living?"

"I respectfully decline . . ."

"Are you familiar with a bar called the Gemini Lounge?"

"I respectfully decline . . ."

"Are you acquainted with a man named Anthony Gaggi?"

"I respectfully decline . . ."

After a while he whispered something to his clerk, who walked the length of that endless table and laid two photographs in front of me. One was a picture of my father, smiling into the camera, another a snapshot of my father and me when I was small. *Where had they gotten these pictures?* Mack continued questioning me, making no reference to the photos lying before me. The clerk glanced at Mack, who nodded slightly and continued speaking as the clerk began laying other photos in a semicircle around the smiling snapshots of me and my dad. These were crime scene photos taken at the time of my father's murder. There were about a dozen of them, taken at various angles while he lay contorted in his own blood in the trunk of our car. There were close-ups of his face and hands, where the bullets had penetrated. I had never seen these photographs before. Clenching my hands to control their shaking, I heard Mack ask, "Who killed your father, Albert?"

The faces of the Gemini Twins flashed in front of my eyes, peering through the darkness at me behind ski masks. *This is war, Al, war*, I reminded myself. I pulled my eyes away from the photos and met Mack's gaze.

"I respectfully decline . . ."

The clerk returned to the far end of the table and sat down as Mack changed direction to a more innocuous series of questions.

"Who did your mother hire to decorate her house?"

What was he talking about? The decorator? The minutes dragged by. At another nod from the prosecutor, the clerk made another journey to the end of the table where I sat. He began arranging new photos around the crime scene pictures of my father's body: Anthony, Joey, Nino, Freddy in his race car, another family snapshot of my father. As the clerk laid each one down, Mack asked me, "Do you recognize the person in this photograph?" Finally the clerk laid down a snapshot of the crew leaving the Gemini. "Who killed your father, Albert?"

All day long it went on. There was a short lunch break, and then it started all over again. More questions, the same questions rephrased and repeated, more photographs. Some were of people I had never seen before; others looked vaguely familiar. One in particular caught my attention. My first thought was "That's Freddy." Yet it didn't look like Freddy. The features were different. Plastic surgery? Jay had told me that Freddy had already been relocated by the witness-protection program. My gut told me it was Freddy DiNome, but I couldn't be sure. Other photos were deeply disturbing. I was shown a series of murder scenes, strangers with mutilated bodies and faces disfigured in death. Piece by piece, a mosaic of horror was constructed in front of me. When the crime scene photos were laid on the table, Mack came down to where I was sitting to point at them, leaning so close to my face I could feel his breath. I could smell his hatred as he asked me to identify the victims in the photos. He clearly believed I knew who they were, but with every question, I became more confused. *Who were these people? What did they have to do with my father?* After what felt like several lifetimes, I was finally dismissed for the day. My entire body was numb. I had taken the Fifth Amendment more times than I can remember.

The next morning Mack called Jay and offered me immunity. A few days later, when the paperwork was completed, I returned to the grand jury room for my second appearance. The questions, the photographs were a repetition of my earlier testimony. I answered politely, vaguely, offering as little information as possible. I identified crew members as "friends of my father's" but said I didn't know what they did for a living. I soon realized that Mack was hoping to trap me into a different reply by continual rephrasing of the same questions, to confuse me or frustrate me into saying something I hadn't planned on. Each time I felt uncertain, I asked to see Jay and made the long walk to the door as the eyes of the jurors followed me. Outside in the hall, I would confer with my lawyer, then open the door and return inside the chamber. Each time I opened it, the door got a little heavier. By the time they finally dismissed me, I felt like an old man. It was over, Jay told me. But I knew by then that it might never be over.

I graduated with the rest of my class, and my mother and sisters were there to smile and wish me well. I made myself smile back at them, and I ached as I watched classmates embrace their fathers and listened to idealistic speeches I could not relate to. Our neighbor the stockbroker arranged a summer job for me in the financial district. It was a kind and courageous gesture on his part, for the stigma of my father's murder had made us pariahs with most of the neighborhood. I worked hard all summer, and in September I began classes at St. John's University in Queens as a business major. It was a beautiful little campus, filled with historic buildings and arching trees, still overseen by the order of priests who had founded it. Yet even there I didn't feel safe. One morning a few weeks into my first semester, I saw the professor look toward the door and say, "May I help you?" in a puzzled voice. I turned with the rest of my class to see two men standing in the doorway. My throat closed. Federal agents.

"We're looking for Albert DeMeo," one of them said, scanning the classroom.

I was on my feet before he finished the sentence. Heading for the hall as quickly as I could, I mumbled something to the professor about going on without me. He resumed the lecture as I stepped into the hallway. One of the agents said, "Mr. Mack wants to see you, Albert. He just has a few more questions."

"Call my lawyer" was my only reply. I quietly retrieved my books from the classroom, called Jay, and met him downtown. I didn't want to prolong this ordeal for another minute.

Two weeks after that it happened again. And again after that. My classmates peered at me curiously, and I could hear them whispering as I walked by. Near the end of my first semester, the dean asked to see me in his office. I entered stoically, expecting the worst, but the face that examined mine over his priestly collar was concerned. "Al, your professors have informed me that you have been taken out of class several times by men who appear to be government agents. Is everything all right? Is there something I could help you with?"

"Thank you, sir, but there's nothing you can do. It's a family matter."

"Would you like me to contact anyone on your behalf?"

"No, thank you, I'll take care of it."

He regarded me thoughtfully, perplexed but unwilling to pry further. At last he said, "Well then, you may go. If you change your mind, you know where to find me."

There was nothing he could do. There was nothing anyone could do to help me. I was one tiny part of a sweeping criminal probe. I understood the rationale for the prosecutions. What bothered me was the methods used to bring them about. It was Machiavelli pure and simple: The end justifies the means. Do whatever you have to do to put these people away, no matter how brutal or unjust. At least the Mob was honest about the way it did things. The government, on the other hand, hid behind a mask of fake piety. The witness-protection program, conceived as a way to protect the innocent, was becoming a retirement program for gangsters, men who were often worse than the defendants they testified against. Sammy "The Bull" Gravano was the most dramatic example. Not only was he responsible for dozens of Mob murders but he swaggered into the courtroom and bragged about them, unrepentant, in front of stunned onlookers. The local papers talked of little else. And when he was finished, he went into early retirement, courtesy of the federal government. The only apparent criterion for the witness-protection program was a willingness to say whatever the government wanted you to say. It didn't seem to matter if it was true, as long as a prosecutor got his conviction. In some instances I knew that individual informants were lying, and I watched a family friend go to prison for something he had never done. His only crime was having a social relationship with my father. I agonized over his sentence, knowing that I might be able to clear him. But to do so would have required that I implicate several other people, and I wasn't willing to do that. To this day I wonder if I made the right decision.

The pressure on me to talk was relentless. Much of the time I could not figure out what they wanted me to say. I had never heard many of the names they brought up, and even when I did recognize a name or incident, my knowledge was very limited. I had been hearing unrelated bits and pieces at the social clubs and the Gemini all my life, but except for the money collections, my father had never shared the daily running of his business with me.

Intellectually, I understood that I was caught up in a process that went far beyond me. My grand jury appearances were only a small part of a far-flung, complex investigation. The heads of all five New York crime families were being systematically prosecuted under Giuliani's leadership. Nothing close to it had ever happened before. During my sophomore year in college, Paul Castellano was murdered just in time to avoid a life sentence in prison. The year I graduated from college, John Gotti, one of my father's first business partners and the man who had murdered Castellano, became a media idol after his own arrest. The Mafia was not only wounded but crippled, the power it had once wielded permanently broken. The sweeping prosecutions of those years were wiping out what was left of my father's world.

An encroaching sense of despair gradually became my daily companion. The passion and persistence of the ongoing federal investigations hounded my every step, literally and figuratively. I had buried my father, but I could not bury the heritage he had left me. My sisters, sheltered during his life from the knowledge of our father's other identity, remained sheltered after his death. Walter Mack never followed through on his threats to subpoena them, and I never told them about my own grand jury appearances. I let them believe that the continual legal intrusions were related to our father's murder investigation. Debra graduated from college with honors and married, putting her career as a textile designer on hold to have children in a home a few miles from where we'd grown up. My younger sister graduated from high school with honors and went on to college as well.

My junior year of college, Mom sold the house my father had built on the water and moved to a new neighborhood. I knew she was desperate to escape the past, to begin a new life free of the pressure and misery of the last few years. I bought a condominium a few miles from my old high school.

The personal toll of those years was tremendous for me. My relationship with my high school girlfriend was only one small casualty. Convinced I would never survive to marry or have children, I lived like a condemned man. When I couldn't escape the stigma of my father's Mafia image, I began to embrace it. During the days I went to class or to work, but at night, I became a wiseguy. I went into stores and ordered everything on the shelves just to prove that I could. I filled my condo with expensive furnishings and every technological gadget money could buy. I showered my friends with more luxuries than they wanted or could possibly use. I took a limo into Manhattan on weekends as I had in the old days, the seats filled with girls for me and my friends and the ice buckets brimming with thousand-dollar bottles of champagne. I was still offered the best tables in restaurants by people who either remembered my father or hoped for some of the cash I flashed around in rolls. On weekends I drank myself into oblivion, often waking in the middle of the night to find a naked stranger in my bed. I didn't remember who the women were, and I didn't care. The only thing that mattered was that I wasn't alone. My greatest fear was being sober and alone.

Christmas of 1987 was one of the lowest points. Isolated and too depressed to accept my sister's invitation to dinner with her husband, I sat alone in my condominium on Christmas Eve, staring at the television screen and drinking to block out the ghosts of Christmases past. When the doorbell rang, I had to concentrate to maneuver to the doorway through the blur. I turned on the porch light and opened the door, and there stood Debra holding an eight-week-old Rottweiler puppy with a big red bow around its neck. With tears in her eyes, Debra put the puppy into my arms and said, "Merry Christmas, Al. I thought you could use a friend."

I put my arms around her and held her for a moment, the puppy squirming in my arms.

"Are you sure you don't want to come for dinner? It's not too late."

"No, that's okay. I think I'd rather hang out here."

Looking at me with concern, she nodded and said she'd better get back home. I wished her Merry Christmas, and as she walked back down the path to her car, I called after her, "I love you, Deb." She smiled wanly and waved back at me as I took the puppy inside to find him something to eat. I named him Luca, after Don Corleone's most trusted aide in *The Godfather*. He became my best friend.

I did not understand what was happening to me. I had not cried once since the day I'd gone to the morgue to identify my father's body. I only knew I had to kill the pain, even if that meant oblivion. Many nights I longed for death; it would be a relief to get it over with. My father had chosen death. I deserved nothing more. I have no idea how I survived those years. I should not have come through alive.

My last year of college brought an event that seemed inconsequential at the time. My mother received a letter from a crime reporter named Jerry Capeci, asking to interview her for a book he was co-writing. Parts of the book would make reference to my father, and he hoped she would supply him with personal information about the family. She called me about the letter, and I told her I would take care of it. I had her lawyer reply, politely declining to take part in the project on the family's behalf, and forgot all about it. It seemed unlikely that my father's auto theft operation would attract much interest in a book about the Mafia when hired killers like Sammy the Bull were still making headlines regularly.

The final important event of that year was my last appearance before a grand jury. I had severed ties with Jay Silverstein by then. With most of my father's old crew dead or in prison, and with a track record of my own demonstrating my unwillingness to share information, the threat of a Mob hit on me was minimal. I had turned instead to a legitimate lawyer, a man who had handled my father's estate and other aspects of his legitimate businesses. Greg was highly respected, competent, and free of Mafia ties, and I was anxious to cleanse myself of the image my Mob lawyer had projected in the courtroom. Greg sought and obtained a renewal of my immunity agreement before agreeing to have me testify. My mother was also subpoenaed this time, but was excused after only twenty minutes of testimony. She invoked spousal privilege when asked about my father's business dealings, and as she really didn't know anything about them, she was quickly dismissed.

On the evening before my final grand jury testimony, after prepping with my attorney all day, I ate dinner at The Palm restaurant in Manhattan with a friend. I was sitting at a table, relaxing over drinks, when I looked up and caught sight of a familiar face. There sat Anthony Senter, one of the Gemini Twins, just four tables away from us. I couldn't believe my past was still following me. He was out on bail pending the investigation I was testifying for. I had not seen him face to face since the night he had run me off the road and pistol-whipped me. He noticed me only seconds after I spotted him. He immediately looked away, pretending he hadn't seen me. I folded my napkin, excused myself, and walked over to Anthony's table. I stood there a moment, then said, "Hi ya, Anthony. How ya doing?"

He looked up at me without replying, white as a sheet. He knew by then that I was well aware he had helped kill my father. I stood there staring down at him. A thousand memories flitted through my mind, ending with my father's face in the morgue, his eye blown out by the man sitting in front of me. For a moment I had an overpowering impulse to grab the steak knife from the table and push it right into Anthony's heart. The words *I should have killed you myself* ran through my mind. I didn't say them aloud. Instead I told him I'd see him around, and I returned to my table to finish my meal. He left the restaurant a few minutes later.

The next day I entered the jury chamber and identified Anthony only as my father's friend, a business associate I used to see around the Gemini when I was a kid. My left temple throbbed as I testified, the fractures Anthony had inflicted still painful under stress. Prosecutors kept me on the stand all day, repeating my previous testimony, but when they finally excused me, they did so without warnings or innuendoes. After conferring with all parties involved, Greg told me that my long legal ordeal seemed to finally be over. The prosecution had no plans to subpoena me again. A few months later I read in the paper that both Anthony and Joey Testa had been given three consecutive life sentences for murdering men I had never heard of. I never saw them again.

eleven

THE ABYSS

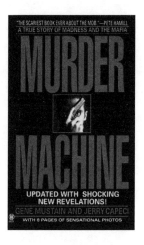

MURDER MACHINE

Blind,
Like one whom sleep comes over in a swoon,
I stumbled into darkness and went down.

—DANTE, *The Inferno*

I had spent every waking moment since I was seven years old learning to live in a world that had ceased to exist by the time I walked out of a courtroom for the last time at age twenty-three. In a sense, it had never existed to begin with. The underworld is as much the product of fiction as of any reality, even in the minds of those who dwell there. On screen, the life of the Mafioso is glamorous and exciting, filled with danger and intense, dark-eyed women. In the real world, the gangster is an exhausted middle-aged man who comes home at dawn to a disillusioned wife and a dog dish that needs cleaning. The shiny maroon Cadillac is the image. The frozen body in the trunk is the reality. I had never been an active player in that universe, but my existence had been trapped in its orbit for as long as I could remember. However illusory, it remained the only world I knew how to function in.

I survived by embracing the hedonism of an existence where every day above ground is a good day. Every meal was my last meal. I lived every moment on the brink of death, addicted to the adrenaline rush that ensures survival. My father had raised me to be a soldier, and I'd spent every day for fifteen years poised for battle. What happens to soldiers when the war is over? They are released into a world for which no one has prepared them. When my father's war finally ended for me, I had no idea what to do next.

All around me, the world was changing. My friend Nick had already married, and soon after, Tommy took a job and moved out of state. One by one, my party companions started careers, moved away, or began families of their own. My sisters were well and happy, with lives of usefulness and fulfillment. I had helped my mother get settled in a house near my older sister, where she could see her grandchildren as often as she wanted. After the long struggle, I was leaving my old life behind at last. I was finally free to do and to be whatever I wanted.

I didn't have the faintest idea where to begin. So I did the one thing I had always been good at; I played a role. This time the role wasn't a wiseguy. It was that of a successful young businessman, a solid citizen. I decided to leave my old identity behind me forever and go into a witness-protection program of my own making. After five summers working on Wall Street under the guidance of my former neighbor, I turned to the stock market for a career. There, free from the old neighborhood and my former classmates, I could reinvent myself as a successful, upwardly mobile stockbroker.

I was able to get a job in the financial district and quickly worked my way up the ranks, landing a job on the floor of the New York Stock Exchange. The intensity, the pace, the high stakes of life on the trading floor gave me an adrenaline rush I hadn't had since my days with my father, and I welcomed it. This time the rush I felt was legitimate, even profitable. Every now and then I felt a ghost walk over my grave when I came across a piece of my past in the newspaper. One Sunday the *Post* reported that Nino Gaggi had died of a heart attack in a prison hospital. A few months later I read that Freddy DiNome had been found hanged in a hotel room half a continent away. Police believed it was suicide. I wondered. Had my father's oldest friend succumbed to despair, or had the witness-protection program failed him? What had it all been for, all those years? All that remained were poverty, imprisonment, and death.

I stayed in touch with Tommy and Nick, but I cultivated new friendships in the financial district as well, where no one knew about my past or my father's Mob connections. When I met a beautiful young girl working her way through college as a waitress, I fell in love on the spot. Carrie was just the sort of woman I had always admired: hardworking, grounded, with clear goals in life. I did not tell her about my father when I began courting her, but I felt obligated to share some information before I proposed to her. One night when we were talking about our families, I told her that my father had run an auto theft operation for the Mafia and that he had been murdered many years earlier. She was sympathetic but suggested that we keep that information to ourselves and quickly changed the subject. I didn't bring it up again. We married in 1991, a formal church wedding with all of our family and friends there. My family was thrilled for me, Carrie's family pleased that she was marrying such an up-and-coming young man. Only Tommy was hesitant, worried that she was more interested in my new image than in me. I didn't care; I liked my new image.

For a while everything seemed to be working perfectly. But it's a strange thing about the past. The harder you try to leave it behind, the more closely it dogs you. I might have been ready to let go of my past, but it had no intention of letting go of me.

It began harmlessly enough, with a resurgence of interest in Mafia movies. Sammy Gravano's revelations and John Gotti's sensational trial and conviction sparked an artistic renaissance for the Mob. The third *Godfather* movie had been released, followed shortly by *GoodFellas*, the ultimate paean to wiseguys. Then, by an odd coincidence, I found myself stationed next to a guy at the Exchange with his own Mafia obsession. Unaware of my personal history, he bragged continually that his son was the driver for the new don of a New York crime family. Every day when I came to work, I was treated to endless descriptions of the crimes his son knew about, the important gangsters his son drove around town. Each day as he told his tales to an admiring throng of my co-workers, I marveled at the man's breathtaking stupidity. If even a portion of what he was saying was true, he was putting his own life and his son's at risk with the Mob and the law by spilling every detail he knew.

For a while my role-playing continued to work. My old identity remained a secret. Each morning I boarded the train from Long Island to Manhattan, got a cup of espresso under the towering arches of the Wall Street exit, bought my copy of the *Wall Street Journal* to read while I had my shoes shined, and joined my colleagues on the floor of the Exchange. In the evenings I took the train back to Long Island, got into the car where Carrie waited at the station, and kissed my beautiful wife hello. It was the best moment of the day for me. I loved the way she smelled. We would drive home together to the quiet of our beautifully appointed home in the suburbs, where Luca greeted us ecstatically at the front door. He had grown from a squirmy, clumsy puppy to nearly one hundred-sixty pounds of solid muscle in the years since Debra brought him to my door, but he was as sweet and affectionate as ever. I had built a two-story home for us less than a mile from my older sister's home, a downsized replica of my family's old home on the water, complete with marble floors and crystal chandeliers. At night, as Carrie lay sleeping in my arms, I would marvel at the place life had finally brought me.

I was rarely happy, but I was safe, and that was enough. I bought Carrie jewelry and let her decorate our home, finding happiness in her excitement. I was still drinking heavily, but I confined my drinking to the nighttime hours. I was always sober by the time I left for work. Carrie couldn't understand my persistent insomnia or the nightmares that sent me to a bottle somewhere between 1:00 and 4:00 A.M., but it was easy enough for her to ignore as long as I continued functioning. The people in my new life saw my hard-earned facade and accepted it as authentic. I was liked and respected by neighbors and colleagues alike. There were days when even to me, my former life with my father seemed unreal, a strange phantom existence that recurred in my consciousness only in the reaches of the night.

A lie is always fragile, and the lie I was living imploded simply and cleanly one gray Manhattan morning. Jerry Capeci, the reporter who had contacted my mother in 1988, and his co-author published their book. I found out about it from an old high school friend who also worked in the financial district. He was the only one of my Wall Street colleagues who knew of my Mafia connections. One evening I got a phone call from him, telling me that a book had just been published about my father. The book was titled *Murder Machine: A True Story of Madness and the Mafia*. According to the advertising blurb, it was based on revelations from my father's old crew. Quietly, without telling Carrie, I went to a Manhattan bookstore the next day and asked the clerk if they stocked the book. She handed it to me without a second glance. Red letters screamed from the black book jacket: "They were the DeMeo gang—the most deadly hit men in organized crime . . . [known as] Murder Machine." An accompanying review by the *New York Post* described the book as "the inside story of a single Brooklyn gang that killed more Americans than the Iraqi army." My whole body went numb. I paid the clerk in cash and got out of there as quickly as I could.

Alone, turning the pages of the book that night, I found myself plunged back nearly ten years, into the same state of shock that had followed my father's murder. Each page was a new agony. My father's name was emblazoned on the cover and included on nearly every page of the text. The photo insert carried pictures of Chris and Anthony and Joey, Uncle Nino, Cousin Joe, and, horrifically, crime scene photos of my father's murder. In the index I found my own

name listed as Albert DeMeo, son of Roy, with page references for
incidents in our family's life. It was overwhelming, bizarre. I read
page after page filled with accounts of our home life by people I had
never met, who had never spoken to anyone present at the occasions
they described. Even more surreal, I found descriptions of what I, my
mother and sisters, and especially my father had been thinking and
feeling through much of our lives. How could these writers possibly
know such things when they had never even met us?

I read detailed descriptions of events that were grossly inaccurate,
events that I had witnessed firsthand. A number of these "factual
accounts" were completely untrue. Most of the information came
from Dominick Montiglio, Nino Gaggi's nephew. I remembered the
Dominick I had known, the wannabe who had always resented his
uncle Nino's reluctance to give him the position in the crew
Dominick believed he deserved. I remembered all the years
Dominick had spent in a drug-induced fog, barely able to function in
the grip of the heroin addiction that destroyed his health, his judgment, and ultimately his personal life. And most of all, I remembered my father talking Nino out of killing Dominick because my
father felt sorry for him, believed that Dominick deserved compassion because of the chemical addiction that consumed him. This was
the "impeccable source" for Capeci's endless accounts of Mafia life
in the seventies and eighties—that and the Gemini Twins, fountains
of truth that they were. As long as they were already in prison for
three murders, why not make it a hundred and three? It sounded so
much more impressive.

Yet it was neither Dominick nor the Twins that angered me most.
What enraged me beyond words, beyond my ability to contain it, was
the book's depiction of my father. In the words of Capeci, my father
had been transformed into a cowardly, hulking creature who killed
for pleasure and groveled in sensory pleasure: a fat, drunken beast
devoid of remorse, incapable of compassion, a preevolutionary

monstrosity. Every sentence about him dripped with contempt and petty, gratuitous insults. Capeci seemed obsessed with my father's weight, the most common epithet attached to him being "the fat bully." I'd rarely seen my father take a drink in all the days and nights I spent with him. He thought alcohol and drugs dulled the senses, a dangerous luxury in the world he inhabited. As for his weight, he worked out daily during his last years, and though he was husky, he was never grossly obese. As for "the fat bully of Brooklyn," as Capeci described him during his teenage years, family photos of Dad show a dark, lean, fit young man during my parents' courtship. What was the point of continually emphasizing Dad's weight except for the sake of insulting him? And my mother—the book referred to her as the "stone cold widow" in the wake of my father's death. I knew the pain she had suffered, still suffered. How dare these strangers speak about my mother with such disrespect? My mind went back to the officers who had arrived at our front door to announce my father's death. "Gina," they had called her, these strangers in our home. They had not even done her the courtesy of calling her Mrs. DeMeo.

And for the first time, I read about my father's murder in the words of the people who had committed it. It confirmed what I already suspected. Paul Castellano had ordered the hit, making my uncle Nino do it himself as a test of loyalty. Nino had trouble pulling the trigger on his old friend and missed his aim, hitting my father in the chest as my father instinctively threw his hands up. That explained the bullet holes I had seen in his hands at the morgue. The story came from the Gemini Twins, who had been in on the hit. They described the shooting with contempt for Nino's weakness, bragging that they had put the fatal bullets in my father's head themselves and stuffed his body in the trunk. Their insolence seemed to leap off the page.

All the old rage came pouring back as I read, and for the first time in years, I wished that I had killed Joey and Anthony myself. Yet the rage wasn't the worst of it. As I continued turning the pages, my anger was gradually transformed into sickened disbelief. I knew that my father had murdered people in the course of his criminal career. I knew he had killed the Colombian student, I suspected he had killed Chris, and I had listened as he considered killing Paul Castellano. I had read articles on Mafia murders from the time I was nine or ten, and I understood the implications of the gun and knife kept hidden in the trunk of the car. My father's profession was dangerous, and sometimes people got killed. Yet I had never seen the killings, never known the details, and had kept the possibilities vague in my mind. The man I knew was careful and compassionate. I had always believed that my father killed only out of grim necessity, only when there was no other way to resolve a situation, and that those who had died at his hands were fellow soldiers in an internecine war. They knew the rules and played the game anyway. Yet however exaggerated and inaccurate this book was, it was impossible to ignore the allegations that my father had been a professional assassin.

The text swam before my eyes as they refused to focus on the words beneath. I felt myself leave my body, and I had the strange sensation that I was watching myself read. The pages overflowed with murder after murder, some of them motivated solely by profit, others involving minor players that no stretch of my imagination could label as fellow soldiers. Faces in the crime scene photos Mack had shown me flitted before my eyes. Was this what he had been getting at? Were these ghastly stories the things he thought I knew? Unbidden pieces of old conversations overheard at the Gemini began to take on horrifying new meanings. There were lurid descriptions of my father's crew disposing of bodies by what the authors called "the Gemini method," draining the blood in the shower and carving them into small pieces with knives in Cousin Joe's kitchen so the victims could not be identified. I used to eat pasta and cannoli in that kitchen as a boy. I suddenly remembered how often Joe's apartment had been freshly repainted. What was the paint covering up? Blood stains?

Worst of all was Chris's murder. The Gemini Twins had been there that night, too. Castellano had told my father that if he didn't kill Chris himself, Big Paul would have my father killed. When Chris got to Cousin Joe's apartment for the usual Friday night division of cash, my father had shot him coming through the door—right by the kitchen table where I had once passed my test of manhood. Only my father's hand was shaking so hard that he missed his aim, and Chris fell to his knees wounded at my father's feet. Anthony and Joey finished Chris off, but not fast enough to keep him from knowing my father was responsible. They dragged Chris's body out to his car while my father remained behind. The parallels were overwhelming. Just as my father had killed Chris, so Nino had killed my father, in the same way and for the same reasons. Not personal, simply survival.

I read all night, sitting in front of my fireplace with Luca, and afterward I sat staring at the pictures of my father in the photo insert. I didn't recognize him. He had lived in my mind every hour since his death, but when I looked at the face staring back at me now, I did not even know who he was.

I could not process what I had just read. I put the book in the back of a drawer, went back to work the next day, and prayed that no one would buy it. I said nothing to Carrie.

A few days later my mother called. Uncle Louis had heard about the book and had brought her a copy. I asked her if she had read it. Her "yes" hung in the air.

"Albert?"

"Yeah, Mom?"

"We can't let your sisters read it."

"Of course not, Mom, absolutely. They don't need to know anything about it. I don't think many people are going to read this piece of trash anyway."

"You really think so, Albert?"

"Sure, Mom. Of course I do. Don't worry about it. Everything will be fine." She pretended to believe me.

I pretended to believe it, too. Maybe I would never have to think about what I'd read again, and I could go on as before, the successful image of a fine young family man.

More than a year passed, and nothing seemed to change. My insomnia was worse than ever, and I found myself short of breath for no apparent reason, but these were minor concerns. Life remained externally calm, and I began to hope that the publication of *Murder Machine* was a temporary ripple rather than the tidal wave I had feared. Then one afternoon on the floor of the New York Stock Exchange, in the twinkling of an eye, I was drowning.

I was standing in front of my computer as usual, absorbed in the daily high stakes gamble as I received, processed, and implemented intricate financial transactions. I never took my attention off the screen in front of me as I responded to the continually shifting columns of figures in front of my eyes. I couldn't afford to. Once, during my first year on the Exchange floor, I had seen a veteran broker drop dead of a heart attack only yards away from me, yet no one had even paused while emergency workers lifted his body onto a stretcher and carried it out a side door. On this particular day, however, I happened to glance idly at a group of co-workers a few yards away as I listened to a message that was being relayed to me on the floor. They were gathered around one of my colleagues, reading over his shoulder as he held a book in front of him at eye level. With a sudden stab in my chest, I recognized the red letters glaring from the black book jacket. I already knew what they said: "the DeMeo gang . . ." A few seconds passed like a lifetime before I was able to drag my eyes back to the screen in front of me. I tried to concentrate once again on the shifting digital display, but my mind had gone completely blank. Against my will, I found my eyes dragged back to the growing group of co-workers gathered whispering around the book. One of them pointed me out, then noticed me watching and quickly looked away.

The littered floor around me started to spin. Gathering the presence of mind to ask the floor manager for a replacement, I rushed to a side door and out into the hallway. A few yards down was the men's room. My stomach felt like it was ripping in two. My heart pounded painfully, and there was a rushing sound in my ears. Clutching my chest with my right arm, I staggered to the nearest elevator and went straight to the small hospital on the top floor of the Exchange. I was certain I was having a heart attack.

After running a series of tests, though, the doctor told me there was nothing wrong with my heart. What I had just experienced, he informed me, was a severe panic attack. I refused to believe him. I never panicked. He gave me medication for my ulcer, then advised me to take a few days off and see my family physician. Most important, he told me, I should tell no one about the diagnosis. Better to let my superiors think it was a heart problem. If anyone found out I was having panic attacks, I would never work on the Exchange again. A panicky broker was a bad risk.

I took his advice and said nothing, even to Carrie. The next day I saw another doctor, who gave me a bottle of Valium with several refills and also advised me to keep quiet about my condition. He didn't need to warn me. I was filled with shame, confused and frightened. I had survived things in life few men have to face and never blinked. What was wrong with me? And why was it happening now? I took a few days off to rest, claiming my ulcer was acting up, and returned to the Exchange the next week. Some of my co-workers now treated me like a celebrity because of the book's revelations; others backed away in suspicion. It was high school all over again: I was the mobster's son. One of them jokingly asked me if I had ever killed anybody. I took my pills, endured their comments and questions, and tried to carry on as if nothing had changed.

Less than two weeks later, the second blow struck. I was soldiering through the days at work by sheer determination, but the nights were another matter. No amount of medication made me sleep, and from midnight to dawn, I wandered from room to room like a restless spirit. One night was particularly bad and, desperate to turn off my thoughts, I switched on the television at about two in the morning. I turned to the Arts and Entertainment channel and was about to sit down when I was stopped in midmotion by the image that took shape. There, on the large screen of the television set, was my father's face, flickering in the darkness. In the background, I was dimly aware of a voice droning a narrative. The voice was familiar. Dominick Montiglio. Sinking onto the couch, I watched in horrified fascination as my father's life passed before my eyes in lurid detail. The shameful narrative had metamorphosed into a nightmare documentary. I couldn't breathe.

There was no escaping this time. The next morning I told Carrie about the documentary and warned my mother and sisters. With the documentary airing, they were certain to hear about it. Carrie shrank from me in humiliation and anger, insisting fiercely that no one must find out about this. But I watched my mother shrink back into the shadow she had become following my father's death. The worst part was Debra. I saw the bewildered pain on my older sister's face as she turned the pages of the book that had started it all. "I don't understand, Al," she told me. "I don't recognize this man. This isn't Daddy. What is this all about? Is any of this true?"

"Some of it."

"Did you know?"

"Parts. Not all of it."

"Where was I when all this was going on?" she cried out in anguish. "Why didn't I know?"

"Daddy didn't want you to know."

I saw her mind casting frantically about, trying to grasp the remnants of her childhood, an illusion that had unraveled in one horrible moment of enlightenment. Finally it caught on a single thread of memory, and she looked up at me with sudden understanding.

"That's why Daddy was crying, wasn't it? After we went away that time? He was crying because he'd killed that boy."

"Yeah."

"Oh, my God," she wept.

I had no words to comfort her. I found myself gazing at the floor in shame, and my mind went back to the day I had innocently asked my father about the worst thing he had ever done. A sense of failure overwhelmed me. I was supposed to be protecting my mother and sisters, yet I was helpless to protect them against this.

Somehow the weeks passed and turned into months. The questions and the stares from my co-workers were more and more frequent as rumors went around the floor. I saw some of them reading *Murder Machine* during breaks. I began making the rounds of doctors, trying to find an explanation for the illness that was crippling me. Each day I found it more difficult to function, and I feared that one day I would not be able to step onto the train that took me daily into the bowels of the city. My body had become a dead thing, and I dragged it behind me like an unwanted burden. Every doctor gave me another medication and the same advice: "Keep your mouth shut. Tell no one what is happening to you. You will never live down the stigma if you do."

I gathered my reserves one last time and decided to take my health back in my own hands. I detested the drugs I had been given and knew I was becoming addicted to the Valium they were prescribing in increasing doses. Against my doctor's advice, I checked myself into the rehab section of the local hospital and went off all of the sedatives and sleeping medications I'd been given. They were not working, and I could not fight my battles when my senses were confused by chemicals. Two weeks later I emerged chemical free and determined to resume some semblance of a normal life. I had survived a long war with the Mob and the government. I told myself that I was not going to be defeated by a couple of hack writers and a Mafia rat.

It is the things you least expect that destroy you. I had learned that lesson with painful clarity in my father's world. I learned it again on the floor of the biggest financial market in the world.

It was 1994, and Rudolph Giuliani had just been elected mayor of New York for the first time. I had not followed the election closely, but I knew the name all right. I had seen it dozens of times over the last ten years, maybe more, a phantom signature at the bottom of every document the New York prosecutors served on me. Giuliani was the head of the investigation that had convened the grand juries at which I'd testified; he was the power behind the faces I saw in the courthouse offices and chambers. Over the years he had come to symbolize every assault on my peace of mind the legal system had made. The fact that I never saw the man face to face only made him loom larger. He was the boogie man in the closet of my anxieties, the name to which my hatred and fear attached itself. And one day, without warning, he was standing in front of me, the flesh-and-blood embodiment of my nightmares.

He had been brought to the Exchange, trailed by news cameras and television reporters, to open the day's activities by ringing the morning bell that sent the market racing. It was an honor and a celebration of his election. The crowds on the floor were jubilant as he made the rounds, shaking hands and smiling for the cameras. In the midst of the excitement and the cheers, I pulled back to my station, intent on ignoring the festivities all around me. There were hundreds of people there that day, yet by a cruel twist of fate, a random surge of the crowd shoved the new mayor right up to my station, and I suddenly found myself looking into the face of the man who had haunted me for a decade. He smiled and held his hand out for me to shake, but I just stood there, staring at him, unable to move. For a moment he paused and looked at me, and in that fraction of a second, I imagined that he was seeing my father's face as he gazed at me. Then it was over, and he moved on, the crowds and the cameras surging forward with him.

I have no clear memory of what happened next. Everything went gray, and suddenly I was eighteen years old again, sitting at a table with one hundred people staring down at me, the mobster's son; and Walter Mack's face, the vein on his neck throbbing with rage and contempt, bent close to mine. I clutched at my work station for support to keep myself from collapsing. Then I wove my way through a sea of sound and confusion and walked off the floor of the Stock Exchange for the last time. The door slammed behind me, and I was falling into darkness. The void opened and swallowed me up.

The day I stumbled out the door of the Stock Exchange for the last time was the beginning of a long journey into the depths of mental illness. The flashback that had knocked me off my feet like a body blow was only the first of many. Night and day they came, a vicious form of déjà vu that made it difficult to breathe. The dual worlds I had been living in since I was seven years old had finally collided with seismic force. The locks on every compartment of my mind were blown off, and all the ghosts came rushing out.

I had taken a leave of absence from work, a leave that turned into a permanent resignation. Ashamed of my failure as a man and a provider, I spent my days cleaning the house over and over, scrubbing and vacuuming, feeling it was never clean enough. It was the age of the day trader, and I continued to trade stocks from a home computer. I also had ongoing income from rental properties and market investments, so financially we were secure. Yet it never felt like enough. I felt useless, lazy. I had to find a way to bring home more money. Yet how could I do that when I couldn't even leave the house in daylight?

So I started going out at night. In the nighttime, while prying eyes were closed in sleep, I could move about unnoticed. I went to the local boatyards, systematically collecting every scrap of recyclable material. Later I remembered the discarded film I had once collected with my father and began searching the roadways and culverts for scrap metal. I filled garbage bags with these treasures and piled my BMW to the roof with the precious refuse. I found a recycling center that was open twenty-four hours a day and began a habit of arriving before dawn, to redeem the merchandise I had collected during the night. If the night attendants thought it was odd that an unshaven man in a luxury automobile was delivering discards in the small hours of the morning, they gave no indication. To them I was just Al, and they accepted me at face value. Under the cover of darkness, in the company of these strangers, I felt safe. Carrie was horrified, mortified at the thought someone in the neighborhood might see me with a car filled with garbage. Despite her embarrassment I continued, for my collections began bringing in several hundred dollars a week in extra income. More important, it made me feel less useless.

Gradually, though, even these nighttime forays became impossible. I became convinced that I was being followed, that the government was looking for me again, that the Mob had taken out a hit on me. My beautiful home, the symbol of my success, became a prison of my own making. Terrified that my wife would be killed in an attack, I armed the house. I had guns everywhere, and I patrolled constantly as I had in the year following the Colombian threat, a loaded gun in my hand and Luca at my side. When the nights came, I would crouch by the windows, gun at the ready, peering through the blinds, soaked with sweat. Fear rustled through the darkness, crept through any window I left unguarded. Everywhere I looked, I saw the faces of my father's old enemies, of the victims I had seen in courtroom photographs, of the families who wanted to kill my family to avenge the lives my father had taken from them. I would not let my mother or sisters come near my house for fear they would be killed, and I told my friends to stay away. Their only hope of safety, I believed, was to keep far away from me.

Carrie was appalled at the change in me, and so was my family. They couldn't understand it. The successful young businessman my wife had married, the strong stoical son and brother who had always protected them, this man was gone. In his place was a terrified child who hid in unlighted rooms during the day, soaked in tears and shaking with terror, afraid of things only he could see. The world I had lived in for most of my life had always remained hidden from them. They had never known about the gun hidden in my clothing on the school grounds when I was twelve, carried to keep my sister safe; about the nights I patrolled the house in my father's absence while the family slept. When they came to visit me in the hospital after Anthony and Joey tried to kill me, they had thought they were visiting the wild son and brother who had run his car off the road in a drunken spree. I had never told them what really happened. They hadn't been there when the government followed me or interrogated me in police stations, and they hadn't been to the morgue to see my father. I had tried to protect them from all that. I had never even told them about my grand jury appearances. So now they looked at me in bewilderment, wondering what was wrong with me. "What are you talking about, Al, what are you talking about? What did Daddy's business have to do with you?" my sisters asked. "Pull yourself together, Al, be a man. What's the matter with you?" my uncles said. They didn't understand, and neither did I. Baffled and repelled by what they saw, they wanted the old Al back, the one who never cried, who didn't seem to be afraid of anything. So did I.

I decided to end everyone's suffering. I was putting my loved ones in jeopardy, I reasoned, for I was the one my enemies wanted to hurt. Once the protector of my mother and sisters, I now believed myself a danger to them. I had become a burden to my wife, unable to function as a provider, and a source of shame and anxiety to her. It seemed clear to me that the only honorable thing I could do for the people I cared about was to leave their lives. And the only way I could do that was to give up my own, which had become a source of misery to me anyway. So I systematically set about doing it.

Like my father, I had always had a number of insurance policies in place, including life policies that included coverage for murder, suicide, and disability. In the back of my mind, I had never expected to live out a normal life span. I knew what to do, for my father had trained me carefully in such matters before he went to his death. Without telling anyone what I was planning, I quietly made certain everything was in order, that the mortgage payments and bills were paid six months ahead, and that the house and car were in Carrie's name. I transferred enough cash into her personal account for her to live on for a year, until all the policies paid off and any assets were out of probate. I even checked to make sure the house was clean and my own belongings were in order. Then when she was out at a friend's house one night for a candle-making party, I locked the house behind me, got in the car, and drove down to the highway to end my life. I wanted to be with my father again, wherever that might be. Hell couldn't be any worse than what I was already living.

The Mob had run me off the road years before when they tried to kill me. Now I would do it to myself. I took the same highway through southeast Long Island I had taken that night long ago. As soon as the road was clear of cars, I accelerated to over 140 miles per hour and veered off into the trees—I was not wearing a seatbelt. A few seconds later my car catapulted over the embankment and through the woods, rolling over several times and eventually coming to rest against some trees. When the noise and confusion finally stopped, I was stunned to find myself still sitting in the driver's seat, dizzy but unhurt. Instead of being relieved, I was angry and disappointed. How could I still be alive? I couldn't even succeed at suicide. I felt trapped in a life that I could neither survive nor relinquish.

Night after night in the weeks that followed, while Carrie slept in the bedroom, I sat in the living room with the barrel of a gun pressed up against my head, Luca's head resting on my knee. The cold metal, the smell of the gunpowder were comforting. They reminded me of my father, of being seven years old and learning to take guns apart in the workshop with him. Most of all, they reminded me that I had the power to end the pain just by flexing my trigger finger. I would execute myself, Mafia-style, with a bullet behind my ear.

I did not want my wife to find my body, so I waited for her to leave me. I knew it wouldn't be much longer. I knew the marriage had disintegrated the night I crawled into bed next to her for comfort, and she pulled away from me with revulsion. We hadn't made love in weeks, and I suspected she was seeing someone else. I didn't blame her. A month after I wrecked the car she left for good, and I chose to make an end of things. Once again, I had planned carefully. I did not want to leave a mess for someone else to clean up, so I decided to do it in the garage. I took a large tarpaulin and laid it out on the garage floor so that the coroner could just wrap me up like so much garbage and put me in the van. "Put me in a garbage bag," my father had told me. Once again I was following his example. Then I collected several towels so that the blood would not splatter all over and make a mess. It never once occurred to me that I was systematically reenacting what I had read about my father's murders at the Gemini, with towels and tarps designed to dispose of blood evidence. I thought only of eliminating a mess for someone else. Then I lay down on the tarp, wrapped the towels around my head, and slid the barrel of the gun in against my skull. I had put only one bullet in the chamber, though I intended to pull the trigger until the gun fired. I wanted the suspense, the adrenaline rush of wondering which chamber it was. The old adrenaline rush. I had never quite adjusted to living without it.

I pulled the trigger. Nothing happened. My hand was shaking, and my trigger finger was slippery with sweat, yet I felt more focused, more confident than I had in months. I prepared myself to empty the next chamber. But just as I did, I heard something moving in the garage. Had my wife returned? I lifted my head slightly and peered at the entrance into the garage from the house.

It was Luca. Sensing something was wrong, he stood looking at me, worry carved into every line around his eyes. I ordered him to go back in the house, but he wouldn't leave. Instead he padded over to where I lay and whimpered. Then he stretched out next to me, shoulders on my chest and head tucked up under my chin. I started to sob. How could I do this while this faithful creature watched? He hadn't done anything wrong, yet he would think it was his fault, for it was his job to protect me. I laid the gun down, put my arms around the dog, and began to stroke his ears, comforting him. My escape would have to wait until another night.

I don't know how much time passed after that. Night blended into day, and with no one there to mark the passage of time, it was all one to me. I lay motionless in the darkened house and waited for death to find me. I thought of my father, lying silently in the dark in our house by the water all those years ago. Luca cried, confused to find his mistress gone and his master immobilized. I knew that if I lay there much longer, I would die. The faces of my mother and sisters floated in front of me, then those of Tommy and Nick. I couldn't let this happen. I dragged my body into the kitchen and struggled onto one elbow until I could reach the phone cord. The receiver came crashing down as I pulled. There in the darkness on the kitchen floor, I dialed Nick's number. When I heard his voice on the other end, I said only, "Come get me."

He didn't hesitate. "I'll be right there," he told me, and he hung up. Within minutes I heard the front door open and Nick's voice calling out for me. I told him where I was. Seeing me there on the floor, he asked no questions. He put my arm over his shoulder and walked me to his car. Too weak to raise my head, I leaned against the seat and closed my eyes. I felt the car vibrate as he drove away into the darkness. Sometime later the car stopped, and I felt him lift me once again. He walked me into the emergency room of the hospital and simply said, "My friend needs help." And they helped me.

The details are fuzzy after that. A doctor looked at me, and after some discussion, I was transferred by ambulance to a locked ward in a nearby mental hospital. I was considered a risk to myself. I signed the papers admitting me. I knew I would die if I didn't. At some point they wheeled me into a room with two beds in it. I heard doors slam and lock behind me. It was dark, but I could hear another man breathing nearby in sleep. Someone handed me a hospital gown and asked if I needed help putting it on. I said no; I just wanted to sleep. A nurse gave me an injection and left me alone to get ready for bed. I looked at the gown and the strange bed on which they had laid me. The orderly had already taken my belt and shoes. My clothing was the only familiar thing in the room. I did not want to take it off and lie naked in this strange place. So I dropped the gown on the floor by the bed, crawled under the blanket, and pulled the covers over my head. All was darkness and silence.

Lying there in that cotton cocoon, I was too depressed to cry. When the medication they had injected me with finally began to take effect, I drifted into a fitful sleep.

twelve

LAZARUS

MY BMW

Our birth is but a sleep and a forgetting:
The Soul that rises with us, our life's Star,
Hath had elsewhere its setting.

—WORDSWORTH, *"Ode: Intimations of Immortality from*
Recollections of Early Childhood"

There's a scripture that says that sometimes a man has to lose his life to find it. I had to let go of a life that had never been mine before I could find a new one. In that horrible place, in that ward filled with the sick and the insane, I began the long, slow process of rebirth.

I had already met a therapist who would become the guide I needed on the long journey out of the darkness. Until then I had always presented myself to Erma as a young stockbroker struggling with depression and a failing marriage. It was only in my hour of extremity that I finally found the courage to confide to her the horrible secret I had been keeping for so long. "My father," I told her, "was a gangster. He was in the Mafia." I paused for her reaction, but she seemed to be waiting for me to continue. She apparently wasn't getting it, so I went on. "He murdered people. Maybe a lot of people." That should be clear enough. I waited once again for the familiar, dreaded reaction: the horror, the revulsion, or worse yet, the fascination. She finally knew who I was—the mobster's son, not the respectable young man she thought I was.

I could see a slight change in her face, but it was not the one I expected. Sadness, concern, and a sense of understanding flitted across her features. "That must have been so hard for you, Al." I was touched and astonished. In that moment I knew that she did not see me as either the stockbroker or the mobster's son; to her I had always been, and always would be, just Al. That tiny, quiet moment was my first step on a long odyssey toward healing.

Incarcerated in that madhouse, the last refuge of the insane and the desperate, I began to put my life in perspective. The first blessing of my sojourn among the mentally wounded was that I finally had a name to put to what was wrong with me. I was suffering from posttraumatic stress disorder, an illness once named "battle fatigue," as it most often afflicts soldiers who have returned from combat. I had the same illness that had once kept Uncle Joe's veteran friend trapped in the mountains. PTSD commonly appears months, even years after the original experiences that caused it. The classic profile is the soldier who serves bravely and well, encountering death and destruction stoically, then returns home to disintegrate emotionally much later, when it is safe to fall apart. The flashbacks, suicide attempts, survivor guilt, and inability to adjust to everyday life that I was experiencing were textbook symptoms. For the first time, I had a diagnosis that made sense to me. I had never served in a military unit, but I had spent most of my childhood and adolescence as a soldier in my father's war.

I finally found the courage to look at my past, and for the first time I felt compassion for the nine-year-old who fired an empty gun at a counterfeit assailant; for the seventh-grader who was charged with the responsibility of protecting his sister's life with a gun; for the fifteen-year-old who prepared to put a gun to his father's stomach and pull the trigger to save his father's life. I began the process of loving and forgiving that boy for all the things he had done, and for all the things he had never done. And I took the first, tentative steps toward forgiving the father who had asked me to do them, and toward mourning his loss. Whatever else he had done, whoever else he had been, he had been my father, and I had loved him more than my own life. And he had loved me. Whatever the world thought of either one of us, I had to hold on to that truth.

I also had to grasp at a new truth. I was not my father. I never had been. It didn't matter what other people saw when they looked at me. What mattered was what I saw when I looked at myself.

When I left the hospital under my own power a few weeks later, I began the slow, painstaking process of creating a new life for myself, a life anchored in truth. I gave almost everything to Carrie as part of the divorce settlement. I didn't want those things anymore. Materialism had become a disease to me, and I wanted only the simplicity and safety of life's basics. I moved into a small apartment near Nick and his wife, not far from the neighborhood where I had lived as a child in Massapequa. I let go of the fancy cars and stopped wearing the diamond watch. Most important, I stopped carrying a gun. I didn't need it anymore.

I began to reassess every aspect of my life. My wife was gone, and I saw now that our marriage had been a sham from the beginning, for the man she had married had never really existed. I also took a long, hard look at my friends. Tommy and Nick remained loyal friends; they had laughed and partied and suffered with me for many years, and I knew they would always be there for me, only a phone call away. Other friends were more troubling. I realized that I had held on to associations with people who had stayed with me for years *because* I was the mobster's son, and that was my primary fascination for them. Those friendships had never been either healthy or authentic, and one by one I began to let them go.

One of the key moments of insight for me was a trip to an Italian ice store near my old neighborhood. It was run by a former member of the organized crime task force who had dedicated a decade of his professional career to prosecuting the New York Mafia and then retired to sell Italian ices on Long Island. An old friend insisted I should visit the store, and finally I did. I had expected to find myself face to face with one of the men who had formerly hounded me, who would regard me with contempt if he realized who I was. It was my determination to get well that empowered me to walk through the door of his establishment that day. Once inside, however, what I found was a virtual shrine to the Mafia. Posters from the *Godfather* and *GoodFellas* movies covered the walls, and the shelves were packed with souvenir memorabilia glorifying the Mob. I purchased a raspberry ice and ate it quietly as I listened to this former police officer regale admirers with tales of "the Life." Listening to him, it was impossible to tell which side of the law he had been on. As I stood there taking it all in, my friend said, "Tell him who you are, Al. He doesn't recognize you. He'll be so excited to hear you're Roy's son." I looked at my friend in disbelief. All those years he had known me, and he didn't understand the first thing about my life.

An even more telling incident occurred a short while later. I no longer drove a car, but I made it a habit to get out of my apartment regularly. My fear of leaving home was gradually abating, but I knew it would come back if I gave in to the urge to hide again. One Saturday morning I walked down to a local doughnut shop to buy a glazed doughnut and a cup of coffee for breakfast. The shop was one I had stopped at occasionally as a kid, and I was forcing myself by then to frequent my old haunts and get reacquainted with the person I once had been. Long Island was then in the process of replacing old gas station tanks with new, more environmentally safe storage units, and the gas station next door to the doughnut shop had been recently torn up. A small article in the local paper had mentioned that human remains were found in one of the old tanks. I hadn't paid much attention to the article, as it didn't seem important at the time.

Standing in line at the crowded counter, waiting to place my order, I gradually became aware of a customer ahead of me talking with the Middle Eastern shop owner while he waited. The voice sounded familiar, and when I looked over, I recognized a guy I had gone to high school with. We had never been friends, but we lived in the same neighborhood and knew one another by name. He was speaking loudly and with great enthusiasm, and everyone in line could hear what he was saying. "You know that body they found in the gas station across the street? I know who probably killed the guy. I bet it was Al DeMeo. We went to school together. His father was a big-time mobster. I'll bet the dead guy is one of Al's."

I couldn't believe what I was hearing. For a moment I wanted to turn and walk right back out the door, but I had never run away from anybody, and I wasn't going to start then. So I made my way behind the line, toward the counter where the two men were chatting, and stepped up in front of my old high school classmate. I was wearing a baseball cap and sunglasses, and I hadn't shaved, so when he first noticed me, he didn't realize who I was. I pulled the cap off and removed my sunglasses, looking him full in the face. As recognition dawned, I saw him go white as a sheet, and for a moment, I thought he might actually faint. All his bravado drained away as he stood there in stunned silence.

I looked at him for a moment and then said, my voice heavy with sarcasm, "Actually, the guy they found isn't one of mine. I've been far too busy taking care of other Mob business all these years to have time to murder anybody. You know how it is. Sometimes you just can't get everything done." And I walked out the door and down the street, back toward my apartment. Suddenly I was overwhelmed with exhaustion.

"All I wanted," I muttered to myself, "was a God-damn doughnut."

I knew I could never make final peace with some scenes of my past until I revisited them. Taking my courage in both hands, I decided to go back. The resulting journey was not only enlightening but some-times bitterly ludicrous.

I took the train into the city one afternoon and got off near Forty-Second Street, where I had once made cash collections for my father in seedy sex malls and sordid theaters. In place of the red light district where my father and I had once hidden from the law, however, I found a thriving theater district showcasing the best of Broadway on clean streets near upscale restaurants. To my infinite amusement, the small venue that had once sold sex toys to Cousin Joe was now a Disney Store, selling Mickey Mouse souvenirs within yards of the theater mounting Disney's *Lion King*.

Another afternoon I took a trip to Brooklyn, where my parents and Debra and I had all been born. My grandparents' house was on a quiet, tree-lined street, well maintained and inhabited by working families. The brick duplex where my father had grown up looked the same as it did in family photos. The Profaci house, however, once a grand mansion, had crumbled into a neglected apartment building, with curtains blowing out unscreened windows and piles of junk on the porch. The open front doorway showed a dim interior and a line of mailboxes on the wall. The splendor that had once filled my grand-mother with envy was a thing of the past. She had died that year, self-ish and cantankerous to the very end. She had her hair done, put on her favorite dress, and announced that she was going to die. True to her word, she woke up dead. My aunt Marie had moved to Florida after my grandmother's passing. She had been a faithful daughter. I hoped that she, too, was finding a new, happier life.

It wasn't far from my parents' neighborhood to the old Gemini Lounge, but it took me a while to find it. I passed it several times be-fore I was certain I had found the right place. To my surprise, it had been transformed into a storefront church. Underneath an adver-tisement showing the hours of service, a prominent banner claimed, "All who enter these doors will be eagerly welcomed." I remembered

the lurid descriptions in *Murder Machine* of the victims who had met
their deaths on the other side of those same doors, and I felt an inex-
plicable desire to laugh. A neighborhood boy, sitting a few yards away
on his bicycle, told me that he went to youth meetings in the basement of the old Gemini. He cheerfully informed me that you could
still see the bullet holes in the concrete walls. Cousin Joe's apartment, however, had been torn out and renovated. It now formed part
of the sanctuary. A redemption of sorts, I mused. Somehow it seemed
fitting. My uncle Joe had recently told me that Joey and Anthony—
who had put the fatal bullets in my father's head and who had once
tried to kill me—had reinvented themselves in prison as a rock band.
Sometimes life really is stranger than fiction.

I also took a taxi to Little Italy with friends to see where my dad
and I had walked the streets when I was a young child. Two guys on a
corner of Mulberry Street were unloading a truck. I wondered if the
goods they carried had "fallen off." The neighborhood had not
changed much, though it was a little more upscale than I remembered it. It still boasted the best espresso in the city. The Ravenite,
where I had visited my uncle Nino, was now a high-end clothing
store run by a Japanese designer. The wooden icon of the pope I remembered from childhood was gone forever. I even felt comfortable
enough to eat a leisurely lunch with friends in my father's favorite
restaurant. The chef still made lobster cream sauce. The food was as
good as I remembered, and though I recognized the maître'd, he
didn't recognize me. Only one vestige of an old habit remained: I sat
at my father's table in the very back by the exit, my back against
the wall.

That same afternoon we drove to Greenwich Village, where my father's pizza parlor once adjoined the occult shop, and Uncle Frank's
restaurant across the street had served me anything I craved. No vestige of the pizza parlor remained, but the restaurant was still there;
and standing in front of it, I felt a chill. Called The Vineyard under

my father's ownership, it had been reincarnated as an upscale Gothic café called The Jekyll and Hyde. On the right of the outdoor dining area was a tall sculpture with skulls gazing down at the diners, death masks to remind them of their own mortality. What disturbed me the most, however, was the quote from Robert Louis Stevenson emblazoned on the front of the building and inscribed on all the napkins and menus:

> In each of us, two natures are at war—the good and the evil. All our lives the fight goes on between them, and one of them must conquer. But in our own hands lies the power to choose—what we want most to be, we are.

My father had made his choice. So had I.

That night I had a dream I'd had many times before. I was on my boat, floating in the bay near Massapequa. It was a beautiful day, the sun dappling the water with slivers of gold as the waves lapped gently against the hull. Toward the stern my father was sitting in a deck chair, a cold drink in his hand. Always before in the dream, he had been sad and silent, but this time he turned and smiled at me. Then he faced the ocean once more. When I looked again, the chair was empty.

THE DARKENED GLASS

1968

For now we see through a glass, darkly;
but then face to face: now I know in part;
but then shall I know even as also I am known.

—1 CORINTHIANS 13:12

One day not long ago, I was rummaging around in the back of a closet and came across an old box. Pulling it out, I sat down on the floor and opened the cardboard flaps to see what was inside.

A faint odor of must rose, and I found myself looking down into a box of my father's clothing. For a moment time spun backward, and I realized I must have packed this box nearly twenty years ago, in the wake of my father's murder, and never given the things away. I stared at the contents for a few moments, then reached tentatively inside and removed a pair of my father's shoes. The leather, stiff with age, felt rigid in my hands.

The shoes were shiny and black, still as pristine as the day my father had cleaned them, identical to hundreds of other beautifully crafted Italian dress shoes I had watched him slip into each day. Always fastidious, my father had kept his shoes as carefully polished as any military officer. He had routinely bought his shoes in lots, often twenty pairs at a time, for he walked so much that he would literally wear them out within weeks. Like other mobsters of his generation, he had early developed the habit of walking the streets while he talked business, constantly alert to the danger of an electronic bug. Hefting it in my palm, I set one shoe on the carpet and turned the other over in my hand.

The sole lay in sharp contrast to the glowing leather upper. It was worn and slightly uneven, stained with the detritus of New York streets. As I looked at it, I wondered what secrets it held. Had it grown thin treading countless miles down Mulberry Street or Flatbush Avenue, during clandestine walks near the Gemini or Ravenite, overhearing what the government was not supposed to? Had it rested on the marble floors of Paul Castellano's palace, its top reflecting the glow of the chandeliers? Had it run from a hit? Was that dark stain a melancholy remnant of someone's life blood? I turned it back over, and there was the shine once again, a brave face for the world to see. I ran my fingers over the shiny surface and reflected that, like my father, his shoes were proud and seemingly unscathed by events on the surface but underneath, stained and worn. I set the shoe on the carpet next to its mate and reached into the box once again.

I pulled out my father's favorite leather jacket. It, too, was black and carefully maintained. Opening the front, I looked at the inner pockets. They were empty now, stretched and worn from their former occupants. I slid my hand into one pocket. My father had kept his .38 revolver there. The fabric was slightly thinner where the handle had once bulged. I removed my hand and touched the other pocket. That was where he had kept the roll of hundreds that he peeled out whenever I wanted candy as a kid.

Rising to my feet, I slipped my arms into the sleeves of the jacket. Then, pulling off my own sneakers, I carefully stepped into my father's shoes and walked awkwardly to the bedroom mirror.

The reflection staring back at me was pale and drawn, melancholy hazel eyes above an unshaven face. The boy who had once shadowed his father's every movement was gone, replaced by a stranger. The broad face and softened chin were those of a man just approaching middle age, but the eyes were those of an old man, haunted and weary. I straightened the jacket on my shoulders, but no amount of adjustment would make it fit properly. I had grown and filled out in the years since my father's death, but the jacket still hung loosely on me. I thought of my father's broad chest, all the hours spent lifting weights to wear off the pounds he could never lose. I placed my hand on the leather covering my chest, and my eyes filled with tears.

My eyes followed the path of my reflection downward, and I stared at my feet. Like the jacket, my father's shoes swam on me. They gaped around my insteps. I looked like a little boy playing dress-up. I lifted my chin and gazed at my reflection once more, half expecting to see my father. But instead, as I looked at the mirrored image, perhaps for the first time in my life, I saw myself, a sad young man wearing his father's clothes. They didn't fit me. They never had. And by the end, my father hadn't wanted them to.

As I gazed at my motley appearance, I thought of the agony of thirty lost years. They say a picture is worth a thousand words, and somehow that living image of myself showed me something that no words had been able to convey. My father had made me who I was, but it was up to me to decide who I was to be. The choice was in my hands. I had my own shoes to wear, my own journeys to take. I had chosen a different journey from my father's. I would love and miss the man until the day I died, but I would not repeat his mistakes. We are each responsible for our own sins, he for his, and I for mine. We are not intended to bear each other's. No one can survive that burden.

I stepped out of the shoes and put them back in the box. I removed the jacket, folded and smoothed it, and placed it carefully on top of the shoes. I closed the cardboard flaps and put the box in the back of the closet once again, where it will lie undisturbed for another twenty years. Then I picked up my own shoes and shut the door behind me.